The GREATEST SPEECHES *of*
Donald J. Trump

The GREATEST SPEECHES *of*
Donald J. Trump

45th President of the United States

Humanix Books
www.humanixbooks.com

Humanix Books

THE GREATEST SPEECHES OF DONALD J. TRUMP
Copyright © 2022 by Humanix Books
All rights reserved.

Humanix Books, P.O. Box 20989, West Palm Beach, FL 33416, USA
www.humanixbooks.com | info@humanixbooks.com

ISBN: 9-781-63006-217-0 (Hardcover)
ISBN: 9-781-63006-219-7 (E-book)

Printed in the United States of America
10 9 8 7 6 5 4 3 2 1

Contents

Introduction   ix
by Craig Shirley

Presidential Announcement Speech   1
Trump Tower, New York, New York
June 16, 2015

Presidential Nomination Acceptance Speech   21
Republican National Convention, Cleveland, Ohio
July 21, 2016

Presidential Victory Speech   37
Hilton Hotel, New York, New York
November 9, 2016

Inaugural Address   43
Washington, DC
January 20, 2017

The Unbreakable Spirit of the Jewish People   49
Israel Museum, Jerusalem, Israel
May 23, 2017

Poland Lives, Poland Prospers, and Poland Prevails   **57**
Krasiński Square, Warsaw, Poland
July 6, 2017

Boy Scout Jamboree   **69**
Summit Bechtel Reserve, Glen Jean, West Virginia
July 24, 2017

Statement on Charlottesville   **83**
The White House, Washington, DC
August 14, 2017

A Time of Both Immense Promise and Great Peril   **87**
U.N. General Assembly, New York, New York
September 19, 2017

Jerusalem Is Israel's Capital   **103**
The White House, Washington, DC
December 6, 2017

A New National Security Strategy   **109**
Ronald Reagan Building, Washington, DC
December 18, 2017

America Is Open for Business   **121**
World Economic Forum, Davos, Switzerland
January 26, 2018

State of the Union Address: A New Tide of Optimism   **129**
US House of Representatives, Washington, DC
January 30, 2018

The US Southern Border and the Government Shutdown   **147**
The White House, Washington, DC
January 19, 2019

State of the Union Address: Courage Together   **153**
US House of Representatives, Washington, DC
February 5, 2019

Toast at a State Dinner with Queen Elizabeth   **171**
Buckingham Palace, London, England
June 3, 2019

Establishment of US Space Command   **175**
The White House, Washington, DC
August 29, 2019

Great Contests, High Stakes, and Clear Choices   **181**
U.N. General Assembly, New York, New York
September 24, 2019

State of the Union Address: Incredible Results   **195**
US House of Representatives, Washington, DC
February 4, 2020

United States Military Academy Graduation   **215**
West Point, New York
June 13, 2020

Campaign Rally   **225**
Tulsa, Oklahoma
June 20, 2020

American Freedom Exists for American Greatness   **259**
Mount Rushmore National Monument, Keystone, South Dakota
July 3, 2020

Presidential Nomination Acceptance Speech   **271**
Republican National Convention, Charlotte, North Carolina
August 27, 2020

Supreme Court Nominee, Amy Coney Barrett   **293**
The White House, Washington, DC
September 26, 2020

On the Violence at the Capitol   **299**
The White House, Washington, DC
January 13, 2021

Farewell Address   **303**
The White House, Washington, DC
January 19, 2021

We've Left It All on the Field   **313**
Joint Base Andrews, Maryland
January 20, 2020

Illustration Credits   **317**

Introduction

Over the years, historians and writers have often referred to the presidential pedestal as "The Bully Pulpit." The term was first coined by Teddy Roosevelt and, contrary to modern usage, means a wonderful platform; a profound and powerful tool by which a president may articulate a grand vision for the future and prosperity of our nation. A message that cannot be corrupted or twisted by pundits or publications who often believe that the right to communicate directly to all Americans is solely their privilege. Indeed, when *The New York Times* reported on his usage of the term, they were not pleased:

> A man may be temperamentally fond of a fight, even of vulgar brawls, but most men have a sobering sense that the power and responsibility of a high office involve the obligation of dignity. Mr. Roosevelt was not sobered, he was not repressed, he was turned loose. His immense egotism exalted in the possession of an office that brought him into the eye of millions, and he was apparently intoxicated with the sense of his power to speak and act.

The shallow and superficial and collectivist *New York Times* bashing a Republican president? What a surprise.

Some things never change.

 It's vitally important that each of us—including presidents—have a chance to speak out for ourselves and not rely on the corrupt filter of *The Washington Post* or NBC, just as the Framers intended in 1787, when they wrote the Constitution. Then, they saw the pamphleteers and broadsheets of the era as valuable allies of the American people. No longer. The national media is mostly the enemy, making presidential speeches even more important.

The bully pulpit is a powerful tool for those leaders with the foresight to recognize its power. Leaders who don't, like Jimmy Carter, have only yelped out from this podium simply because they did not understand presidential power. Who can forget the now notorious "Malaise Speech" by Carter, blaming Americans for high inflation, long gas lines, high interest rates, and all the other problems America faced in that steamy, hot summer of 1979?

Other presidents who rightly roared over the years include Franklin Roosevelt, John Kennedy, Ronald Reagan, and Donald Trump. They may not have always been right—as FDR was incorrect about the Great Depression needing more government regulations—but they spoke with verve and conviction.

And FDR was right about the threats from Nazi Germany and the Empire of Japan.

President Theodore Roosevelt spoke often of the presidency as a bully pulpit. The president has the rare ability to speak to the nation at will, and to disseminate information supporting his point of view, as when the old Bull Moose pointed out in his speech on the six duties of American citizenship, long before he was president. They included the "Big Stick" foreign policy, as well noting that Americans should be good people and, especially, act as a political watchdog over the system. Great presidents think great thoughts even before they become president. Donald Trump was such a watchdog, as when he took on the liberals of the high-tech industry, who are a direct threat to the American way of life.

Some presidents—like Lyndon Johnson—confuse the bully pulpit with the pulpit of a bully. He was a small man, and as a result, a bully.

Other presidents evolved in office. Men such as Abraham Lincoln, Harry Truman, and John Kennedy all developed and "grew" in office. The Abraham Lincoln of 1861 was not the Abraham Lincoln of 1865, when he appealed to the nation to bind up its wounds. He'd gone from a hack politician who won the presidency with a mere plurality, to one of our most important presidents. JFK blundered badly in the Bay of Pigs in Cuba of 1961 but performed magnificently during the Cuban Missile Crisis of 1962. Truman was over his head in 1944, but was commanding the seas by 1950.

Sometimes presidents suffer for using the executive podium, as in the many cases of Richard Nixon, who only seemed to make the Watergate scandal even worse, as he did when he blundered by saying, "The American people need to know if their president is a crook. Well, I am not a crook." At the time, no one was accusing Nixon of being a crook. He was pleading his innocence when no one was accusing him of being guilty. Nixon had a history of flying off the handle, as he did when he once said to the media, in the third person, they "won't have Nixon to kick around anymore." Some, like Joe Biden, are just plain disasters, in over his head. In the context of history, he will rank with our poorer presidents like Franklin Pierce, James Buchanan, and Herbert Hoover.

Others, like Reagan, were more surefooted. Reagan was a reader, a writer, a thinker, and a listener. A true intellectual. He wrote many of his own speeches, even as he had the best speechwriters in the history of the presidency. They came up with phrases such as "Mr. Gorbachev, tear down this wall!" Historians rank his Farewell Address alongside Washington's and Eisenhower's as the best farewell remarks in the history of the presidency.

The Constitution established a relatively weak chief executive. The Framers were understandably fearful of granting too much power to one man, having just been the victims of King George II and King George III. This was made clear in the *Federalist Papers* when Alexander Hamilton, James Madison, and John Jay made the case against the Articles of Confederation, and for a new constitution, as they did in Federalist 59 and 70. They argued for the need for a stronger central government but also argued for the need to regulate the presidency.

The greatest power the president exercises with regularity is the power to persuade Congress and the American people that his agenda should be implemented. Over the course of the twentieth century, technology has permitted the president's words to move faster, not just to the American people, but around the world.

Donald Trump is a historical anomaly. He is the first person to be elected to the presidency without having served in government or the military. However, he has understood the bully pulpit better than most career politicians. Mr. Trump emerged in the New York media as a brash, second-generation real estate developer. His projects were proclaimed to be the biggest and the best in the greatest city in the world. He was used to getting things done and leapfrogging over bureaucracy. Over time, he became a media celebrity. He parlayed his business acumen and showmanship into the hit reality television show *The Apprentice*. His demands for accountability and swift terminations with "You're fired!" gave a preview into his administration.

On June 16, 2015, Donald Trump famously descended the escalator in Trump Tower to announce his seemingly longshot candidacy for the presidency. He began the speech by commenting on the size of the crowd. He immediately listed ways in which the United States was losing to both China and Japan. One of his most controversial statements was "The US has become a dumping ground for everybody else's problems." And he rightly pointed out those problems, which Washington politicians sweep, with regularity, under the nation's rug. Trump was refreshing in his frankness, talking about things that others ducked.

This book is a compilation of President Donald Trump's best presidential speeches. Trump is *sui generis*—Latin for *unique* or *one's own class*.

I am known for being a Reagan biographer and presidential historian, and I find Trump's take on the conservative philosophy, republicanism, and America interesting. People don't always agree with him, but at least he gets them thinking. Is he a reader of the philosophy of John Locke? No. Does he feel conservatism instinctively? The answer is a resounding yes! He says what's on his mind, much like Harry Truman. Truman suffered in the short term for his bluntness but now ranks firmly in the second tier of American presidents. And he had to follow Roosevelt!

Trump is blunt-spoken in an era of untrue niceties. Many are sick of the false platitudes of the mainstream media and the political establishment. Instead, Trump would paraphrase the words of Thomas Paine in *Common Sense.* Now is the time to try peoples' souls. Today, we have collectivist politicians telling us that more taxes and more regulation will lead to more prosperity. We have collectivist politicians telling us that reducing police forces will result in less crime. Yeah, and two plus two equals five. Trump is like a breath of fresh air, bringing common sense to the national debate.

Right from the beginning, Trump took the bull by the horns, saying forthrightly in his Inaugural Address: "We the citizens of America are now joined in a great national effort to rebuild our country and restore its promise for all of our people. Together, we will determine the course of America, and the world, for many, many years to come. We will face challenges. We will confront hardships, but we will get the job done." He was making clear that the period of Obama celebrityhood was over, and it was time to get this nation moving again.

Later, he said, "I'm calling on all members of Congress to put the safety of the American people first." One can argue whether this is the proper role of the national government, except in times of national crisis. But one cannot argue intent.

And who can argue with the results? A booming economy, peace breaking out in the Middle East, standing up to communist China, the border crisis mostly healed, a vaccine found for the Chinese-inspired Wuhan plague that has killed millions of our fellow Americans, our military strength restored, a solid plan to declare victory and leave Afghanistan honorably. His tweets aside, he accomplished a lot.

Trump will never be known as a great speechifier like Kennedy, or "The Great Communicator" Reagan, but he did communicate important thoughts. Trump talked about a secure border, as did Reagan. Trump talked about the need to get this country moving again, as did JFK. Trump talked about cleaning up Washington, a worthy goal. Maybe the establishment has some things twisted. Maybe it is that Donald Trump didn't talk about things so farfetched, but that the establishment that has become so farfetched.

Maybe Trump was talking about some good old-fashioned common sense that this nation has gotten away from, and that we desperately need to hear again.

Here are some of Trump's best speeches. Best thoughts for "we the people."

Sine die.

Craig Shirley
Ben Lomond, Virgina

Presidential Announcement Speech

TRUMP TOWER, NEW YORK CITY, NEW YORK

June 16, 2015

Wow! Whoa. That is some group of people. Thousands.

So nice. Thank you very much. That's really nice. Thank you. It's great to be at Trump Tower. It's great to be in a wonderful city, New York. And it's an honor to have everybody here. This is beyond anybody's expectations. There's been no crowd like this.

And I can tell, some of the candidates, they went in. They didn't know the air conditioner didn't work. They sweated like dogs. They didn't know the room was too big, because they didn't have anybody there.

How are they going to beat ISIS? I don't think it's gonna happen. Our country is in serious trouble. We don't have victories anymore. We used to have victories, but we don't have them. When was the last time anybody saw us beating, let's say, China in a trade deal? They kill us. I beat China all the time. All the time.

When did we beat Japan at anything? They send their cars over by the millions, and what do we do? When was the last time you saw a Chevrolet in Tokyo? It doesn't exist, folks. They beat us all the time.

When do we beat Mexico at the border? They're laughing at us, at our stupidity. And now they are beating us economically. They are not our friend, believe me. But they're killing us economically.

The US has become a dumping ground for everybody else's problems.

Thank you. It's true, and these are the best and the finest. When Mexico sends its people, they're not sending their best. They're not sending you. They're not sending you. They're sending people that have lots of problems, and they're bringing those problems to us. They're bringing drugs. They're bringing crime. They're rapists. And some, I assume, are good people.

But I speak to border guards and they tell us what we're getting. And it only makes common sense. It only makes common sense. They're sending us not the right people.

It's coming from more than Mexico. It's coming from all over South and Latin America, and it's coming probably—probably—from the Middle East. But we don't know. Because we have no protection, and we have no competence. We don't know what's happening. And it's got to stop, and it's got to stop fast.

Islamic terrorism is eating up large portions of the Middle East. They've become rich. I'm in competition with them.

They just built a hotel in Syria. Can you believe this? They built a hotel. When I have to build a hotel, I pay interest. They don't have to pay interest because they took the oil that, when we left Iraq, I said we should've taken. So now ISIS has the oil, and what they don't have, Iran has. And in nineteen—and I will tell you this, and I said it very strongly, years ago, I said—and I love the military, and I want to have the strongest military that we've ever had, and we need it more now than ever. But I said, "Don't hit Iraq," because you're going to totally destabilize the Middle East. Iran is going to take over the Middle East. Iran and somebody else will get the oil, and it turned out that Iran is now taking over Iraq. Think of it. Iran is taking over Iraq, and they're taking it over big league.

We spent two trillion dollars in Iraq. Two trillion dollars. We lost thousands of lives, thousands in Iraq. We have wounded soldiers, who I love, I love—they're great—all over the place, thousands and thousands of wounded soldiers. And we have nothing. We can't even go there. We have nothing. And every time we give Iraq equipment, the first time a bullet goes off in the air, they leave it.

Last week, I read twenty-three hundred Humvees—these are big vehicles—were left behind for the enemy. Two thousand? You would say maybe two, maybe four? Twenty-three hundred sophisticated vehicles, they ran, and the enemy took them.

Last quarter, it was just announced, our gross domestic product—a sign of strength, right? But not for us. It was below zero. Whoever heard of this? It's never below zero.

Our labor participation rate was the worst since 1978. But think of it, GDP below zero, horrible labor participation rate.

And our real unemployment is anywhere from eighteen to twenty percent. Don't believe the 5.6. Don't believe it. That's right. A lot of people up there can't get jobs. They can't get jobs, because there are no jobs, because China has our jobs and Mexico has our jobs. They all have jobs.

But the real number, the real number is anywhere from eighteen to nineteen, and maybe even twenty-one percent, and nobody talks about it, because it's a statistic that's full of nonsense.

Our enemies are getting stronger and stronger, by the way, and we as a country are getting weaker. Even our nuclear arsenal doesn't work.

It came out recently they have equipment that is thirty years old. They don't know if it worked. And I thought it was horrible when it was broadcast on television, because, boy, does that send signals to Putin and all of the other people that look at us and they say, "That is a group of people, and that is a nation that truly has no clue. They don't know what they're doing. They don't know what they're doing."

We have a disaster called the big lie: Obamacare. Obamacare.

Yesterday, it came out that costs are going for people up twenty-nine, thirty-nine, forty-nine, and even fifty-five percent. And deductibles are through the roof. You have to be hit by a tractor—literally, a tractor—to use it, because the deductibles are so high, it's virtually useless. It's virtually useless. It is a disaster.

And remember the five billion-dollar website? Five billion dollars we spent on a website, and to this day it doesn't work. A five billion-dollar website.

I have so many websites. I have them all over the place. I hire people, they do a website. It costs me three dollars. Five billion-dollar website.

Well, you need somebody, because politicians are all talk, no action. Nothing's gonna get done. They will not bring us—believe me—to the promised land. They will not.

As an example, I've been on the circuit making speeches, and I hear my fellow Republicans. And they're wonderful people. I like them. They all want me to support them. They don't know how to bring it about. They come up to my office. I'm meeting with three of them in the next week. And they don't know—"Are you running? Are you not running? Could we have your support? What do we do? How do we do it?"

I like them. And I hear their speeches. And they don't talk jobs, and they don't talk China. When was the last time you heard China is killing us? They're devaluing their currency to a level that you wouldn't believe. It makes it impossible for our companies to compete. Impossible. They're killing us.

But you don't hear that from anybody else. You don't hear it from anybody else. And I watch the speeches. I watch the speeches of these people, and they say the sun will rise, the moon will set, all sorts of wonderful things will happen. And people are saying, "What's going on? I just want a job. Just get me a job. I don't need the rhetoric. I want a job."

And that's what's happening. And it's going to get worse, because remember, Obamacare really kicks in in '16, 2016. Obama is going to be out playing golf. He might be on one of my courses. I would invite him. I actually would say I have the best courses in the world, so I'd say—you what? . . . if he wants to. I have one right next to the White House, right on the Potomac. If he'd like to play, that's fine. In fact, I'd love him to leave early and play. That would be a very good thing.

But Obamacare kicks in in 2016. Really big league. It is going to be amazingly destructive. Doctors are quitting. I have a friend who's a doctor, and he said to me the other day, "Donald, I never saw anything like it. I have more accountants than I have nurses.

It's a disaster. My patients are beside themselves. They had a plan that was good. They have no plan now."

We have to repeal Obamacare, and it can be—and—and it can be replaced with something much better for everybody. Let it be for everybody. But much better and much less expensive for people and for the government. And we can do it.

So I've watched the politicians. I've dealt with them all my life. If you can't make a good deal with a politician, then there's something wrong with you. You're certainly not very good. And that's what we have representing us. They will never make America great again. They don't even have a chance. They're controlled fully. They're controlled fully by the lobbyists, by the donors, and by the special interests, fully.

Yes, they control them. Hey, I have lobbyists. I have to tell you. I have lobbyists that can produce anything for me. They're great. But you know what? It won't happen. It won't happen. Because we have to stop doing things for some people. But for this country, it's destroying our country. We have to stop, and it has to stop now.

Now, our country needs—our country needs a truly great leader, and we need a truly great leader now. We need a leader that wrote *The Art of the Deal*. We need a leader that can bring back our jobs, can bring back our manufacturing, can bring back our military, can take care of our vets. Our vets have been abandoned.

And we also need a cheerleader.

You know, when President Obama was elected, I said, "Well, the one thing I think he'll do well—I think he'll be a great cheerleader for the country. I think he'd be a great spirit."

He was vibrant. He was young. I really thought that he would be a great cheerleader.

He's not a leader. That's true. You're right about that.

But he wasn't a cheerleader. He's actually a negative force. He's been a negative force. He wasn't a cheerleader; he was the opposite.

We need somebody that can take the brand of the United States and make it great again. It's not great again.

We need—we need somebody—we need somebody that literally will take this country and make it great again. We can do that.

And, I will tell you, I love my life. I have a wonderful family. They're saying, "Dad, you're going to do something that's going to be so tough."

You know, all of my life, I've heard that a truly successful person, a really, really successful person, and even modestly successful, cannot run for public office. Just can't happen. And yet that's the kind of mindset that you need to make this country great again.

So ladies and gentlemen . . . I am officially running . . . for president of the United States, and we are going to make our country great again.

It can happen. Our country has tremendous potential. We have tremendous people.

We have people that aren't working. We have people that have no incentive to work. But they're going to have incentive to work, because the greatest social program is a job. And they'll be proud, and they'll love it, and they'll make much more than they would've ever made, and they'll be—they'll be doing so well, and we're going to be thriving as a country. Thriving. It can happen.

I will be the greatest jobs president that God ever created. I tell you that.

I'll bring back our jobs from China, from Mexico, from Japan, from so many places. I'll bring back our jobs, and I'll bring back our money.

Right now, think of this: We owe China 1.3 trillion dollars. We owe Japan more than that. So they come in, they take our jobs, they take our money, and then they loan us back the money, and we pay them in interest, and then the dollar goes up, so their deal's even better.

How stupid are our leaders? How stupid are these politicians to allow this to happen? How stupid are they?

I'm going to tell you—thank you. I'm going to tell you a couple of stories about trade, because I'm totally against the trade bill for a number of reasons.

Number one, the people negotiating don't have a clue. Our president doesn't have a clue. He's a bad negotiator.

He's the one that did Bergdahl. We get Bergdahl, they get five killer terrorists that everybody wanted over there.

We get Bergdahl. We get a traitor. We get a no-good traitor, and they get the five people that they wanted for years, and those people are now back on the battlefield trying to kill us. That's the negotiator we have.

Take a look at the deal he's making with Iran. He makes that deal, Israel maybe won't exist very long. It's a disaster, and we have to protect Israel. But. . . .

So we need people. I'm a free trader. But the problem with free trade is you need really talented people to negotiate for you. If you don't have talented people, if you don't have great leadership, if you don't have people that know business, not just a political hack that got the job because he made a contribution to a campaign—which is the way all jobs, just about, are gotten—free trade is terrible.

Free trade can be wonderful if you have smart people, but we have people that are stupid. We have people that aren't smart. And we have people that are controlled by special interests. And it's just not going to work.

So here's a couple of stories happened recently. A friend of mine is a great manufacturer. And you know, China comes over, and they dump all their stuff, and I buy it. I buy it because, frankly, I have an obligation to buy it, because they devalue their currency so brilliantly. They just did it recently, and nobody thought they could do it again.

But with all our problems with Russia, with all our problems with everything—everything—they got away with it again. And it's impossible for our people here to compete.

So I want to tell you this story. A friend of mine who's a great manufacturer, calls me up a few weeks ago. He's very upset. I said, "What's your problem?"

He said, "You know, I make great product."

And I said, "I know. I know that because I buy the product."

He said, "I can't get it into China. They won't accept it. I sent a boat over, and they actually sent it back. They talked about environmental. They talked about all sorts of crap that had nothing to do with it."

I said, "Oh, wait a minute, that's terrible. Does anyone know this?"

He said, "Yeah, they do it all the time with other people."

I said, "They send it back?"

"Yeah. So I finally got it over there, and they charged me a big tariff. They're not supposed to be doing that. I told them."

Now, they do charge you tariff on trucks, when we send trucks and other things over there. Ask Boeing. They wanted Boeing's secrets. They wanted their patents and all their secrets before they agreed to buy planes from Boeing.

Hey, I'm not saying they're stupid. I like China. I sell apartments for—I just sold an apartment for fifteen million dollars to somebody from China. Am I supposed to dislike them? I own a big chunk of the Bank of America Building at 1290 Avenue of the Americas, that I got from China in a war. Very valuable.

I love China. The biggest bank in the world is from China. You know where their United States headquarters is located? In this building, in Trump Tower. I love China. People say, "Oh, you don't like China?" No, I love them. But their leaders are much smarter than our leaders, and we can't sustain ourself with that. There's too much. It's like—it's like, take the New England Patriots and Tom Brady and have them play your high-school football team. That's the difference between China's leaders and our leaders.

They are ripping us. We are rebuilding China. We're rebuilding many countries. China, you go there now—roads, bridges, schools . . . you never saw anything like it. They have bridges that make the George Washington Bridge look like small potatoes. And they're all over the place.

We have all the cards, but we don't know how to use them. We don't even know that we have the cards, because our leaders don't understand the game. We could turn off that spigot by charging them tax until they behave properly.

Now they're going militarily. They're building a military island in the middle of the South China Sea! A military island! Now, our country could never do that, because we'd have to get environmental clearance, and the environmentalists wouldn't let our country—we would never build in an ocean. They built it in about one year, this massive military port.

They're building up their military to a point that is very scary. You have a problem with ISIS. You have a bigger problem with China.

And in my opinion, the new China, believe it or not, in terms of trade, is Mexico.

So this man tells me about the manufacturing. I say, "That's a terrible story. I hate to hear it."

But I have another one—Ford.

So Mexico takes a company—a car company that was going to build in Tennessee—rips it out. Everybody thought the deal was dead. Reported it in *The Wall Street Journal* recently. Everybody thought it was a done deal. It's going in, and that's going to be it, going into Tennessee. Great state, great people.

All of a sudden, at the last moment, this big car manufacturer, foreign, announces they're not going to Tennessee. They're gonna spend their billion dollars in Mexico instead. Not good.

Now, Ford announces a few weeks ago that Ford is going to build a 2.5 billion-dollar car and truck and parts manufacturing plant in Mexico. Two point five billion. It's going to be one of the largest in the world. Ford. Good company.

So I announced that I'm running for president. I would . . .

One of the early things I would do, probably before I even got in—and I wouldn't even use—you know, I have—I know the smartest negotiators in the world. I know the good ones. I know the bad ones. I know the overrated ones. You get a lot of them that are overrated. They're not good. They think they are. They get good stories, because the newspapers get buffaloed. But they're not good.

But I know the negotiators in the world, and I put them one for each country. Believe me, folks. We will do very, very well. Very, very well.

But I wouldn't even waste my time with this one. I would call up the head of Ford, who I know. If I was president, I'd say, "Congratulations. I understand that you're building a nice 2.5 billion-dollar car factory in Mexico and that you're going to take your cars and sell them to the United States, zero tax. Just flow them across the border."

And you say to yourself, *How does that help us?* Right? *How does that help us? Where is that good?* It's not.

So I would say, "Congratulations. That's the good news. Let me give you the bad news. Every car and every truck and every part manufactured in this plant that comes across the border, we're going to charge you a thirty-five-percent tax, and that tax is going to be paid simultaneously with the transaction. And that's it."

Now, here's what is going to happen. If it's not me in the position, it's one of these politicians that we're running against—you know, the four hundred people that we're all running against. And here's what's going to happen. They're not so stupid. They know it's not a good thing, and they may even be upset by it. But then they're going to get a call from their donors, or probably from the lobbyist for Ford, and say, "You can't do that to Ford, because Ford takes care of me and I take care of you, and you can't do that to Ford."

And guess what? No problem. They're going to build in Mexico. They're going to take away thousands of jobs. It's very bad for us.

So under President Trump, here's what would happen:

The head of Ford will call me back, I would say, within an hour after I told them the bad news. But it could be he'd want to be cool, and he'll wait until the next day. You know, they want to be a little cool.

And he'll say, "Please, please, please." He'll beg for a little while, and I'll say, "No interest." Then he'll call all sorts of political people, and I'll say, "Sorry, fellas. No interest." Because I don't need anybody's money. It's nice. I don't need anybody's money. I'm using my own money. I'm not using the lobbyists. I'm not using donors. I don't care. I'm really rich. "I'll show you that in a second.

And I'm not even saying that [to brag]. That's the kind of mindset, that's the kind of thinking, you need for this country.

So—because we got to make the country rich.

It sounds crass. Somebody said, "Oh, that's crass." It's not crass.

We got eighteen trillion in debt. We got nothing but problems.

We got a military that needs equipment all over the place. We got nuclear weapons that are obsolete.

We've got nothing. We've got Social Security that's going to be destroyed if somebody like me doesn't bring money into the country. All these other people want to cut the hell out of it. I'm not going to cut it at all. I'm going to bring money in, and we're going to save it.

But here's what's going to happen: After I'm called by thirty friends of mine who contributed to different campaigns, after I'm called by all of the special interests and by the—the donors and by the lobbyists—and they have zero chance at convincing me, zero—I'll get a call the next day from the head of Ford. He'll say, "Please reconsider." I'll say, "No."

He'll say, "Mister President, we've decided to move the plant back to the United States, and we're not going to build it in Mexico." That's it. They have no choice. They have no choice.

There are hundreds of things like that. I'll give you another example: Saudi Arabia, they make a billion dollars a day. A billion dollars a day. I love the Saudis. Many are in this building. They make a billion dollars a day. Whenever they have problems, we send over the ships. We say, "We're gonna protect." What are we doing? They've got nothing but money.

If the right person asked them, they'd pay a fortune. They wouldn't be there except for us.

And believe me, you look at the border with Yemen. You remember Obama a year ago, Yemen was a great victory. Two weeks later, the place was blown up. Everybody got out—and they kept our equipment. They always keep our equipment. We ought to send used equipment, right? They always keep our equipment. We ought to send some real junk, because frankly, it would be— we ought to send our surplus. We're always losing this gorgeous brand-new stuff.

But look at that border with Saudi Arabia. Do you really think that these people are interested in Yemen? Saudi Arabia without us is gone. They're gone.

And I'm the one that made all of the right predictions about Iraq. You know, all of these politicians that I'm running against now—it's so nice to say I'm running, as opposed to if I run, if I run. I'm running.

But all of these politicians that I'm running against now, they're trying to disassociate. I mean, you looked at Bush—it took him five days to answer the question on Iraq. He couldn't answer the question. He didn't know. I said, "Is he intelligent?"

Then I looked at Rubio. He was unable to answer the question, *Is Iraq a good thing or bad thing?* He didn't know. He couldn't answer the question.

How are these people gonna lead us? How are we gonna—how are we gonna go back and make it great again? We can't. They don't have a clue. They can't lead us. They can't. They can't even answer simple questions. It was terrible.

But Saudi Arabia is in big, big trouble. Now, thanks to fracking and other things, the oil is all over the place. And I used to say it . . . there are ships at sea—and this was during the worst crisis—that were loaded up with oil, and the cartel kept the price up, because again, they were smarter than our leaders. They were smarter than our leaders.

There is so much wealth out there that can make our country so rich again, and therefore make it great again. Because we need money. We're dying. We're dying. We need money. We have to do it. And we need the right people.

So Ford will come back. They'll all come back. And I will say this—this is going to be an election, in my opinion, that's based on competence.

Somebody said to me the other day—a reporter, a very nice reporter, "But Mister Trump, you're not a nice person."

[Woman in the audience yells, "We don't need NICE!"] That's true. But actually I am. I think I am a nice person. People that know me, like me. Does my family like me? I think so, right. Look at my family. I'm proud of my family.

By the way, speaking of my family—Melania, Barron, Kai, Donnie, Don, Vanessa, Tiffany, Ivanka did a great job. Did she do a great job?

Great. Jared, Laura, and Eric—I'm very proud of my family. They're a great family.

So the reporter said to me the other day, "But Mister Trump, you're not a nice person. How can you get people to vote for you?"

I said, "I don't know." I said, "I think that, number one, I am a nice person. I give a lot of money away to charities and other things. I think I'm actually a very nice person."

But I said, "This is going to be an election that's based on competence, because people are tired of these nice people. And they're tired of being ripped off by everybody in the world. And they're tired of spending more money on education than any nation in the world per capita, than any nation in the world, and we are twenty-sixth in the world. Twenty-five countries are better than us in education. And some of them are like Third World countries. But we're becoming a Third World country because of our infrastructure, our airports, our roads, everything. So one of the things I did—and I said, "You know what I'll do. I'll do it." Because a lot of people said, "He'll never run. Number one, he won't want to give up his lifestyle."

They're right about that, but I'm doing it.

Number two, I'm a private company, so nobody knows what I'm worth. And the one thing is that when you run, you have to announce and certify to all sorts of governmental authorities your net worth.

So I said, "That's OK. I'm proud of my net worth. I've done an amazing job."

I started off—thank you—I started off in a small office with my father in Brooklyn and Queens, and my father said—and I loved my father. I learned so much. He was a great negotiator. I learned so much just sitting at his feet, playing with blocks, listening to him negotiate with subcontractors. But I learned a lot.

But he used to say, "Donald, don't go into Manhattan. That's the big leagues. We don't know anything about that. Don't do it."

I said, "I gotta go into Manhattan. I gotta build those big buildings. I gotta do it, Dad. I've gotta do it."

And after four or five years in Brooklyn, I ventured into Manhattan and did a lot of great deals: The Grand Hyatt Hotel. I was responsible for the convention center on the west side.

I did a lot of great deals, and I did them early and young. And now I'm building all over the world, and I love what I'm doing.

But they all said—a lot of the pundits on television: "Well, Donald will never run, and one of the main reasons is he's private, and he's probably not as successful as everybody thinks."

So I said to myself, *You know, nobody's ever going to know unless I run, because I'm really proud of my success. I really am.*

I've employed—I've employed tens of thousands of people over my lifetime. That means medical. That means education. That means everything.

So a large accounting firm and my accountants have been working for months, because it's big and complex, and they've put together a statement, a financial statement, just a summary. But everything will be filed eventually with the government, and we don't need extensions or anything. We'll be filing it right on time. We don't need anything.

And it was even reported incorrectly yesterday, because they said, "He had assets of nine billion." So I said, "No, that's the wrong number. That's the wrong number. Not assets."

So they put together this. And before I say it, I have to say this. I made it the old-fashioned way. It's real estate. You know, it's real estate. It's labor, and it's unions—good and some bad—and lots of people that aren't in unions. And it's all over the place and building all over the world.

And I have assets—big accounting firm, one of the most highly respected. Nine billion two hundred and forty million dollars.

And I have liabilities of about five hundred [million dollars]. That's long-term debt, very low interest rates.

In fact, one of the big banks came to me and said, "Donald, you don't have enough borrowings. Could we loan you four billion dollars?" I said, "I don't need it! I don't want it! And I've been there! I don't want it!"

But in two seconds, they give me whatever I wanted. So I have a total net worth—and now with the increase, it'll be well over ten billion dollars. But here, a total net worth of eight billion—net worth, not assets, not—a net worth, after all debt, after all expenses, the greatest assets—Trump Tower, 1290 Avenue of the Americas, Bank of America building in San Francisco, 40 Wall Street, sometimes referred to as the Trump building right opposite the New York [Stock Exchange]—many other places all over the world.

So the total is 8,737,540,000 dollars.

Now I'm not doing that . . . I'm not doing that to brag, because you know what? I don't have to brag. I don't have to, believe it or not.

I'm doing that to say that that's the kind of thinking our country needs. We need that thinking. We have the opposite thinking. We have losers. We have losers. We have people that don't have it. We have people that are morally corrupt. We have people that are selling this country down the drain.

So I put together this statement, and the only reason I'm telling you about it today is because we really do have to get going. Because if we have another three or four years—you know, we're at eight trillion now. We're soon going to be at twenty trillion dollars.

According to the economists—who I'm not big believers in, but nevertheless, this is what they're saying—that twenty-four trillion dollars—we're very close—that's the point of no return. Twenty-four trillion dollars. We will be there soon. That's when we become Greece. That's when we become a country that's unsalvageable. And we're gonna be there very soon. We're gonna be there very soon.

So just to sum up, I would do various things very quickly. I would repeal and replace the big lie, Obamacare.

I would build a great wall, and nobody builds walls better than me, believe me. And I'll build them very inexpensively. I will build a great, great wall on our southern border. And I will have Mexico pay for that wall.

Mark my words. Nobody would be tougher on ISIS than Donald Trump. Nobody.

I will find—within our military, I will find the General Patton, or I will find General MacArthur. I will find the right guy. I will find the guy that's going to take that military and make it really work. Nobody, nobody will be pushing us around.

I will stop Iran from getting nuclear weapons. And we won't be using a man like Secretary Kerry that has absolutely no concept of negotiation, who's making a horrible and laughable deal, who's just being tapped along as they make weapons right now, and then goes into a bicycle race at seventy-two years old, and falls and breaks his leg. I won't be doing that. And I promise I will never be in a bicycle race. That, I can tell you.

I will immediately terminate President Obama's illegal executive order on immigration. Immediately.

Fully support and back up the Second Amendment.

Now, it's very interesting. Today I heard it—through stupidity, in a very, very hard core prison, interestingly named Clinton—two vicious murderers, two vicious people escaped, and nobody knows where they are. And a woman was on television this morning, and she said, "You know, Mister Trump," and she was telling other people, and I actually called her, but she said, "You know, Mister Trump, I always was against guns. I didn't want guns. And now since this happened"—it's up in the prison area—"my husband and I are finally in agreement, because he wanted the guns. We now have a gun on every table. We're ready to start shooting."

I said, "Very interesting." So protect the Second Amendment.

End—end Common Core. Common Core should—it is a disaster. Bush is totally in favor of Common Core. I don't see how he can possibly get the nomination. He's weak on immigration. He's in favor of Common Core. How the hell can you vote for this guy? You just can't do it. We have to end—education has to be local.

Rebuild the country's infrastructure. Nobody can do that like me. Believe me. It will be done on time, on budget, way below cost, way below what anyone ever thought.

I look at these roads being built all over the country, and I say, "I can build those things for one-third." What they do is unbelievable. How bad.

You know, we're building on Pennsylvania Avenue—the Old Post Office, we're converting it into one of the world's great hotels. It's gonna be the best hotel in Washington, DC. We got it from the General Services Administration in Washington. The Obama administration. We got it. It was the most highly sought after—or one of them—but I think the most highly sought after project in the history of General Services. We got it. People were shocked Trump got it.

Well, I got it for two reasons. Number one, we're really good. Number two, we had a really good plan. And I'll add in the third: we had a great financial statement. Because the General Services—who are terrific people, by the way, and talented people—they wanted to do a great job. And they wanted to make sure it got built.

So we have to rebuild our infrastructure, our bridges, our roadways, our airports. You come into LaGuardia Airport, it's like we're in a Third World country. You look at the patches and the forty-year-old floor. They throw down asphalt, and they throw. . . . You look at these airports, we are like a Third World country. And I come in from China, and I come in from Qatar, and I come in from different places, and they have the most incredible airports in the world. You come to back to this country, and you have LAX—disaster. You have all of these disastrous airports. We have to rebuild our infrastructure.

Save Medicare, Medicaid, and Social Security without cuts. Have to do it.

Get rid of the fraud. Get rid of the waste and abuse, but save it. People have been paying it for years. And now many of these candidates want to cut it. You save it by making the United States—by making us rich again. By taking back all of the money that's being lost.

Renegotiate our foreign trade deals. Reduce our eighteen trillion dollars in debt, because believe me, we're in a bubble. We have artificially low interest rates. We have a stock market that frankly has been good to me. But I still hate to see what's happening. We have a stock market that is so bloated.

Be careful of a bubble, because what you've seen in the past might be small potatoes compared to what happens. So be very, very careful.

And strengthen our military, and take care of our vets. So, so important.

Sadly, the American dream is dead. But if I get elected president, I will bring it back bigger and better and stronger than ever before, and we will make America great again.

Thank you. Thank you very much.

Presidential Nomination Acceptance Speech

REPUBLICAN NATIONAL CONVENTION, CLEVELAND, OHIO

July 21, 2016

Friends, delegates, and fellow Americans:

I humbly and gratefully accept your nomination for the presidency of the United States. USA! USA! USA! USA!

Who would have believed that when we started this journey on June sixteenth, last year, we—I say *we* because we are a team—would have received almost fourteen million votes, the most in the history of the Republican Party and that the Republican Party would get sixty percent more votes than it received eight years ago. Who would have believed this? The Democrats, on the other hand, received twenty percent fewer votes than they got four years ago. Not so good. Not so good.

Together, we will lead our party back to the White House, and we will lead our country back to safety, prosperity, and peace. We will be a country of generosity and warmth. But we will also be a country of law and order.

Our convention occurs at a moment of crisis for our nation. The attacks on our police and the terrorism of our cities threaten our very way of life. Any politician who does not grasp this danger is not fit to lead our country.

Americans watching this address tonight have seen the recent images of violence in our streets and the chaos in our communities. Many have witnessed this violence personally. Some have even been its victims.

I have a message for all of you: The crime and violence that today afflicts our nation will soon—and I mean very soon—come to an end. Beginning on January twentieth of 2017, safety will be restored.

The most basic duty of government is to defend the lives of its citizens. Any government that fails to do so is a government unworthy to lead.

It is finally time for a straightforward assessment of the state of our nation. I will present the facts, plainly and honestly. We cannot afford to be so politically correct anymore.

So if you want to hear the corporate spin, the carefully crafted lies, and the media myths—the Democrats are holding their convention next week. Go there.

But here, at our convention, there will be no lies. We will honor the American people with the truth and nothing else.

These are the facts:

Decades of progress made in bringing down crime are now being reversed by this administration's rollback of criminal enforcement.

Homicides last year increased by seventeen percent in America's fifty largest cities. That's the largest increase in twenty-five years.

In our nation's capital, killings have risen by fifty percent. They are up nearly sixty percent in nearby Baltimore.

In the president's hometown of Chicago, more than two thousand people have been the victims of shootings this year alone. And almost four thousand have been killed in the Chicago area since he took office.

The number of police officers killed in the line of duty has risen by almost fifty percent compared to this point last year.

Nearly one hundred eighty thousand illegal immigrants with criminal records—ordered deported from our country—are tonight roaming free to threaten peaceful citizens.

The number of new illegal immigrant families who have crossed the border so far this year already exceeds the entire total of 2015.

They are being released by the tens of thousands into our communities, with no regard for the impact on public safety or resources.

One such border crosser was released and made his way to Nebraska. There, he ended the life of an innocent young girl named Sarah Root. She was twenty-one years old and was killed the day after graduating from college with a 4.0 grade point average—number one in her class. Her killer was then released a second time, and he is now a fugitive from the law. I've met Sarah's beautiful family. But to this administration, their amazing daughter was just one more American life that wasn't worth protecting. One more child to sacrifice on the altar of open borders.

What about our economy? Again, I will tell you the plain facts that have been edited out of your nightly news and your morning newspaper:

Nearly four in ten African American children are living in poverty, while fifty-eight percent of African American youth are now not employed.

Two million more Latinos are in poverty today than when President Obama took his oath of office less than eight years ago.

Another fourteen million people have left the workforce entirely.

Household incomes are down more than four thousand dollars since the year 2000. That is sixteen years ago.

Our trade deficit in goods reached—think of this—our trade deficit is eight hundred billion dollars. Think of that. Eight hundred billion dollars last year alone. We're gonna fix that.

The budget is no better. President Obama has almost doubled our national debt to more than nineteen trillion dollars, and growing.

Yet, what do we have to show for it? Our roads and bridges are falling apart, our airports are in Third World condition, and forty-three million Americans are on food stamps.

Now let us consider the state of affairs abroad. Not only have our citizens endured domestic disaster, but they have lived through one international humiliation after another. One after another.

We all remember the images of our sailors being forced to their knees by their Iranian captors at gunpoint. This was just prior to the signing of the Iran deal, which gave back to Iran one hundred fifty billion dollars and gave us absolutely nothing. It will go down in history as one of the worst deals ever negotiated.

Another humiliation came when President Obama drew a red line in Syria, and the whole world knew it meant absolutely nothing.

In Libya, our consulate—the symbol of American prestige around the globe—was brought down in flames.

America is far less safe, and the world is far less stable, than when Obama made the decision to put Hillary Clinton in charge of America's foreign policy. ["Lock her up!"] Let's defeat her in November, OK? I am certain that it was a decision that President Obama truly regrets.

Her bad instincts and her bad judgment—something pointed out by Bernie Sanders—are what caused so many of the disasters unfolding today. Let's review the record:

In 2009, pre-Hillary, ISIS was not even on the map. Libya was stable. Egypt was peaceful. Iraq was seeing really a big, big reduction in violence. Iran was being choked by sanctions. Syria was somewhat under control.

After four years of Hillary Clinton, what do we have? ISIS has spread across the region and the entire world. Libya is in ruins, and our ambassador and his staff were left helpless to die at the hands of savage killers. Egypt was turned over to the radical Muslim Brotherhood, forcing the military to retake control. Iraq is in chaos. Iran is on the path to nuclear weapons. Syria is engulfed in a civil war, and a refugee crisis now threatens the West. After fifteen years of wars in the Middle East, after trillions of dollars spent and thousands of lives lost, the situation is worse than it has ever been before.

This is the legacy of Hillary Clinton: death, destruction, terrorism, and weakness.

But Hillary Clinton's legacy does not have to be America's legacy. The problems we face now—poverty and violence at home, war and destruction abroad—will last only as long as we continue relying on the same politicians who created them in the first place. A change in leadership is required to produce a change in outcomes.

Tonight, I will share with you my plan for action for America. The most important difference between our plan and that of our opponents, is that our plan will put America first! Americanism, not globalism, will be our credo.

As long as we are led by politicians who will not put America first, then we can be assured that other nations will not treat America with respect—the respect that we deserve. The American people will come first once again.

My plan will begin with safety at home, which means safe neighborhoods, secure borders, and protection from terrorism. There can be no prosperity without law and order.

On the economy, I will outline reforms to add millions of new jobs and trillions in new wealth that can be used to rebuild America.

A number of these reforms that I will outline tonight will be opposed by some of our nation's most powerful special interests. That is because these interests have rigged our political and economic system for their exclusive benefit. Believe me, it is for their benefit.

Big business, elite media, and major donors are lining up behind the campaign of my opponent because they know she will keep our rigged system in place. They are throwing money at her because they have total control over every single thing she does. She is their puppet, and they pull the strings. That is why Hillary Clinton's message is that things will never change. Never ever.

My message is that things have to change, and they have to change right now. Every day, I wake up determined to deliver a better life for the people all across this nation that had been ignored, neglected, and abandoned.

I have visited the laid-off factory workers, and the communities crushed by our horrible and unfair trade deals. These are the forgotten men and women of our country. And they are forgotten, but but they're not gonna be forgotten long. These are people who work hard but no longer have a voice. I am your voice!

I have embraced crying mothers who have lost their children because our politicians put their personal agendas before the national good.

I have no patience for injustice. No tolerance for government incompetence, of which there is so much. No sympathy for leaders who fail their citizens. When innocent people suffer, because our political system lacks the will, or the courage, or the basic decency to enforce our laws—or still worse, has sold out to some corporate lobbyist for cash—I am not able to look the other way. And I won't look the other way.

And when a secretary of state illegally stores her emails on a private server, deletes thirty-three thousand of them so the authorities can't see her crime, puts our country at risk, lies about it in every different form, and faces no consequence—I know that corruption has reached a level like never ever before in our country.

When the FBI director says that the secretary of state was "extremely careless" and "negligent" in handling our classified secrets, I also know that these terms are minor compared to what she actually did. They were just used to save her from facing justice for her terrible, terrible crimes.

In fact, her single greatest accomplishment may be committing such an egregious crime and getting away with it, especially when others who have done far less have paid so dearly.

When that same secretary of state rakes in millions and millions of dollars trading access and favors to special interests and foreign powers, I know the time for action has come.

I have joined the political arena so that the powerful can no longer beat up on people who cannot defend themselves.

Nobody knows the system better than me, which is why I alone can fix it. I have seen firsthand how the system is rigged against our citizens, just like it was rigged against Bernie Sanders. He never had a chance.

But his supporters will join our movement, because we will fix his biggest single issue: trade deals that strip our country of its jobs and strip us of our wealth as a country.

Millions of Democrats will join our movement, because we are going to fix the system so it works fairly and justly for each and every American.

In this cause, I am proud to have at my side the next vice president of the United States: Governor Mike Pence of Indiana. And a great guy. We will bring the same economic success to America that Mike brought to Indiana, which is amazing. He is a man of character and accomplishment. He is the man for the job.

The first task for our new administration will be to liberate our citizens from the crime and terrorism and lawlessness that threatens our communities.

America was shocked to its core when our police officers in Dallas were so brutally executed. Immediately after Dallas, we have seen continued threats and violence against our law enforcement officials. Law officers have been shot or killed in recent days in Georgia, Missouri, Wisconsin, Kansas, Michigan, and Tennessee.

On Sunday, more police were gunned down in Baton Rouge, Louisiana. Three were killed, and three were very badly injured. An attack on law enforcement is an attack on all Americans.

I have a message to every last person threatening the peace on our streets and the safety of our police: When I take the oath of office next year, I will restore law and order to our country. Believe me. Believe me.

I will work with, and appoint, the best prosecutors and law enforcement officials in the country to get the job properly done. In this race for the White House, I am the law and order candidate.

The irresponsible rhetoric of our president, who has used the pulpit of the presidency to divide us by race and color has made America a more dangerous environment than, frankly, I have ever seen, and anybody in this room has ever watched or seen.

This administration has failed America's inner cities. Remember, it has failed America's inner cities. It's failed them on education. It's failed them on jobs. It's failed them on crime. It's failed them in every way and on every single level.

When I am president, I will work to ensure that all of our kids are treated equally and protected equally. Every action I take, I will ask myself: Does this make life better for young Americans in Baltimore, in Chicago, in Detroit, and in Ferguson, who have really, in every way, folks, the same right to live out their dreams as any other child in America? Any other child?

To make life safe for all of our citizens, we must also address the growing threats we face from outside the country. We are going to defeat the barbarians of ISIS. And we are going to defeat them fast.

Once again, France is the victim of brutal Islamic terrorism. Men, women, and children viciously mowed down. Lives ruined. Families ripped apart. A nation in mourning. The damage and devastation that can be inflicted by Islamic radicals has been proven over and over. At the World Trade Center, at an office party in San Bernardino, at the Boston Marathon, at a military recruiting center in Chattanooga, Tennessee. And many, many other locations.

Only weeks ago, in Orlando, Florida, forty-nine wonderful Americans were savagely murdered by an Islamic terrorist. This time, the terrorist targeted the LGBTQ community.

No good. And we're going to stop it. As your president, I will do everything in my power to protect our LGBTQ citizens from the violence and oppression of a hateful foreign ideology. Believe me.

And I have to say, as a Republican, it is so nice to hear you cheering for what I just said. Thank you.

To protect us from terrorism, we need to focus on three things.

We must have the best—absolutely the best—gathering of intelligence anywhere in the world. The best.

We must abandon the failed policy of nation-building and regime change that Hillary Clinton pushed in Iraq, Libya, in Egypt, and Syria.

Instead, we must work with all of our allies who share our goal of destroying ISIS and stamping out Islamic terrorism and doing it now, doing it quickly. We're going to win. We're going to win fast. This includes working with our greatest ally in the region, the State of Israel.

Recently, I have said that NATO was obsolete because it did not properly cover terror, and also that many of the member countries were not paying their fair share. As usual, the United States has been picking up the cost. Shortly thereafter, it was announced that NATO will be setting up a new program in order to combat terrorism. A true step in the right direction.

Lastly, and very importantly, we must immediately suspend immigration from any nation that has been compromised by terrorism until such time as proven vetting mechanisms have been put in place. We don't want them in our country!

My opponent has called for a radical five hundred fifty percent increase—think of this . . . this is not believable, but this is what is happening—a five hundred fifty percent increase in Syrian refugees, on top of existing massive refugee flows coming into our country already, under the leadership of President Obama.

She proposes this despite the fact that there's no way to screen these refugees in order to find out who they are or where they come from. I only want to admit individuals into our country who will support our values and love our people! Anyone who endorses violence, hatred, or oppression is not welcome in our country, and never ever will be!

Decades of record immigration have produced lower wages and higher unemployment for our citizens, especially for African American and Latino workers. We are going to have an immigration system that works, but one that works for the American people.

On Monday, we heard from three parents whose children were killed by illegal immigrants: Mary Ann Mendoza, Sabine Durden, and my friend Jamiel Shaw. They are just three brave representatives of many thousands who have suffered so gravely.

Of all my travels in this country, nothing has affected me more—nothing even close, I have to tell you—than the time I have spent with the mothers and fathers who have lost their children to violence spilling across our borders, which we can solve. We have to solve it. These families have no special interests to represent them. There are no demonstrators to protect them, and certainly none to protest on their behalf.

My opponent will never meet with them or share in their pain. Believe me. Instead, my opponent wants sanctuary cities. But where was sanctuary for Kate Steinle? Where was sanctuary for the children of Mary Ann, and Sabine, and Jamiel? Where was the sanctuary for all of the other—oh, it's so sad to even be talking about this. We can solve it so quickly. Where was sanctuary for all the other Americans who have been so brutally murdered, and who have suffered so horribly? These wounded American families have been alone, but they are not alone any longer.

Tonight, this candidate, and this whole nation, stand in their corner to support them, to send them our love, and to pledge in their honor that we will save countless more families from suffering and the same awful fate.

We are going to build a great border wall to stop illegal immigration, to stop the gangs and the violence, and to stop the drugs from pouring into our communities.

I have been honored to receive the endorsement of America's Border Patrol agents and will work directly with them to protect the integrity of our lawful, lawful, lawful immigration system. Lawful.

By ending catch-and-release on the border, we will stop the cycle of human smuggling and violence. Illegal border crossings will go down. We will stop it. It won't be happening very much anymore. Believe me.

Peace will be restored by enforcing the rules for the millions who overstay their visas. Our laws will finally receive the respect that they deserve.

Tonight, I want every American whose demands for immigration security have been denied, and every politician who has denied them, to listen very, very closely to the words I am about to say: On January twentieth of 2017, the day I take the oath of office, Americans will finally wake up in a country where the laws of the United States are enforced.

We are going to be considerate and compassionate to everyone. But my greatest compassion will be for our own struggling citizens. USA! USA! USA! USA!

My plan is the exact opposite of the radical and dangerous immigration policy of Hillary Clinton. Americans want relief from uncontrolled immigration, which is what we have now. Communities want relief. Yet Hillary Clinton is proposing mass amnesty, mass immigration, and mass lawlessness.

Her plan will overwhelm your schools and hospitals, further reduce your jobs and wages, and make it harder for recent immigrants to escape the tremendous cycle of poverty they are going through right now, and make it almost impossible for them to join the middle class.

I have a different vision for our workers. It begins with a new, fair trade policy that protects our jobs and stands up to countries that cheat—of which there are many.

It's been a signature message of my campaign from day one, and it will be a signature feature of my presidency from the moment I take the oath of office. I have made billions of dollars in business making deals. Now I'm going to make our country rich again. Using the greatest businesspeople in the world—which our country has—I'm going to turn our bad trade agreements into great trade agreements.

America has lost nearly one-third of its manufacturing jobs since 1997, following the enactment of disastrous trade deals supported by Bill and Hillary Clinton. Remember, it was Bill Clinton who signed NAFTA, one of the worst economic deals ever made by our country or frankly, any other country. Never ever again.

I am going to bring our jobs back our jobs to Ohio and Pennsylvania and New York and Michigan and all of America, and I am not going to let companies move to other countries, firing their employees along the way, without consequence. Not going to happen anymore.

My opponent, on the other hand, has supported virtually every trade agreement that has been destroying our middle class. She supported NAFTA, and she supported China's entrance into the World Trade Organization—another one of her husband's colossal mistakes and disasters. She supported the job-killing trade deal with South Korea. She supported the Trans-Pacific Partnership, which will not only destroy our manufacturing, but it will make America subject to the rulings of foreign governments. And it is not going to happen.

I pledge to never sign any trade agreement that hurts our workers or that diminishes our freedom and independence. We will never ever sign bad trade deals. America first again! American first!

Instead, I will make individual deals with individual countries. No longer will we enter into these massive transactions with many countries that are thousands of pages long, and which no one from our country even reads or understands. We are going to enforce all trade violations against any country that cheats. This includes stopping China's outrageous theft of intellectual property, along with their illegal product dumping, and their devastating currency manipulation. They are the greatest that ever came about. They are the greatest currency manipulators ever.

Our horrible trade agreements with China, and many others, will be totally renegotiated. That includes renegotiating NAFTA to get a much better deal for America, and we will walk away if we don't get that kind of a deal. Our country is going to start building and making things again.

Next comes the reform of our tax laws, regulations, and energy rules. While Hillary Clinton plans a massive—and I mean massive—tax increase, I have proposed the largest tax reduction of any candidate who has run for president this year, Democrat or Republican. Middle-income Americans will experience profound relief, and taxes will be greatly simplified for everyone. I mean everyone.

America is one of the highest taxed nations in the world. Reducing taxes will cause new companies and new jobs to come roaring back into our country. Believe me. It will happen, and it will happen fast.

Then we are going to deal with the issue of regulation, one of the greatest job killers of them all. Excessive regulation is costing our country as much as two trillion dollars a year, and we will end it very quickly.

We are going to lift the restrictions on the production of American energy. This will produce more than twenty trillion dollars in job-creating economic activity over the next four decades.

My opponent, on the other hand, wants to put the great miners and steelworkers of our country out of work and out of business. That will never happen with Donald J. Trump as president. Our steelworkers and our miners are going back to work again.

With these new economic policies, trillions of dollars will start flowing into our country. This new wealth will improve the quality of life for all Americans. We will build the roads, highways, bridges, tunnels, airports, and the railways of our tomorrow. This, in turn, will create millions of more jobs.

We will rescue kids from failing schools by helping their parents send them to a safe school of their choice. My opponent would rather protect bureaucrats than serve American children. That is what she is doing, and that is what she has done.

We will repeal and replace disastrous Obamacare. You will be able to choose your own doctor again.

And we will fix TSA at the airports, which is a total disaster.

We are going to work with all of our students who are drowning in debt, to take the pressure off these young people just starting out in their adult lives. Tremendous problem.

We will completely rebuild our depleted military. And the countries that we are protecting at a massive cost to us will be asked to pay their fair share.

We will take care of our great veterans like they have never been taken care of before. My just-released ten-point plan has received tremendous veteran support. We will guarantee those who serve this country will be able to visit the doctor or hospital of their choice without waiting five days on a line and dying.

My opponent dismissed the VA scandal—one more sign of how out of touch she really is.

We are going to ask every department head in government to provide a list of wasteful spending projects that we can eliminate in my first one hundred days. The politicians have talked about this for years, but I'm going to do it. [Yes you will!]

We are going to appoint justices of the United States Supreme Court, who will uphold our laws and our Constitution. The replacement of our beloved Justice Scalia will be a person of similar views, principles, and judicial philosophies. Very important. This will be one of the most important issues decided by this election.

My opponent wants to essentially abolish the Second Amendment. I, on the other hand, received the early and strong endorsement of the National Rifle Association and will protect the right of all Americans to keep their families safe.

At this moment, I would like to thank the evangelical and religious community because—I will tell you what—the support that they have given me—and I'm not sure I totally deserve it—has been so amazing, and has had such a big reason for me being here tonight. True. So true. They have much to contribute to our politics, yet our laws prevent you from speaking your minds from your own pulpits. An amendment, pushed by Lyndon Johnson, many years ago, threatens religious institutions with a loss of their tax-exempt status if they openly advocate their political views. Their voice has been taken away. I am going to work very hard to repeal that language and to protect free speech for all Americans.

We can accomplish these great things and so much more. All we need to do is start believing in ourselves and in our country again. Start believing. It is time to show the whole world that America is back, bigger and better and stronger than ever before.

In this journey, I'm so lucky to have at my side, my wife, Melania, and my wonderful children, Don, Ivanka, Eric, Tiffany, and Barron. You will always be my greatest source of pride and joy. And by the way, Melania and Ivanka, did they do a job?

My dad, Fred Trump, was the smartest and hardest-working man I ever knew. I wonder sometimes what he'd say if he were here to see this and to see me tonight. It's because of him that I learned, from my youngest age, to respect the dignity of work and the dignity of working people.

He was a guy most comfortable in the company of bricklayers, and carpenters, and electricians, and I have a lot of that in me also. I love those people.

Then there's my mother, Mary. She was strong, but also warm and fair-minded. She was a truly great mother. She was also one of the most honest and charitable people that I have ever known, and a great, great judge of character. She could pick them out from anywhere.

To my sisters, Mary Anne and Elizabeth, my brother Robert, and my late brother, Fred: I will always give you my love. You are most special to me.

I have loved my life in business. But now, my sole and exclusive mission is to go to work for our country, to go to work for you. It is time to deliver a victory for the American people. We don't win anymore, but we are going to start winning again! But to do that, we must break free from the petty politics of the past.

America is a nation of believers, dreamers, and strivers that is being led by a group of censors, critics, and cynics. Remember, all of the people telling you, you can't have the country you want, are the same people that wouldn't stand, I mean, they said Trump doesn't have a chance of being here tonight. Not a chance—the same people. Oh, we love defeating those people, don't we? Don't we love defeating those people? Love it, love it, love it.

No longer can we rely on those same people in the media and politics, who will say anything to keep our rigged system in place. Instead, we must choose to believe in America.

We don't have much time, but history is watching. It's waiting to see if we will rise to the occasion, and if we will show the whole world that America is still free and independent and strong.

I am asking for your support tonight so that I can be your champion in the White House. And I will be your champion.

My opponent asks her supporters to recite a three-word loyalty pledge. It reads: "I'm with her."

I choose to recite a different pledge. My pledge reads: "I'm with you, the American people."

I am your voice. So to every parent who dreams for their child, and every child who dreams for their future, I say these words to you tonight: I am with you, and I will fight for you, and I will win for you.

To all Americans tonight, in all of our cities and all of our towns, I make this promise:

We will make America strong again.

We will make America proud again.

We will make America safe again.

And we will make America great again!

God bless you, and goodnight! I love you!

Presidential Victory Speech

HILTON HOTEL, NEW YORK CITY, NEW YORK

November 9, 2016

Thank you. Thank you very much, everybody. Sorry to keep you waiting. Complicated business. Complicated. Thank you very much.

I've just received a call from Secretary Clinton. She congratulated us—it's about us—on our victory. And I congratulated her and her family on a very, very hard-fought campaign. I mean, she fought very hard. Hillary has worked very long and very hard over a long period of time, and we owe her a major debt of gratitude for her service to our country. I mean that very sincerely.

Now it is time for America to bind the wounds of division. Have to get together. To all Republicans and Democrats and Independents across this nation, I say it is time for us to come together as one united people. It is time.

I pledge to every citizen of our land that I will be president for all Americans, and this is so important to me. For those who have chosen not to support me in the past—of which there were a few people—I'm reaching out to you for your guidance and your help so that we can work together and unify our great country.

As I've said from the beginning, ours was not a campaign but rather an incredible and great movement made up of millions of hard-working men and women who love their country and want a better, brighter future for themselves and for their family.

It is a movement comprised of Americans from all races, religions, backgrounds, and beliefs, who want and expect our government to serve the people—and serve the people it will.

Working together, we will begin the urgent task of rebuilding our nation and renewing the American dream. I've spent my entire life in business, looking at the untapped potential in projects and in people, all over the world.

That is now what I want to do for our country. Tremendous potential. I've gotten to know our country so well. Tremendous potential. It is going to be a beautiful thing. Every single American will have the opportunity to realize his or her fullest potential.

The forgotten men and women of our country will be forgotten no longer.

We are going to fix our inner cities and rebuild our highways, bridges, tunnels, airports, schools, hospitals. We're going to rebuild our infrastructure, which will become, by the way, second to none. And we will put millions of our people to work as we rebuild it.

We will also finally take care of our great veterans, who have been so loyal, and I've gotten to know so many over this eighteen-month journey. The time I've spent with them during this campaign has been among my greatest honors. Our veterans are incredible people.

We will embark upon a project of national growth and renewal. I will harness the creative talents of our people, and we will call upon the best and brightest to leverage their tremendous talent for the benefit of all. It is going to happen.

We have a great economic plan. We will double our growth and have the strongest economy anywhere in the world. At the same time, we will get along with all other nations willing to get along with us. We will be. We will have great relationships. We expect to have great, great relationships.

No dream is too big, no challenge is too great. Nothing we want for our future is beyond our reach.

America will no longer settle for anything less than the best. We must reclaim our country's destiny and dream big and bold and daring. We have to do that. We're going to dream of things for our country—and beautiful things and successful things—once again.

I want to tell the world community that, while we will always put America's interests first, we will deal fairly with everyone, with everyone. All people and all other nations.

We will seek common ground, not hostility. Partnership, not conflict.

And now, I would like to take this moment to thank some of the people who really helped me with this, what they are calling tonight a very, very historic victory.

First, I want to thank my parents, who I know are looking down on me right now. Great people. I've learned so much from them. They were wonderful in every regard. I had truly great parents.

I also want to thank my sisters, Marianne and Elizabeth, who are here with us tonight. Where are they? They're here someplace. They're very shy, actually.

And my brother Robert, my great friend. Where is Robert? Where is Robert? My brother Robert.

And they should all be on this stage, but that's OK. They're great.

And also, my late brother, Fred. Great guy. Fantastic guy. Fantastic family. I was very lucky.

Great brothers, sisters. Great, unbelievable parents.

To Melania, and Don, and Ivanka, and Eric, and Tiffany, and Barron: I love you, and I thank you. And especially for putting up with all of those hours. This was tough. This was tough. This political stuff is nasty, and it is tough.

So I want to thank my family very much. Really fantastic. Thank you all. Thank you all. Lara, unbelievable job. Unbelievable. Vanessa, thank you. Thank you very much. What a great group.

You've all given me such incredible support, and I will tell you that we have a large group of people. You know, they kept saying we have a small staff. Not so small. Look at all of the people that we have. Look at all of these people.

And Kellyanne, and Chris, and Rudy, and Steve, and David. We have got tremendously talented people up here, and I want to tell you it's been very, very special.

I want to give a very special thanks to our former mayor, Rudy Giuliani. He's unbelievable. Unbelievable. He traveled with us, and he went through meetings, and Rudy never changes. Where is Rudy. Where is he?

Governor Chris Christie, folks, was unbelievable. Thank you, Chris. The first man, first senator, first major, major politician. Let me tell you, he is highly respected in Washington, because he is as smart as you get. Senator Jeff Sessions. Where is Jeff? A great man. Another great man. Very tough competitor. He was not easy. He was not easy. Who is that? Is that the mayor that showed up? Oh, Rudy got up here.

Another great man who has been really a friend to me. But I'll tell you, I got to know him as a competitor, because he was one of the folks that was negotiating to go against those Democrats— Doctor Ben Carson. Where's Ben? Where is Ben? By the way, Mike Huckabee is here someplace, and he is fantastic. Mike and his family, Sarah, thank you very much. General Mike Flynn. Where is Mike? And General Kellogg. We have over two hundred generals and admirals that have endorsed our campaign, and they are special people, and it's really an honor.

We have twenty-two Congressional Medal of Honor recipients. We have just tremendous people. A very special person who—believe me, I'd read reports that I wasn't getting along with him. I never had a bad second with him. He's an unbelievable star. He is . . . that's right. How did you possibly guess? So let me tell you about Reince. I've said, "Reince—" and I know it. I know it. Look at all of those people over there. I know, "because you can't be called a superstar, like Secretariat. If Secretariat came in second, Secretariat would not have that big beautiful bronze bust at the track at Belmont."

But I'll tell you Reince is really a star, and he is the hardest-working guy. And in a certain way, I did this. Reince, come up here. Where is Reince? Get over here, Reince.

Boy, oh boy, oh boy. It's about time you did this, Reince. My God. Say a few words. Nah, come here. Say something. [Reince Priebus offers brief remarks.]

Amazing guy. Our partnership with the RNC was so important to the success and what we've done, so I also have to say, I've gotten to know some incredible people. The Secret Service people. They're tough, and they're smart, and they're sharp, and I don't want to mess around with them, I can tell you. And when I want to go and wave to a big group of people and they rip me down and put me back down in the seat—but they are fantastic people, so I want to thank the Secret Service.

And law enforcement in New York City, they're here tonight. These are spectacular people. Sometimes underappreciated, unfortunately, but we appreciate them. We know what they go through.

So it's been what they call a "historic event." But to be really historic, we have to do a great job, and I promise you that I will not let you down. We will do a great job. We will do a great job. I look very much forward to being your president, and hopefully at the end of two years, or three years, or four years, or maybe even eight years—you will say so many of you worked so hard for us, you will say that—you will say that that was something that you were—really were very proud to do, and I can only say that while the campaign is over, our work on this movement is now really just beginning. We're going to get to work immediately for the American people, and we're going to be doing a job that hopefully you will be so proud of your president. You will be so proud. Again, it's my honor.

It's an amazing evening. It's been an amazing two-year period, and I love this country. Thank you.

Thank you very much. Thank you to Mike Pence.

Inaugural Address

WASHINGTON, DC

January 20, 2017

Chief Justice Roberts, President Carter, President Clinton, President Bush, President Obama, fellow Americans, and people of the world:

Thank you. We the citizens of America are now joined in a great national effort to rebuild our country and restore its promise for all of our people. Together, we will determine the course of America, and the world, for many, many years to come. We will face challenges. We will confront hardships, but we will get the job done.

Every four years, we gather on these steps to carry out the orderly and peaceful transfer of power, and we are grateful to President Obama and First Lady Michelle Obama for their gracious aid throughout this transition. They have been magnificent. Thank you.

Today's ceremony, however, has very special meaning, because today we are not merely transferring power from one administration to another, or from one party to another, but we are transferring power from Washington, DC, and giving it back to you, the people.

For too long, a small group in our nation's capital has reaped the rewards of government, while the people have borne the cost. Washington flourished, but the people did not share in its wealth. Politicians prospered, but the jobs left and the factories closed. The establishment protected itself, but not the citizens of our country. Their victories have not been your victories. Their triumphs have not been your triumphs. And while they celebrated in our nation's capital, there was little to celebrate for struggling families all across our land. That all changes, starting right here and right now, because this moment is your moment—it belongs to you. It belongs to everyone gathered here today, and everyone watching all across America. This is your day. This is your celebration, and this, the United States of America, is your country.

What truly matters is not which party controls our government, but whether our government is controlled by the people. January 20th, 2017, will be remembered as the day the people became the rulers of this nation again. The forgotten men and women of our country will be forgotten no longer. Everyone is listening to you now. You came by the tens of millions to become part of a historic movement, the likes of which the world has never seen before. At the center of this movement is a crucial conviction that a nation exists to serve its citizens. Americans want great schools for their children, safe neighborhoods for their families, and good jobs for themselves. These are just and reasonable demands of righteous people and a righteous public, but for too many of our citizens a different reality exists. Mothers and children trapped in poverty in our inner cities; rusted-out factories scattered like tombstones across the across the landscape of our nation; an education system flush with cash, but which leaves our young and beautiful students deprived of all knowledge; and the crime, and the gangs, and the drugs that have stolen too many lives and robbed our country of so much unrealized potential. This American carnage stops right here and stops right now.

We are one nation, and their pain is our pain. Their dreams are our dreams, and their success will be our success. We share one heart, one home, and one glorious destiny. The Oath of Office I take today is an oath of allegiance to all Americans. For many decades, we've enriched foreign industry at the expense of American industry, subsidized the armies of other countries while allowing for the very sad depletion of our military. We've defended other nations' borders while refusing to defend our own. And spent trillions and trillions of dollars overseas, while America's infrastructure has fallen into disrepair and decay. We've made other countries rich, while the wealth, strength, and confidence of our country has dissipated over the horizon. One by one, the factories shuddered and left our shores, with not even a thought about the millions and millions of American workers that were left behind. The wealth of our middle class has been ripped from their homes and then redistributed all across the world.

But that is the past, and now we are looking only to the future. We assembled here today are issuing a new decree to be heard in every city, in every foreign capital, and in every hall of power. From this day forward, a new vision will govern our land. From this day forward, it's going to be only America first. America first.

Every decision on trade, on taxes, on immigration, on foreign affairs will be made to benefit American workers and American families. We must protect our borders from the ravages of other countries making our products, stealing our companies, and destroying our jobs. Protection will lead to great prosperity and strength. I will fight for you with every breath in my body, and I will never, ever let you down. America will start winning again—winning like never before. We will bring back our jobs. We will bring back our borders. We will bring back our wealth, and we will bring back our dreams. We will build new roads, and highways, and bridges, and airports, and tunnels, and railways, all across our wonderful nation. We will get our people off of welfare and back to work, rebuilding our country with American hands and American labor.

We will follow two simple rules: buy American, and hire American. We will seek friendship and goodwill with the nations of the world, but we do so with the understanding that it is the right of all nations to put their own interests first. We do not seek to impose our way of life on anyone, but rather to let it shine as an example. We will shine for everyone to follow. We will reinforce old alliances and form new ones, and unite the civilized world against radical Islamic terrorism, which we will eradicate completely from the face of the earth.

At the bedrock of our politics will be a total allegiance to the United States of America, and through our loyalty to our country, we will rediscover our loyalty to each other. When you open your heart to patriotism, there is no room for prejudice. The Bible tells us how good and pleasant it is when God's people live together in unity. We must speak our minds openly, debate our disagreements, but always pursue solidarity. When America is united, America is totally unstoppable. There should be no fear. We are protected, and we will always be protected. We will be protected by the great men and women of our military and law enforcement. And most importantly, we will be protected by God.

Finally, we must think big and dream even bigger. In America, we understand that a nation is only living as long as it is striving. We will no longer accept politicians who are all talk and no action, constantly complaining but never doing anything about it. The time for empty talk is over. Now arrives the hour of action. Do not allow anyone to tell you that it cannot be done. No challenge can match the heart and fight and spirit of America. We will not fail. Our country will thrive and prosper again.

We stand at the birth of a new millennium, ready to unlock the mysteries of space, to free the earth from the miseries of disease, and to harness the energies, industries, and technologies of tomorrow. A new national pride will stir our souls, lift our sights, and heal our divisions. It's time to remember that old wisdom our soldiers will never forget—that whether we are black, or brown, or white, we all bleed the same red blood of patriots. We all enjoy the same glorious freedoms, and we all salute the same, great American flag. And whether a child is born in the urban sprawl of Detroit or the windswept plains of Nebraska, they look up at the at the same night sky, they fill their heart with the same dreams, and they are infused with the breath of life by the same almighty creator.

So to all Americans, in every city near and far, small and large, from mountain to mountain, from ocean to ocean: hear these words: You will never be ignored again. Your voice, your hopes, and your dreams will define our American destiny. And your courage and goodness and love will forever guide us along the way. Together, we will make America strong again.

We will make America wealthy again.

We will make America proud again.

We will make America safe again.

And, yes, together, we will make America great again.

Thank you. God bless you. And God bless America. Thank you. God bless America.

The Unbreakable Spirit of the Jewish People

ISRAEL MUSEUM, JERUSALEM, ISRAEL

May 23, 2017

Thank you to Prime Minister Netanyahu. And I also want to thank Sara for hosting us last night in really a very unforgettable dinner. We had a great time. We talked about a lot of very, very important things. And thank you to Ambassador David Friedman and Mrs. Friedman for joining us, along with a number of very good friends who have come from our country to yours as we reaffirm the unshakable bond between the United States of America and Israel. Thank you.

It is a privilege to stand here in this national museum, in the ancient city of Jerusalem, to address the Israeli people—and all people in the Middle East who yearn for security, prosperity, and peace.

Jerusalem is a sacred city. Its beauty, splendor, and heritage are like no other place on earth. The ties. What a heritage. What a heritage.

The ties of the Jewish people to this Holy Land are ancient and eternal. They date back thousands of years, including the reign of King David, whose star now flies proudly on Israel's white and blue flag.

Yesterday, I visited the Western Wall and marveled at the monument to God's presence and man's perseverance. I was humbled to place my hand upon the wall and to pray in that holy space for wisdom from God.

I also visited and prayed at the Church of the Holy Sepulchre, a site revered by Christians throughout the world. I laid a wreath at Yad Vashem, honoring, remembering, and mourning the six million Jews who were murdered in the Holocaust. I pledged right then and there what I pledge again today: The words "never again!"

Israel is a testament to the unbreakable spirit of the Jewish people. From all parts of this great country, one message resounds—and that is the message of hope.

Down through the ages, the Jewish people have suffered persecution, oppression, and even those who have sought their destruction. But through it all, they have endured—and in fact they have thrived.

I stand in awe of the accomplishments of the Jewish people, and I make this promise to you: My administration will always stand with Israel.

Through your hardships, you have created one of the most abundant lands anywhere in the world. A land that is rich not only in history, culture, and opportunity, but especially in spirit.

This museum, where we are gathered today, tells the story of that spirit—from the two holy temples to the glorious heights of Masada, we see an incredible story of faith and perseverance. That faith is what inspired Jews to believe in their destiny, to overcome their despair, and to build—right here—a future that others dared not even to dream.

In Israel, not only are Jews free to till the soil, teach their children, and pray to God in the ancient land of their fathers—and they love this land, and they love God—but Muslims, Christians, and people of all faiths are free to live and worship according to their conscience, and to follow their dreams right here.

Today, gathered with friends, I call upon all people—Jews, Christians, Muslims, and every faith, every tribe, every creed—to draw inspiration from this ancient city, to set aside our sectarian differences, to overcome oppression and hatred, and to give all children the freedom and hope and dignity written into our souls.

Earlier this week, I spoke at a very historic summit in Saudi Arabia. I was hosted by King Salman, a very wise man. There,

I urged our friends in the Muslim world to join us in creating stability, safety, and security. And I was deeply encouraged by the desire of many leaders to join us in cooperation toward these shared and vital goals. Conflict cannot continue forever—the only question is when nations will decide that they have had enough—enough bloodshed, enough killing.

That historic summit represents a new opportunity for people throughout the Middle East to overcome sectarian and religious divisions, to extinguish the fires of extremism and to find common ground and shared responsibility in making the future of this region so much better than it is right now. Change must come from within. It can *only* come from within.

No mother or father wants their children to grow up in a world where terrorists roam free, schoolchildren are murdered, and their loved ones are taken. No child is born with prejudice in their heart. No one should teach young boys and girls to hate and to kill.

No civilized nation can tolerate the massacre of innocents with chemical weapons.

My message to that summit was the same message I have for you: We must build a coalition of partners who share the aim of stamping out extremism and violence—and providing our children a peaceful and hopeful future.

But a hopeful future for children in the Middle East requires the world to fully recognize the vital role of the State of Israel. And on behalf of the United States, we pledge to stand by you and defend our shared values, so that together we can defeat terrorism and create safety for all of God's children.

Israelis have experienced firsthand the hatred and terror of radical violence. Israelis are murdered by terrorists wielding knives and bombs. Hamas and Hezbollah launch rockets into Israeli communities where schoolchildren have to be trained to hear the sirens and to run to the bomb shelters not with fear but with speed. ISIS targets Jewish neighborhoods, synagogues, and storefronts. And Iran's leaders routinely call for Israel's destruction. Not with Donald J. Trump. Believe me.

Despite these challenges, Israel is thriving as a sovereign nation—and no international body should question the contributions Israel makes to the region and indeed the world.

Today, let us pray for that peace—and for a more hopeful future across the Middle East.

There are those who present a false choice. They say that we must choose between supporting Israel and supporting Arab and Muslim nations in the region. That is completely wrong. All decent people want to live in peace, and all humanity is threatened by the evils of terrorism. Diverse nations can unite around the goal of protecting innocent life, upholding human dignity, and promoting peace and stability in the region. My administration is committed to pursuing such a coalition, and we have already made substantial progress during this trip.

We know, for instance, that both Israelis and Palestinians seek lives of hope for their children. And we know that peace is possible if we put aside the pain and disagreements of the past, and commit together to finally resolving this crisis which, has dragged on for nearly half a century or more.

As I have repeatedly said, I am personally committed to helping Israelis and Palestinians achieve a peace agreement. And I had a meeting this morning with President Abbas and can tell you that the Palestinians are ready to reach for peace. I know you've heard it before. I am telling you—that's what I do—they are ready to reach for peace. In my meeting with my very good friend, Benjamin, I can tell you also that he is reaching for peace. He wants peace. He loves people. He especially loves the Israeli people. Benjamin Netanyahu wants peace.

Making peace, however, will not be easy. We all know that. Both sides will face tough decisions. But with determination, compromise, and the belief that peace is possible, Israelis and Palestinians can make a deal. But even as we work toward peace, we will build strength to defend our nations.

The United States is firmly committed to keep Iran from developing a nuclear weapon and halting their support of terrorists and militias. So we are telling you, right now, that Iran will not have nuclear weapons.

America's security partnership with Israel is stronger than ever. Under my administration, you see the difference. Big, big, beautiful difference—including the Iron Dome missile-defense program, which has been keeping the Israeli people safe from short-range rockets launched by Hezbollah and Hamas, and David's sling, which guards against long-range missiles. It is my hope that someday very soon, Israeli children will never need to rush towards shelters again as sirens ring out loud and clear.

Finally, the United States is proud that Israeli Air Force pilots are flying the incredible new American F-35 planes. There is nothing in the world like them to defend their nation. And it was wonderful to see these mighty aircraft in the skies over Israel recently as you celebrated the sixty-ninth anniversary of Israel's independence.

But even as we strengthen our partnership in practice, let us always remember our highest ideals. Let us never forget that the bond between our two nations is woven together in the hearts of our people—and their love of freedom, hope, and dignity for every man and every woman.

Let us dream of a future where Jewish, Muslim, and Christian children can grow up together and live together in trust, harmony, tolerance, and respect. The values that are practiced in Israel have inspired millions and millions of people all across the world.

The conviction of Theodor Herzl rings true today: "Whatever we attempt there for our own benefit will redound mightily and beneficially to the good of all mankind."

As we stand in Jerusalem, we see pilgrims of all faiths coming to this land to walk on this hallowed ground.

Jews place the prayers from their hearts, in the stone blocks of the beautiful Western Wall.

Christians pray in the pews of an ancient church.

Muslims answer the call to prayer at their holy sites.

This city, like no other place in the world, reveals the longing of human hearts—to know and to worship God.

Jerusalem stands as a reminder that life can flourish against any odds.

When we look around this city, so beautiful, and we see people of all faiths engaged in reverent worship, and schoolchildren learning side by side, and men and women lifting up the needy and forgotten, we see that God's promise of healing has brought goodness to so many lives. We see that the people of this land had the courage to overcome the oppression and injustice of the past—and to live in the freedom God intends for every person on this earth.

Today, in Jerusalem, we pray and we hope that children around the world will be able to live without fear, to dream without limits, and to prosper without violence. I ask this land of promise to join with me to fight our common enemies, to pursue our shared values, and to protect the dignity of every child of God.

Thank you. God bless you. God bless the State of Israel. And God bless the United States. Thank you very much. Thank you. Thank you.

Poland Lives, Poland Prospers, and Poland Prevails

KRASIŃSKI SQUARE, WARSAW, POLAND

July 6, 2017

Melania is the best ambassador. We've come to your nation to deliver a very important message: America loves Poland, and America loves the Polish people.

The Poles have not only greatly enriched this region, but Polish Americans have also greatly enriched the United States. And I was truly proud to have their support in the 2016 election.

It is a profound honor to stand in this city, by this monument to the Warsaw Uprising, and to address the Polish nation that so many generations have dreamed of—a Poland that is safe, strong, and free.

President Duda and your wonderful First Lady, Agata, have welcomed us with the tremendous warmth and kindness for which Poland is known around the world. Thank you. My sincere—and I mean sincerely thank both of them. And to Prime Minister Szydlo, a very special thanks also.

We are also pleased that former president Lech Wałęsa so famous for leading the Solidarity movement, has joined us today, also. Thank you. Thank you. Thank you.

On behalf of all Americans, let me also thank the entire Polish people for the generosity you have shown in welcoming our soldiers to your country. These soldiers are not only brave defenders of freedom but also symbols of America's commitment to your security and your place in a strong and democratic Europe.

We are proudly joined on stage by American, Polish, British, and Romanian soldiers. Thank you. Thank you. Great job.

President Duda and I have just come from an incredibly successful meeting with the leaders participating in the Three Seas Initiative. To the citizens of this great region, America is eager to expand our partnership with you. We welcome stronger ties of trade and commerce as you grow your economies. And we are committed to securing your access to alternate sources of energy so Poland and its neighbors are never again held hostage to a single supplier of energy.

Mister President, I congratulate you, along with the president of Croatia, on your leadership of this historic Three Seas Initiative. Thank you.

This is my first visit to Central Europe as president, and I am thrilled that it could be right here at this magnificent, beautiful piece of land. It is beautiful. Poland is the geographic heart of Europe. But more importantly, in the Polish people, we see the soul of Europe. Your nation is great because your spirit is great and your spirit is strong.

For two centuries, Poland suffered constant and brutal attacks. But while Poland could be invaded and occupied, and its borders even erased from the map, it could never be erased from history or from your hearts. In those dark days, you have lost your land, but you never lost your pride.

So it is with this true admiration that I can say today, that from the farms and villages of your countryside to the cathedrals and squares of your great cities, Poland lives, Poland prospers, and Poland prevails.

Despite every effort to transform you, oppress you, or destroy you, you endured and overcame. You are the proud nation of Copernicus. Think of that—Chopin, Saint John Paul II. Poland is a land of great heroes. And you are a people who know the true value of what you defend.

The triumph of the Polish spirit, over centuries of hardship, gives us all hope for a future in which good conquers evil, and peace achieves victory over war.

For Americans, Poland has been a symbol of hope since the beginning of our nation. Polish heroes and American patriots fought side by side in our War of Independence and in many wars that followed. Our soldiers still serve together today in Afghanistan and Iraq, combating the enemies of all civilization.

For America's part, we have never given up on freedom and independence as the right and destiny of the Polish people. And we never, ever will.

Our two countries share a special bond forged by unique histories and national characters. It's a fellowship that exists only among people who have fought and bled and died for freedom.

The signs of this friendship stand in our nation's capital. Just steps from the White House, we've raised statues of men with names like Pułaski and Kościuszko. The same is true in Warsaw, where street signs carry the name of George Washington, and a monument stands to one of the world's greatest heroes—Ronald Reagan.

And so I am here today not just to visit an old ally, but to hold it up as an example for others who seek freedom, and who wish to summon the courage and the will to defend our civilization. The story of Poland is the story of a people who have never lost hope, who have never been broken, and who have never, ever forgotten who they are.

This is a nation more than one thousand years old. Your borders were erased for more than a century and only restored just one century ago.

In 1920, in the Miracle of Vistula, Poland stopped the Soviet Army bent on European conquest. Then, nineteen years later, in 1939, you were invaded yet again, this time by Nazi Germany from the west, and the Soviet Union from the east. That's trouble. That's tough.

Under a double occupation, the Polish people endured evils beyond description: the Katyn forest massacre, the occupations, the Holocaust, the Warsaw Ghetto, and the Warsaw Ghetto Uprising, the destruction of this beautiful capital city, and the deaths of nearly one in five Polish people. A vibrant Jewish population—the largest in Europe—was reduced to almost nothing after the Nazis systematically murdered millions of Poland's Jewish citizens, along with countless others, during that brutal occupation.

In the summer of 1944, the Nazi and Soviet armies were preparing for a terrible and bloody battle right here in Warsaw. Amid that hell on earth, the citizens of Poland rose up to defend their homeland. I am deeply honored to be joined on stage today by veterans and heroes of the Warsaw Uprising.

What great spirit. We salute your noble sacrifice and we pledge to always remember your fight for Poland and for freedom. Thank you. Thank you.

This monument reminds us that more than one hundred fifty thousand Poles died during that desperate struggle to overthrow oppression.

From the other side of the river, the Soviet armed forces stopped and waited. They watched as the Nazis ruthlessly destroyed the city, viciously murdering men, women, and children. They tried to destroy this nation forever by shattering its will to survive.

But there is a courage and a strength deep in the Polish character that no one could destroy. The Polish martyr, Bishop Michael Kozal, said it well: "More horrifying than a defeat of arms is a collapse of the human spirit."

Through four decades of communist rule, Poland and the other captive nations of Europe endured a brutal campaign to demolish freedom, your faith, your laws, your history, your identity—indeed, the very essence of your culture and your humanity. Yet through it all, you never lost that spirit. Your oppressors tried to break you, but Poland could not be broken.

And when the day came on June second, 1979, and one million Poles gathered around Victory Square for their very first mass with their Polish pope—that day, every communist in Warsaw must have known that their oppressive system would soon come crashing down. They must have known it at the exact moment during Pope John Paul the Second's sermon, when a million Polish men, women, and children suddenly raised their voices in a single prayer. A million Polish people did not ask for wealth. They did not ask for privilege. Instead, one million Poles sang three simple words: "We want God."

In those words, the Polish people recalled the promise of a better future. They found new courage to face down their oppressors, and they found the words to declare that Poland would be Poland once again.

As I stand here today before this incredible crowd, this faithful nation, we can still hear those voices that echo through history. Their message is as true today as ever. The people of Poland, the people of America, and the people of Europe still cry out, "We want God."

Together, with Pope John Paul II, the Poles reasserted their identity as a nation devoted to God. And with that powerful declaration of who you are, you came to understand what to do and how to live. You stood in solidarity against oppression, against a lawless secret police, against a cruel and wicked system that impoverished your cities and your souls. And you won. Poland prevailed. Poland will always prevail.

You were supported in that victory over communism by a strong alliance of free nations in the West that defied tyranny. Now, among the most committed members of the NATO Alliance, Poland has resumed its place as a leading nation of a Europe that is strong, whole, and free.

A strong Poland is a blessing to the nations of Europe, and they know that. A strong Europe is a blessing to the West and to the world. One hundred years after the entry of American forces into World War One, the transatlantic bond between the United States and Europe is as strong as ever. And maybe, in many ways, even stronger.

This continent no longer confronts the specter of communism. But today we're in the West, and we have to say, there are dire threats to our security and to our way of life. You see what's happening out there. They are threats. We will confront them. We will win. But they are threats.

We are confronted by another oppressive ideology—one that seeks to export terrorism and extremism all around the globe.

America and Europe have suffered one terror attack after another. We're going to get it to stop.

During a historic gathering in Saudi Arabia, I called on the leaders of more than fifty Muslim nations to join together to drive out this menace, which threatens all of humanity. We must stand united against these shared enemies to strip them of their territory, and their funding, and their networks, and any form of ideological support that they may have. While we will always welcome new citizens who share our values and love our people, our borders will always be closed to terrorism and extremism of any kind.

We are fighting hard against radical Islamic terrorism, and we will prevail. We cannot accept those who reject our values and who use hatred to justify violence against the innocent.

Today, the West is also confronted by the powers that seek to test our will, undermine our confidence, and challenge our interests. To meet new forms of aggression, including propaganda, financial crimes, and cyberwarfare, we must adapt our alliance to compete effectively in new ways and on all new battlefields.

We urge Russia to cease its destabilizing activities in Ukraine and elsewhere, and its support for hostile regimes—including Syria and Iran—and to instead join the community of responsible nations in our fight against common enemies and in defense of civilization itself.

Finally, on both sides of the Atlantic, our citizens are confronted by yet another danger—one firmly within our control. This danger is invisible to some but familiar to the Poles: the steady creep of government bureaucracy that drains the vitality and wealth of the people. The West became great not because of paperwork and regulations, but because people were allowed to chase their dreams and pursue their destinies.

Americans, Poles, and nations of Europe value individual freedom and sovereignty. We must work together to confront forces, whether they come from inside or out, from the South or the East, that threaten, over time, to undermine these values and to erase the bonds of culture, faith, and tradition that make us who we are. If left unchecked, these forces will undermine our courage, sap our spirit, and weaken our will to defend ourselves and our societies.

But just as our adversaries and enemies of the past learned here in Poland, we know that these forces, too, are doomed to fail if we want them to fail. And we do, indeed, want them to fail. They are doomed not only because our alliance is strong, our countries are resilient, and our power is unmatched. Through all of that, you have to say everything is true. Our adversaries, however, are doomed because we will never forget who we are. And if we don't forget who are, we just can't be beaten. Americans will never forget. The nations of Europe will never forget. We are the fastest and the greatest community. There is nothing like our community of nations. The world has never known anything like our community of nations.

We write symphonies. We pursue innovation. We celebrate our ancient heroes, embrace our timeless traditions and customs, and always seek to explore and discover brand-new frontiers.

We reward brilliance. We strive for excellence, and cherish inspiring works of art that honor God. We treasure the rule of law, and protect the right to free speech and free expression.

We empower women as pillars of our society and of our success. We put faith and family, not government and bureaucracy, at the center of our lives. And we debate everything. We challenge everything. We seek to know everything so that we can better know ourselves.

And above all, we value the dignity of every human life, protect the rights of every person, and share the hope of every soul to live in freedom. That is who we are. Those are the priceless ties that bind us together as nations, as allies, and as a civilization.

What we have, what we inherited from our—and you know this better than anybody, and you see it today with this incredible group of people—what we've inherited from our ancestors has never existed to this extent before. And if we fail to preserve it, it will never, ever exist again. So we cannot fail.

This great community of nations has something else in common: in every one of them, it is the people, not the powerful, who have always formed the foundation of freedom and the cornerstone of our defense. The people have been that foundation here in Poland—as they were right here in Warsaw—and they were the foundation from the very, very beginning in America.

Our citizens did not win freedom together, did not survive horrors together, did not face down evil together, only to lose our freedom to a lack of pride and confidence in our values. We did not, and we will not. We will never back down.

As long as we know our history, we will know how to build our future. Americans know that a strong alliance of free, sovereign, and independent nations is the best defense for our freedoms and for our interests. That is why my administration has demanded that all members of NATO finally meet their full and fair financial obligation.

As a result of this insistence, billions of dollars more have begun to pour into NATO. In fact, people are shocked. But billions and billions of dollars more are coming in from countries that, in my opinion, would not have been paying so quickly.

To those who would criticize our tough stance, I would point out that the United States has demonstrated not merely with words, but with its actions, that we stand firmly behind Article Five, the mutual defense commitment.

Words are easy, but actions are what matters. And for its own protection—and you know this, everybody knows this, everybody has to know this—Europe must do more. Europe must demonstrate that it believes in its future by investing its money to secure that future.

That is why we applaud Poland for its decision to move forward this week on acquiring from the United States the battle-tested Patriot air and missile defense system. The best anywhere in the world. That is also why we salute the Polish people for being one of the NATO countries that has actually achieved the benchmark for investment in our common defense. Thank you. Thank you, Poland. I must tell you, the example you set is truly magnificent, and we applaud Poland. Thank you.

We have to remember that our defense is not just a commitment of money—it is a commitment of will. Because, as the Polish experience reminds us, the defense of the West ultimately rests not only on means, but also on the will of its people to prevail and be successful and get what you have to have. The fundamental question of our time is whether the West has the will to survive. Do we have the confidence in our values to defend them at any cost? Do we have enough respect for our citizens to protect our borders? Do we have the desire and the courage to preserve our civilization in the face of those who would subvert and destroy it?

We can have the largest economies and the most lethal weapons anywhere on earth. But if we do not have strong families and strong values, then we will be weak, and we will not survive. If anyone forgets the critical importance of these things, let them come to one country that never has. Let them come to Poland. And let them come here, to Warsaw, and learn the story of the Warsaw Uprising.

When they do, they should learn about Jerusalem Avenue. In August of 1944, Jerusalem Avenue was one of the main roads running east and west through this city, just as it is today.

Control of that road was crucially important to both sides in the battle for Warsaw. The German military wanted it as their most direct route to move troops and to form a very strong front. And for the Polish Home Army, the ability to pass north and south across that street was critical to keep the center of the city, and the Uprising itself, from being split apart and destroyed.

Every night, the Poles put up sandbags amid machine gun fire—and it was horrendous fire—to protect a narrow passage across Jerusalem Avenue. Every day, the enemy forces knocked them down again and again and again. Then the Poles dug a trench. Finally, they built a barricade. And the brave Polish fighters began to flow across Jerusalem Avenue. That narrow passageway, just a few feet wide, was the fragile link that kept the Uprising alive.

Between its walls, a constant stream of citizens and freedom fighters made their perilous—just perilous—sprints. They ran across that street, they ran through that street, they ran under that street—all to defend this city. "The far side was several yards away," recalled one young Polish woman named Greta. That mortality, and that life was so important to her. In fact, she said, "The mortally dangerous sector of the street was soaked in blood. It was the blood of messengers, liaison girls, and couriers."

Nazi snipers shot at anybody who crossed. Anybody who crossed, they were being shot at. Their soldiers burned every building on the street, and they used the Poles as human shields for their tanks in their effort to capture Jerusalem Avenue. The enemy never ceased its relentless assault on that small outpost of civilization. And the Poles never ceased its defense.

The Jerusalem Avenue passage required constant protection, repair, and reinforcement, but the will of its defenders did not waver, even in the face of death. And to the last days of the Uprising, the fragile crossing never, ever failed. It was never, ever forgotten. It was kept open by the Polish people.

The memories of those who perished in the Warsaw Uprising cry out across the decades, and few are clearer than the memories of those who died to build and defend the Jerusalem Avenue crossing. Those heroes remind us that the West was saved with the blood of patriots—that each generation must rise up and play their part in its defense, and that every foot of ground, and every last inch of civilization, is worth defending with your life.

Our own fight for the West does not begin on the battlefield—it begins with our minds, our wills, and our souls. Today, the ties that unite our civilization are no less vital, and demand no less defense, than that bare shred of land on which the hope of Poland once totally rested. Our freedom, our civilization, and our survival depend on these bonds of history, culture, and memory.

And today, as ever, Poland is in our heart, and its people are in that fight. Just as Poland could not be broken, I declare today, for the world to hear, that the West will never, ever be broken. Our values will prevail. Our people will thrive. And our civilization will triumph.

So together, let us all fight like the Poles—for family, for freedom, for country, and for God.

Thank you. God bless you. God bless the Polish people. God bless our allies. And God bless the United States of America. Thank you. God bless you. Thank you very much.

Boy Scout Jamboree

SUMMIT BECHTEL RESERVE, GLEN JEAN, WEST VIRGINIA

July 24, 2017

Thank you, everybody. Thank you very much. I am thrilled to be here! Thrilled.

And if you think that was an easy trip, you're wrong. But I am thrilled.

Nineteenth Boy Scout Jamboree. Wow! And to address such a tremendous group. Boy, you have a lot of people here. The press will say it's about two hundred people.

It looks like about forty-five thousand people. You set a record today.

You set a record. That's a great honor, believe me.

Tonight, we put aside all of the policy fights in Washington, DC you've been hearing about, with the fake news and all of that. We're going to put that aside. And instead, we're going to talk about success, about how all of you amazing young Scouts can achieve your dreams. What to think of—what I've been thinking about. You want to achieve your dreams. I said, who the hell wants to speak about politics when I'm in front of the Boy Scouts, right?

There are many great honors that come with the job of being president of the United States. But looking out at this incredible gathering of mostly young patriots—mostly young—I'm especially proud to speak to you as the honorary president of the Boy Scouts of America.

You are the young people of character, integrity, who will serve as leaders of our communities, and uphold the sacred values of our nation.

I want to thank Boy Scouts president, Randall Stephenson; chief Scout executive, Michael Surbaugh; Jamboree chairman, Ralph de la Vega; and the thousands of volunteers who have made this a life-changing experience for all of you. And when they asked me to be here, I said, "Absolutely yes."

Finally—and we can't forgot these people—I especially want to salute the moms and the dads and troop leaders who are here tonight. Thank you for making scouting possible. Thank you, Mom and Dad, troop leaders.

When you volunteer for the Boy Scouts, you are not only shaping young lives, you are shaping the future of America.

The United States has no better citizens than its Boy Scouts. No better.

The values, traditions, and skills you learn here will serve you throughout your lives. And just as importantly, they will serve your families, your cities—and in the future and in the present, will serve your country.

The Scouts believe in putting America first.

You know, I go to Washington, and I see all these politicians, and I see the swamp, and it's not a good place. In fact, today, I said we ought to change it from the word *swamp* to the word *cesspool*. Or perhaps to the word *sewer*.

But it's not good. Not good. And I see what's going on. And believe me, I'd much rather be with you. That, I can tell you.

I'll tell you, the reason that I love this, and the reason that I really wanted to be here, is because as president, I rely on former Boy Scouts every single day. And so do the American people.

It's amazing how many Boy Scouts we have at the highest level of our great government. Many of my top advisers in the White House were Scouts. Ten members of my cabinet were Scouts. Can you believe that? Ten.

Secretary of State Rex Tillerson is not only a Boy Scout, he is your former national president.

The vice president of the United States, Mike Pence—a good guy—was a Scout, and it meant so much to him.

Some of you here tonight might even have camped out in this yard when Mike was the governor of Indiana. But the scouting was very, very important.

And by the way, where are our Indiana scouts tonight?

I wonder if the television cameras will follow you? They don't like doing that when they see these massive crowds. They don't like doing that. Hi, folks.

There's a lot of love in this big, beautiful place. A lot of love. And a lot of love for our country. And a lot of love for our country.

Secretary of the Interior Ryan Zinke is here tonight. Come here, Ryan. Ryan is an Eagle Scout from Big Sky Country in Montana. Pretty good.

And by the way, he is doing a fantastic job. He makes sure that we leave our national parks and federal lands better than we found them, in the best scouting tradition. So thank you very much, Ryan.

Secretary of Energy Rick Perry of Texas, an Eagle Scout from the great state.

The first time he came to the National Jamboree was in 1964. He was very young then. And Rick told me just a little while ago, it totally changed his life.

So Rick, thank you very much for being here. And we're doing—we're doing a lot with energy. And very soon, Rick, we will be an energy exporter. Isn't that nice? An energy exporter.

In other words, we'll be selling our energy instead of buying it from everybody all over the globe. So that's good. We will be energy dominant.

And I'll tell you what, the folks in West Virginia—who were so nice to me—boy, have we kept our promise. We are going on and on. So we love West Virginia. We want to thank you.

Where's West Virginia, by the way?

Thank you.

Secretary Tom Price is also here today. Dr. Price still lives the Scout Oath, helping to keep millions of Americans strong and healthy, as our secretary of Health and Human Services. And he's doing a great job. And hopefully he's going to get the votes tomorrow to start our path toward killing this horrible thing known as Obamacare that's really hurting us.

By the way, are you going to get the votes? He better get them. He better get them. Oh, he better. Otherwise, I'll say, "Tom, you're fired!" I'll get somebody.

He better get Senator Capito to vote for it. He better get the other senators to vote for it. It's time.

You know, after seven years of saying, "Repeal and replace Obamacare," we have a chance to now do it. They better do it. Hopefully, they'll do it.

As we can see just by looking at our government—in America, Scouts lead the way. And another thing I've noticed—and I've noticed it all my life—there is a tremendous spirit with being a Scout. More so than almost anything I can think of. So whatever is going on, keep doing it. It's incredible to watch, believe me.

Each of these leaders will tell that you their road to American success—and you have to understand, their American success—and they are a great, great story—was paved with the patriotic American values and traditions they learned in the Boy Scouts. And some day, many years from now, when you look back on all of the adventures in your lives, you will be able to say the same: "I got my start as a Scout, just like these incredibly great people that are doing such a good job for our country. So that's going to happen."

Boy Scout values are American values. And great Boy Scouts become great, great Americans.

As the Scout Law says, A Scout is trustworthy, loyal. . . . We could use some more loyalty, I will tell that you that.

That was very impressive. You've heard that before. But here, you learn the rewards of hard work and perseverance. Never, ever give up. Never quit. Persevere. Never, ever quit. You learn the satisfaction of building a roaring campfire, reaching a mountain summit, or earning a merit badge after mastering a certain skill. There's no better feeling than an achievement that you've earned with your own sweat, tears, resolve, hard work. There's nothing like it. Do you agree with that?

I'm waving to people back there so small I can't even see them. Man, this is a lot of people. Turn those cameras back there, please. That is so incredible.

By the way, what do you think the chances are that this incredible, massive crowd—record-setting—is going to be shown on television tonight? One percent or zero?

The fake media will say, "President Trump spoke"—you know what is—"President Trump spoke before a small crowd of Boy Scouts today." That's some—that is some crowd. Fake media. Fake news.

Thank you. And I'm honored by that. By the way, all of you people that—can't even see you. So thank you. I hope you can hear.

Through scouting, you also learned to believe in yourself—so important—to have confidence in your ability and to take responsibility for your own life. When you face down new challenges—and you will have plenty of them—develop talents you never thought possible, and lead your teammates through daring trials, you discover that you can handle anything. And you learn it by being a Scout. It's great. You can do anything. You can be anything you want to be. But in order to succeed, you must find out what you love to do. You have to find your passion, no matter what they tell you. By the way, just a question. Did President Obama ever come to a Jamboree? . . .

And we'll be back. We'll be back. The answer is no. But we'll be back.

In life, in order to be successful—and you people are well on the road to success—you have to find out what makes you excited, what makes you want to get up each morning and go to work? You have to find it. If you love what you do and dedicate yourself to your work, then you will gain momentum. And look, you have to. You need the word *momentum*. You will gain that momentum. And each success will create another success. The word *momentum*.

I'll tell you a story that's very interesting for me. When I was young, there was a man named William Levitt—Levittowns. You have some here. You have some in different states. Anybody ever hear of Levittown?

And he was a very successful man. Became unbelievable. He was a home builder, became an unbelievable success and got more and more successful. And he'd build homes, and at night he'd go to these major sites with teams of people, and he'd scour the sites for nails and sawdust and small pieces of wood. And they cleaned the site, so when the workers came in the next morning, the sites would be spotless and clean. And he did it properly. And he did this for twenty years, and then he was offered a lot of money for his company, and he sold his company for a tremendous amount of money—at the time, especially. This is a long time ago. Sold his company for a tremendous amount of money. And he went out and bought a big yacht, and he had a very interesting life. I won't go any more than that, because you're Boy Scouts, so I'm not going to tell you what he did.

Should I tell you? Should I tell you?

Oh, you're Boy Scouts, but you know life. You know life.

So look at you. Who would think this is the Boy Scouts, right?

So he had a very, very interesting life. And the company that bought his company was a big conglomerate, and they didn't know anything about building homes, and they didn't know anything about picking up the nails and the sawdust and selling it, and the scraps of wood. This was a big conglomerate based in New York City.

And after about a ten-year period, they were losing a lot with it. It didn't mean anything to them, and they couldn't sell it. So they called William Levitt up, and they said, "Would you like to buy back your company?" And he said, "Yes, I would." He so badly wanted it. He got bored with this life of yachts and sailing and all of the things he did in the South of France and other places.

You won't get bored, right? You know, truthfully, you're workers. You'll get bored, too, believe me. Of course, having a few good years like that isn't so bad.

But what happened is, he bought back his company, and he bought back a lot of empty land, and he worked hard at getting zoning, and he worked hard on starting to develop. And in the end, he failed, and he failed badly. Lost all of his money. He went personally bankrupt, and he was now much older. And I saw him at a cocktail party. And it was very sad, because the hottest people in New York were at this party. It was the party of Steve Ross. Steve Ross, who was one of the great people. He came up and discovered—really, founded Time Warner—and he was a great guy. He had a lot of successful people at the party.

And I was doing well, so I got invited to the party. I was very young. And I go in, but I'm in the real estate business. And I see a hundred people, some of whom I recognize, and they're big in the entertainment business.

And I see, sitting in the corner was a little old man who was all by himself. Nobody was talking to him. I immediately recognized that that man was the once-great William Levitt of Levittown, and I immediately went over. I wanted to talk to him more than the Hollywood, show-business, communications people.

So I went over and talked to him, and I said, "Mister Levitt, I'm Donald Trump."

He said, "I know."

I said, "Mister Levitt, how are you doing?"

He goes, "Not well. Not well at all."

And I knew that. But he said, "Not well at all."

And he explained what was happening, and how bad it's been, and how hard it's been.

And I said, "What exactly happened? Why did this happen to you? You're one of the greats ever in our industry. Why did this happen to you?"

And he said, "Donald, I lost my momentum. I lost my momentum." A word you never hear when you're talking about success—when some of these guys that never made ten cents, they're on television giving you things about how you're going to be successful, and the only thing they ever did was a book and a tape. But I tell you—I'll tell you, it was very sad, and I never forgot that moment.

And I thought about it, and it's exactly true. He lost his momentum. Meaning, he took this period of time off—long years—and then when he got back, he didn't have that same momentum.

In life, I always tell this to people: You have to know whether or not you continue to have the momentum. And if you don't have it, that's OK, because you're going to go on, and you're going to learn, and you're going to do things that are great. But you have to know about the word *momentum*.

But the big thing: Never quit. Never give up. Do something you love. When you do something you love as a Scout, I see that you love it. But when you do something that you love, you'll never fail. What you're going to do is give it a shot again and again and again. You're ultimately going to be successful.

And remember this, you're not working. Because when you're doing something that you love, like I do—of course I love my business, but this is a little bit different. Who thought this was going to happen. We're, you know, having a good time. We're doing a good job. Doing a good job.

But when you do something that you love, remember this—it's not work. So you'll work twenty-four-seven. You're going to work all the time. And at the end of the year, you're not really working. You don't think of it as work. When you're not doing something that you like, or when you're forced into doing something that you really don't like, that's called *work*, and it's hard work, and tedious work.

So as much as you can, do something that you love, work hard, and never, ever give up, and you're going to be tremendously successful. Tremendously successful.

Now, with that, I have to tell you, our economy is doing great. Our stock market has picked up since the election, November eighth. Do we remember that day? Was that a beautiful day? What a day.

Do you remember that famous night on television, November eighth, where they said—these dishonest people—where they said, "There is no path to victory for Donald Trump. They forgot about the forgotten people."

By the way, they're not forgetting about the forgotten people anymore. They're going crazy trying to figure it out. But I told them, far too late. It's far too late.

But you remember that incredible night with the maps—and the Republicans are red, and the Democrats are blue. And that map was so red, it was unbelievable. And they didn't know what to say. And you know, we have a tremendous disadvantage in the Electoral College. Popular vote is much easier. We have—because New York, California, Illinois . . . you have to practically run the East Coast. And we did. We won Florida. We won South Carolina. We won North Carolina. We won Pennsylvania.

We won and won. So when they said, there is no way to victory. There is no way to two-seventy. You know, I went to Maine four times, because it's one vote. And we won. We won. One vote. I went there because I kept hearing we're at two-sixty-nine. But then Wisconsin came in. Many, many years. Michigan came in.

So—and we worked hard there. You know, my opponent didn't work hard there, because she was told—she was told she was going to win Michigan. And I said, well, wait a minute. The car industry is moving to Mexico. Why is she going to move—she's there. Why are they allowing it to move? And by the way, do you see those car industry—do you see what's happening? They're coming back to Michigan. They're coming back to Ohio. They're starting to peel back in.

And we go to Wisconsin, now—Wisconsin hadn't been won in many, many years by a Republican. But we go to Wisconsin, and we had tremendous crowds. And I'd leave these massive crowds, I'd say, "Why are we going to lose this state?"

The polls, that's also fake news. They're fake polls. But the polls are saying—but we won Wisconsin.

So I have to tell you, what we did, in all fairness, is an unbelievable tribute to you and all of the other millions and millions of people that came out and voted for Make America Great Again.

And I'll tell you what, we are indeed making America great again.

And I'll tell you what, we are indeed making America great again. What's going on is incredible. We had the best jobs report in sixteen years. The stock market, on a daily basis, is hitting an all-time high.

We're going to be bringing back, very soon, trillions of dollars from companies that can't get their money back into this country, and that money is going to be used to help rebuild America. We're doing things that nobody ever thought was possible, and we've just started. It's just the beginning, believe me.

You know, in the Boy Scouts you learn right from wrong, correct? You learn to contribute to your communities, to take pride in your nation, and to seek out opportunities to serve. You pledge to help other people at all times.

In the Scout Oath, you pledge on your honor to do your best and to do your duty to God and your country.

And by the way, under the Trump administration, you'll be saying, "Merry Christmas again when you go shopping, believe me."

Merry Christmas.

They've been downplaying that little beautiful phrase. You're going to be saying, "Merry Christmas again, folks."

But the words *duty, country,* and *God* are beautiful words. In other words, basically what you're doing is you're pledging to be a great American patriot.

For more than a century, that is exactly what our Boy Scouts have been. Last year, you gave more than fifteen million hours of service to helping people in your communities. Incredible. That's an incredible stat.

All of you here tonight will contribute more than a hundred thousand hours of service by the end of this Jamboree. One hundred thousand.

When natural disaster strikes, when people face hardship, when the beauty and glory of our outdoor spaces must be restored and taken care of, America turns to the Boy Scouts because we know that the Boy Scouts never, ever, ever let us down.

Just like you know you can count on me, we know we can count on you, because we know the values that you live by.

Your values are the same values that have always kept America strong, proud, and free.

And by the way, do you see the billions and billions and billions of additional money that we're putting back into our military? Billions of dollars.

New planes, new ships, great equipment for our people that are so great to us. We love our vets. We love our soldiers. And we love our police, by the way.

Firemen, police. We love our police. Those are all special people. Uniformed services.

Two days ago, I traveled to Norfolk, Virginia, to commission an American aircraft carrier into the fleet of the United States Navy. It's the newest, largest, and most advanced aircraft carrier anywhere in the world, and it's named for an Eagle Scout—the USS *Gerald R. Ford*.

Everywhere it sails, that great Scout's name will be feared and revered, because that ship will be a symbol of American power, prestige, and strength.

Our nation honors President Gerald R. Ford today because he lived his life the scouting way. Boy Scouts celebrate American patriots, especially the brave members of our Armed Forces. Thank you very much. Thank you. Thank you.

American hearts are warmed every year when we read about Boy Scouts placing thousands and thousands of flags next to veterans' grave sites all across the country. By honoring our heroes, you help to ensure that their memory never, ever dies. You should take great pride in the example you set for every citizen of our country to follow.

Generations of American Boy Scouts have sworn the same oath and lived according to the same law. You inherit a noble American tradition. And as you embark on your lives, never cease to be proud of who you are and the principles you hold dear and stand by. Wear your values as your badge of honor. What you've done, few have done before you. What you've done is incredible.

What you've done is admired by all. So I want to congratulate you, Boy Scouts.

Let your scouting oath guide your path from this day forward. Remember your duty, honor your history, take care of the people God put into your life, and love and cherish your great country.

You are very special people. You're special in the lives of America. You're special to me. But if you do what we say, I promise you that you will live scouting's adventure every single day of your life, and you will win, win, win, and help people in doing so.

Your lives will have meaning and purpose and joy. You will become leaders, and you will inspire others to achieve the dreams they once thought were totally impossible. Things that you said could never, ever happen are already happening for you. And if you do these things, and if you refuse to give in to doubt or to fear, then you will help to make America great again, you will be proud of yourself, be proud of the uniform you wear, and be proud of the country you love.

And never, ever forget: America is proud of you.

This is a very, very special occasion for me. I've known so many Scouts over the years. Winners. I've known so many great people. They've been taught so well, and they love the heritage. But this is very special for me.

And I just want to end by saying—very importantly—God bless you. God bless the Boy Scouts. God Bless the United States of America. Go out, have a great time in life, compete, and go out and show me that there is nobody, nobody like a Boy Scout.

Thank you very much, everybody.

Statement on Charlottesville

THE WHITE HOUSE, WASHINGTON, DC

August 14, 2017

I'm in Washington today to meet with my economic team about trade policy and major tax cuts and reform. We are renegotiating trade deals and making them good for the American worker, and it's about time. The economy is now strong. The stock market continues to hit record highs. Unemployment is at a sixteen-year low, and businesses are more optimistic than ever before. Companies are moving back to the United States and bringing many thousands of jobs with them. We have already created over one million jobs since I took office.

We will be discussing economic issues in greater detail later this afternoon, but based on the events that took place over the weekend in Charlottesville, Virginia, I would like to provide the nation with an update on the ongoing federal response to the horrific attack and violence that was witnessed by everyone. I just met with FBI Director Christopher Wray, and Attorney General Jeff Sessions. The Department of Justice has opened a civil rights investigation into the deadly car attack that killed one innocent American and wounded twenty others. To anyone who acted criminally in this weekend's racist violence, you will be held accountable. Justice will be delivered.

As I said on Saturday, we condemn, in the strongest possible terms, this egregious display of bigotry, hatred, and violence. It has no place in America. And as I have said many times before, no matter the color of our skin, we all live under the same laws, we all salute the same great flag, and we are all made by the same almighty God. We must love each other, show affection for each other, and unite together in condemnation of hatred, bigotry, and violence. We must discover the bonds of love and loyalty that bring us together as Americans. Racism is evil, and those who cause violence in its name are criminals and thugs, including the KKK, neo-Nazis, white supremacists, and other hate groups that are repugnant to everything we hold dear as Americans.

We are a nation founded on the truth that all of us are created equal. We are equal in the eyes of our creator, we are equal under the law, and we are equal under our Constitution. Those who spread violence in the name of bigotry strike at the very core of America.

Two days ago, a young American woman, Heather Heyer, was tragically killed. Her death fills us with grief, and we send her family our thoughts, our prayers, and our love. We also mourn the two Virginia state troopers who died in service to their community, their commonwealth, and their country. Troopers H. Jay Cullen and Berke Bates exemplify the very best of America, and our hearts go out to their families, their friends, and every member of American law enforcement.

These three fallen Americans embody the goodness and decency of our nation. In times such as these, America has always shown its true character, responding to hate with love, division with unity, and violence with an unwavering resolve for justice. As a candidate, I promised to restore law and order to our country, and our federal law enforcement agencies are following through on that pledge. We will spare no resource in fighting so that every American child can grow up free from violence and fear. We will defend and protect the sacred rights of all Americans, and we will work together so that every citizen in this blessed land is free to follow their dreams in their hearts, and to express the love and joy in their souls.

Thank you. God bless you. And God bless America.

A Time of Both Immense Promise and Great Peril

U.N. GENERAL ASSEMBLY, NEW YORK, NEW YORK

September 19, 2017

Mister Secretary General, Mister President, world leaders, and distinguished delegates:

Welcome to New York. It is a profound honor to stand here in my home city, as a representative of the American people, to address the people of the world.

As millions of our citizens continue to suffer the effects of the devastating hurricanes that have struck our country, I want to begin by expressing my appreciation to every leader in this room who has offered assistance and aid. The American people are strong and resilient, and they will emerge from these hardships more determined than ever before.

Fortunately, the United States has done very well since Election Day last November eighth. The stock market is at an all-time high—a record. Unemployment is at its lowest level in sixteen years. And because of our regulatory and other reforms, we have more people working in the United States today than ever before. Companies are moving back, creating job growth the likes of which our country has not seen in a very long time. And it has just been announced that we will be spending almost seven hundred billion dollars on our military and defense.

Our military will soon be the strongest it has ever been. For more than seventy years, in times of war and peace, the leaders of nations, movements, and religions have stood before this assembly. Like them, I intend to address some of the very serious threats before us today, but also the enormous potential waiting to be unleashed.

We live in a time of extraordinary opportunity. Breakthroughs in science, technology, and medicine are curing illnesses and solving problems that prior generations thought impossible to solve. But each day also brings news of growing dangers that threaten everything we cherish and value. Terrorists and extremists have gathered strength and spread to every region of the planet. Rogue regimes represented in this body not only support terrorists, but threaten other nations, and their own people, with the most destructive weapons known to humanity.

Authority and authoritarian powers seek to collapse the values, the systems, and alliances that prevented conflict and tilted the world toward freedom since World War Two.

International criminal networks traffic drugs, weapons, people; force dislocation and mass migration; threaten our borders; and new forms of aggression exploit technology to menace our citizens.

To put it simply, we meet at a time of both immense promise and great peril. It is entirely up to us whether we lift the world to new heights or let it fall into a valley of disrepair.

We have it in our power, should we so choose, to lift millions from poverty, to help our citizens realize their dreams, and to ensure that new generations of children are raised free from violence, hatred, and fear.

This institution was founded in the aftermath of two world wars to help shape this better future. It was based on the vision that diverse nations could cooperate to protect their sovereignty, preserve their security, and promote their prosperity.

It was in the same period, exactly seventy years ago, that the United States developed the Marshall Plan to help restore Europe. Those three beautiful pillars—they're pillars of peace, sovereignty, security, and prosperity.

The Marshall Plan was built on the noble idea that the whole world is safer when nations are strong, independent, and free. As

President Truman said in his message to Congress at that time: "Our support of European recovery is in full accord with our support of the United Nations. The success of the United Nations depends upon the independent strength of its members."

To overcome the perils of the present, and to achieve the promise of the future, we must begin with the wisdom of the past. Our success depends on a coalition of strong and independent nations that embrace their sovereignty to promote security, prosperity, and peace for themselves and for the world.

We do not expect diverse countries to share the same cultures, traditions, or even systems of government. But we do expect all nations to uphold these two core sovereign duties: to respect the interests of their own people, and the rights of every other sovereign nation. This is the beautiful vision of this institution, and this is the foundation for cooperation and success.

Strong, sovereign nations let diverse countries with different values, different cultures, and different dreams not just coexist, but work side by side on the basis of mutual respect.

Strong, sovereign nations let their people take ownership of the future and control their own destiny. And strong, sovereign nations allow individuals to flourish in the fullness of the life intended by God.

In America, we do not seek to impose our way of life on anyone, but rather to let it shine as an example for everyone to watch. This week gives our country a special reason to take pride in that example. We are celebrating the two hundred thirtieth anniversary of our beloved Constitution—the oldest constitution still in use in the world today.

This timeless document has been the foundation of peace, prosperity, and freedom for the Americans, and for countless millions around the globe whose own countries have found inspiration in its respect for human nature, human dignity, and the rule of law.

The greatest in the United States Constitution is its first three beautiful words. They are: "We the people."

Generations of Americans have sacrificed to maintain the promise of those words, the promise of our country, and of our great history. In America, the people govern, the people rule, and the people are sovereign. I was elected not to take power, but to give power to the American people, where it belongs.

In foreign affairs, we are renewing this founding principle of sovereignty. Our government's first duty is to its people, to our citizens—to serve their needs, to ensure their safety, to preserve their rights, and to defend their values.

As President of the United States, I will always put America first—just like you, as the leaders of your countries, will always, and should always, put your countries first.

All responsible leaders have an obligation to serve their own citizens, and the nation-state remains the best vehicle for elevating the human condition.

But making a better life for our people also requires us to work together in close harmony and unity to create a more safe and peaceful future for all people.

The United States will forever be a great friend to the world, and especially to its allies. But we can no longer be taken advantage of, or enter into a one-sided deal where the United States gets nothing in return. As long as I hold this office, I will defend America's interests above all else.

But in fulfilling our obligations to our own nations, we also realize that it's in everyone's interest to seek a future where all nations can be sovereign, prosperous, and secure.

America does more than speak for the values expressed in the United Nations Charter. Our citizens have paid the ultimate price to defend our freedom, and the freedom of many nations represented in this great hall. America's devotion is measured on the battlefields, where our young men and women have fought and sacrificed alongside of our allies, from the beaches of Europe to the deserts of the Middle East to the jungles of Asia.

It is an eternal credit to the American character that, even after we and our allies emerged victorious from the bloodiest war in history, we did not seek territorial expansion, or attempt to oppose and impose our way of life on others. Instead, we helped build institutions, such as this one, to defend the sovereignty, security, and prosperity for all.

For the diverse nations of the world, this is our hope. We want harmony and friendship, not conflict and strife. We are guided by outcomes, not ideology. We have a policy of principled realism, rooted in shared goals, interests, and values.

That realism forces us to confront a question facing every leader and nation in this room. It is a question we cannot escape or avoid. We will slide down the path of complacency, numb to the challenges, threats, and even wars, that we face. Or do we have enough strength and pride to confront those dangers today, so that our citizens can enjoy peace and prosperity tomorrow?

If we desire to lift up our citizens, if we aspire to the approval of history, then we must fulfill our sovereign duties to the people we faithfully represent. We must protect our nations, their interests, and their futures. We must reject threats to sovereignty, from the Ukraine to the South China Sea. We must uphold respect for law, respect for borders, and respect for culture, and the peaceful engagement these allow. And just as the Founders of this body intended, we must work together and confront together those who threaten us with chaos, turmoil, and terror.

The scourge of our planet today is a small group of rogue regimes that violate every principle on which the United Nations is based. They respect neither their own citizens nor the sovereign rights of their countries.

If the righteous many do not confront the wicked few, then evil will triumph. When decent people and nations become bystanders to history, the forces of destruction only gather power and strength.

No one has shown more contempt for other nations, and for the wellbeing of their own people, than the depraved regime in North Korea. It is responsible for the starvation deaths of millions of North Koreans, and for the imprisonment, torture, killing, and oppression of countless more.

We were all witness to the regime's deadly abuse when an innocent American college student, Otto Warmbier, was returned to America, only to die a few days later. We saw it in the assassination of the dictator's brother using banned nerve agents in an international airport. We know it kidnapped a sweet thirteen-year-old Japanese girl from a beach in her own country to enslave her as a language tutor for North Korea's spies.

If this is not twisted enough, now North Korea's reckless pursuit of nuclear weapons and ballistic missiles threatens the entire world with unthinkable loss of human life.

It is an outrage that some nations would not only trade with such a regime, but would arm, supply, and financially support a country that imperils the world with nuclear conflict. No nation on earth has an interest in seeing this band of criminals arm itself with nuclear weapons and missiles.

The United States has great strength and patience, but if it is forced to defend itself or its allies, we will have no choice but to totally destroy North Korea. Rocket Man is on a suicide mission for himself and for his regime. The United States is ready, willing, and able, but hopefully this will not be necessary. That's what the United Nations is all about. That's what the United Nations is for. Let's see how they do.

It is time for North Korea to realize that the denuclearization is its only acceptable future. The United Nations Security Council recently held two unanimous fifteen-to-zero votes, adopting hard-hitting resolutions against North Korea. And I want to thank China and Russia for joining the vote to impose sanctions, along with all of the other members of the Security Council. Thank you to all involved.

But we must do much more. It is time for all nations to work together to isolate the Kim regime until it ceases its hostile behavior.

We face this decision not only in North Korea. It is far past time for the nations of the world to confront another reckless regime—one that speaks openly of mass murder, vowing death to America, destruction to Israel, and ruin for many leaders and nations in this room.

The Iranian government masks a corrupt dictatorship behind the false guise of a democracy. It has turned a wealthy country, with a rich history and culture, into an economically depleted rogue state whose chief exports are violence, bloodshed, and chaos. The longest-suffering victims of Iran's leaders are, in fact, its own people.

Rather than use its resources to improve Iranian lives, its oil profits go to fund Hezbollah and other terrorists that kill innocent Muslims and attack their peaceful Arab and Israeli neighbors. This wealth, which rightly belongs to Iran's people, also goes to shore up Bashar al-Assad's dictatorship, fuel Yemen's civil war, and undermine peace throughout the entire Middle East.

We cannot let a murderous regime continue these destabilizing activities while building dangerous missiles, and we cannot abide by an agreement if it provides cover for the eventual construction of a nuclear program. The Iran deal was one of the worst and most one-sided transactions the United States has ever entered into. Frankly, that deal is an embarrassment to the United States, and I don't think you've heard the last of it—believe me.

It is time for the entire world to join us in demanding that Iran's government end its pursuit of death and destruction. It is time for the regime to free all Americans, and citizens of other nations, that they have unjustly detained. And above all, Iran's government must stop supporting terrorists, begin serving its own people, and respect the sovereign rights of its neighbors.

The entire world understands that the good people of Iran want change, and other than the vast military power of the United States, that Iran's people are what their leaders fear the most. This is what causes the regime to restrict Internet access, tear down satellite dishes, shoot unarmed student protestors, and imprison political reformers.

Oppressive regimes cannot endure forever, and the day will come when the Iranian people will face a choice. Will they continue down the path of poverty, bloodshed, and terror? Or will the Iranian people return to the nation's proud roots as a center of civilization, culture, and wealth, where their people can be happy and prosperous once again?

The Iranian regime's support for terror is in stark contrast to the recent commitments of many of its neighbors to fight terrorism and halt its financing.

In Saudi Arabia early last year, I was greatly honored to address the leaders of more than fifty Arab and Muslim nations. We agreed that all responsible nations must work together to confront terrorists and the Islamist extremism that inspires them.

We will stop radical Islamic terrorism, because we cannot allow it to tear up our nation, and indeed, to tear up the entire world.

We must deny the terrorists safe haven, transit, funding, and any form of support for their vile and sinister ideology. We must drive them out of our nations. It is time to expose and hold responsible those countries who support and finance terror groups like al-Qaeda, Hezbollah, the Taliban, and others that slaughter innocent people.

The United States and our allies are working together throughout the Middle East to crush the loser terrorists and stop the re-emergence of safe havens they use to launch attacks on all of our people.

Last month, I announced a new strategy for victory in the fight against this evil in Afghanistan. From now on, our security interests will dictate the length and scope of military operations, not arbitrary benchmarks and timetables set up by politicians.

I have also totally changed the rules of engagement in our fight against the Taliban and other terrorist groups. In Syria and Iraq, we have made big gains toward lasting defeat of ISIS. In fact, our country has achieved more against ISIS in the last eight months than it has in many, many years combined.

We seek the de-escalation of the Syrian conflict, and a political solution that honors the will of the Syrian people. The actions of the criminal regime of Bashar al-Assad, including the use of chemical weapons against his own citizens—even innocent children—shock the conscience of every decent person. No society can be safe if banned chemical weapons are allowed to spread.

That is why the United States carried out a missile strike on the airbase that launched the attack.

We appreciate the efforts of United Nations agencies that are providing vital humanitarian assistance in areas liberated from ISIS, and we especially thank Jordan, Turkey, and Lebanon for their role in hosting refugees from the Syrian conflict.

The United States is a compassionate nation, and has spent billions and billions of dollars in helping to support this effort. We seek an approach to refugee resettlement that is designed to help these horribly treated people, and which enables their eventual return to their home countries, to be part of the rebuilding process.

For the cost of resettling one refugee in the United States, we can assist more than ten in their home region. Out of the goodness of our hearts, we offer financial assistance to hosting countries in the region, and we support recent agreements of the G20 nations that will seek to host refugees as close to their home countries as possible. This is the safe, responsible, and humanitarian approach.

For decades, the United States has dealt with migration challenges here in the Western Hemisphere. We have learned that, over the long term, uncontrolled migration is deeply unfair to both the sending and the receiving countries.

For the sending countries, it reduces domestic pressure to pursue needed political and economic reform, and drains them of the human capital necessary to motivate and implement those reforms.

For the receiving countries, the substantial costs of uncontrolled migration are borne overwhelmingly by low-income citizens whose concerns are often ignored by both media and government.

I want to salute the work of the United Nations in seeking to address the problems that cause people to flee from their homes. The United Nations and African Union led peacekeeping missions to have invaluable contributions in stabilizing conflicts in Africa. The United States continues to lead the world in humanitarian assistance, including famine prevention and relief in South Sudan, Somalia, and northern Nigeria and Yemen.

We have invested in better health and opportunity all over the world through programs like PEPFAR, which funds AIDS relief; the President's Malaria Initiative; the Global Health Security Agenda; the Global Fund to End Modern Slavery; and the Women Entrepreneurs Finance Initiative, part of our commitment to empowering women all across the globe.

We also thank the Secretary-General for recognizing that the United Nations must reform if it is to be an effective partner in confronting threats to sovereignty, security, and prosperity. Too often, the focus of this organization has not been on results, but on bureaucracy and process.

In some cases, states that seek to subvert this institution's noble aims have hijacked the very systems that are supposed to advance them. For example, it is a massive source of embarrassment to the United Nations that some governments with egregious human rights records sit on the U.N. Human Rights Council.

The United States is one out of a hundred ninety-three countries in the United Nations, and yet we pay twenty-two percent of the entire budget, and more. In fact, we pay far more than anybody realizes. The United States bears an unfair cost burden. But, to be fair, if it could actually accomplish all of its stated goals, especially the goal of peace, this investment would easily be well worth it.

Major portions of the world are in conflict. And some, in fact, are going to hell. But the powerful people in this room, under the guidance and auspices of the United Nations, can solve many of these vicious and complex problems.

The American people hope that one day soon, the United Nations can be a much more accountable and effective advocate for human dignity and freedom around the world. In the meantime, we believe that no nation should have to bear a disproportionate share of the burden, militarily or financially. Nations of the world must take a greater role in promoting secure and prosperous societies in their own regions.

That is why in the Western Hemisphere, the United States has stood against the corrupt and destabilizing regime in Cuba, and embraced the enduring dream of the Cuban people to live in freedom. My administration recently announced that we will not lift sanctions on the Cuban government until it makes fundamental reforms.

We have also imposed tough, calibrated sanctions on the socialist Maduro regime in Venezuela, which has brought a once thriving nation to the brink of total collapse.

The socialist dictatorship of Nicolas Maduro has inflicted terrible pain and suffering on the good people of that country. This corrupt regime destroyed a prosperous nation by imposing a failed ideology that has produced poverty and misery everywhere it has been tried. To make matters worse, Maduro has defied his own people, stealing power from their elected representatives to preserve his disastrous rule.

The Venezuelan people are starving, and their country is collapsing. Their democratic institutions are being destroyed. This situation is completely unacceptable, and we cannot stand by and watch.

As a responsible neighbor and friend, we, and all others, have a goal. That goal is to help them regain their freedom, recover their country, and restore their democracy. I would like to thank leaders in this room for condemning the regime and providing vital support to the Venezuelan people.

The United States has taken important steps to hold the regime accountable. We are prepared to take further action if the government of Venezuela persists on its path to impose authoritarian rule on the Venezuelan people.

We are fortunate to have incredibly strong and healthy trade relationships with many of the Latin American countries gathered here today. Our economic bond forms a critical foundation for advancing peace and prosperity for all of our people and all of our neighbors.

I ask every country represented here today to be prepared to do more to address this very real crisis. We call for the full restoration of democracy and political freedoms in Venezuela.

The problem in Venezuela is not that socialism has been poorly implemented, but that socialism has been faithfully implemented. From the Soviet Union to Cuba to Venezuela, wherever true socialism or communism has been adopted, it has delivered anguish and devastation and failure. Those who preach the tenets of these discredited ideologies only contribute to the continued suffering of the people who live under these cruel systems.

America stands with every person living under a brutal regime. Our respect for sovereignty is also a call for action. All people deserve a government that cares for their safety, their interests, and their wellbeing, including their prosperity.

In America, we seek stronger ties of business and trade with all nations of goodwill. But this trade must be fair, and it must be reciprocal.

For too long, the American people were told that mammoth multinational trade deals, unaccountable international tribunals, and powerful global bureaucracies were the best way to promote their success. But as those promises flowed, millions of jobs vanished, and thousands of factories disappeared. Others gamed the system and broke the rules. And our great middle class, once the bedrock of American prosperity, was forgotten and left behind. But they are forgotten no more, and they will never be forgotten again.

While America will pursue cooperation and commerce with other nations, we are renewing our commitment to the first duty of every government: the duty of our citizens. This bond is the source of America's strength, and that of every responsible nation represented here today.

If this organization is to have any hope of successfully confronting the challenges before us, it will depend—as President Truman said some seventy years ago—on the "independent strength of its members." If we are to embrace the opportunities of the future and overcome the present dangers together, there can be no substitute for strong, sovereign, and independent nations—nations that are rooted in their histories and invested in their destinies. Nations that seek allies to befriend, not enemies to conquer. And most important of all, nations that are home to patriots, to men and women who are willing to sacrifice for their countries, their fellow citizens, and for all that is best in the human spirit.

In remembering the great victory that led to this body's founding, we must never forget that those heroes who fought against evil, also fought for the nations that they loved.

Patriotism led the Poles to die to save Poland, the French to fight for a free France, and the Brits to stand strong for Britain.

Today, if we do not invest ourselves, our hearts, and our minds in our nations, if we will not build strong families, safe communities, and healthy societies for ourselves, no one can do it for us.

We cannot wait for someone else—for faraway countries or far-off bureaucracies. We can't do it. We must solve our problems, to build our prosperity, to secure our future, or we will be vulnerable to decay, domination, and defeat.

The true question for the United Nations today, for people all over the world who hope for better lives for themselves and their children, is a basic one: Are we still patriots? Do we love our nations enough to protect their sovereignty and to take ownership of their futures? Do we revere them enough to defend their interests, preserve their cultures, and ensure a peaceful world for their citizens?

One of the greatest American patriots, John Adams, wrote that the American Revolution was "effected before the war commenced. The Revolution was in the minds and hearts of the people."

That was the moment when America awoke, when we looked around and understood that we were a nation. We realized who we were, what we valued, and what we would give our lives to defend. From its very first moments, the American story is the story of what is possible when people take ownership of their future.

The United States of America has been among the greatest forces for good in the history of the world, and the greatest defenders of sovereignty, security, and prosperity for all.

Now we are calling for a great reawakening of nations, for the revival of their spirits, their pride, their people, and their patriotism.

History is asking us whether we are up to the task. Our answer will be a renewal of will, a rediscovery of resolve, and a rebirth of devotion. We need to defeat the enemies of humanity and unlock the potential of life itself.

Our hope is a word and world of proud, independent nations that embrace their duties, seek friendship, respect others, and make common cause in the greatest shared interest of all: a future of dignity and peace for the people of this wonderful earth.

This is the true vision of the United Nations, the ancient wish of every people, and the deepest yearning that lives inside every sacred soul.

So let this be our mission, and let this be our message to the world: We will fight together, sacrifice together, and stand together for peace, for freedom, for justice, for family, for humanity, and for the almighty God who made us all.

Thank you. God bless you. God bless the nations of the world. And God bless the United States of America. Thank you very much.

Jerusalem Is Israel's Capital

THE WHITE HOUSE, WASHINGTON, DC

December 6, 2017

When I came into office, I promised to look at the world's challenges with open eyes and very fresh thinking. We cannot solve our problems by making the same failed assumptions and repeating the same failed strategies of the past. All challenges demand new approaches.

My announcement today marks the beginning of a new approach to conflict between Israel and the Palestinians. In 1995, Congress adopted the Jerusalem Embassy Act, urging the federal government to relocate the American embassy to Jerusalem, and to recognize that that city—and so importantly—is Israel's capital.

This act passed Congress by an overwhelming bipartisan majority and was reaffirmed by unanimous vote of the Senate only six months ago. Yet, for over twenty years, every previous American president has exercised the law's waiver, refusing to move the US Embassy to Jerusalem or to recognize Jerusalem as Israel's capital city.

Presidents issued these waivers under the belief that delaying the recognition of Jerusalem would advance the cause of peace. Some say they lacked courage, but they made their best judgments based on facts as they understood them at the time.

Nevertheless, the record is in. After more than two decades of waivers, we are no closer to a lasting peace agreement between

Israel and the Palestinians. It would be folly to assume that repeating the exact same formula would now produce a different or better result.

Therefore, I have determined that it is time to officially recognize Jerusalem as the capital of Israel. While previous presidents have made this a major campaign promise, they failed to deliver. Today, I am delivering.

I've judged this course of action to be in the best interests of the United States of America and the pursuit of peace between Israel and the Palestinians. This is a long overdue step to advance the peace process and to work towards a lasting agreement.

Israel is a sovereign nation with the right—like every other sovereign nation—to determine its own capital. Acknowledging this as a fact is a necessary condition for achieving peace.

It was seventy years ago that the United States, under President Truman, recognized the State of Israel. Ever since then, Israel has made its capital in the city of Jerusalem, the capital the Jewish people established in ancient times.

Today, Jerusalem is the seat of the modern Israeli government. It is the home of the Israeli parliament, the Knesset, as well as the Israeli Supreme Court. It is the location of the official residence of the prime minister and the president. It is the headquarters of many government ministries. For decades, visiting American presidents, secretaries of state, and military leaders have met their Israeli counterparts in Jerusalem, as I did on my trip to Israel earlier this year.

Jerusalem is not just the heart of three great religions, but it is now also the heart of one of the most successful democracies in the world. Over the past seven decades, the Israeli people have built a country where Jews, Muslims, and Christians—and people of all faiths—are free to live and worship according to their conscience and according to their beliefs. Jerusalem is today—and must remain—a place where Jews pray at the Western Wall, where Christians walk the Stations of the Cross, and where Muslims worship at Al-Aqsa Mosque.

However, through all of these years, presidents representing the United States have declined to officially recognize Jerusalem as Israel's capital. In fact, we have declined to acknowledge any Israeli capital at all. But today, we finally acknowledge the obvious: that Jerusalem is Israel's capital. This is nothing more or less than a recognition of reality. It is also the right thing to do. It's something that has to be done.

That is why, consistent with the Jerusalem Embassy Act, I am also directing the State Department to begin preparation to move the American Embassy from Tel Aviv to Jerusalem. This will immediately begin the process of hiring architects, engineers, and planners so that a new embassy, when completed, will be a magnificent tribute to peace.

In making these announcements, I also want to make one point very clear: this decision is not intended in any way to reflect a departure from our strong commitment to facilitate a lasting peace agreement. We want an agreement that is a great deal for the Israelis and a great deal for the Palestinians.

We are not taking a position on any final status issues, including the specific boundaries of the Israeli sovereignty in Jerusalem, or the resolution of contested borders. Those questions are up to the parties involved. The United States remains deeply committed to helping facilitate a peace agreement that is acceptable to both sides. I intend to do everything in my power to help forge such an agreement.

Without question, Jerusalem is one of the most sensitive issues in those talks. The United States would support a two-state solution if agreed to by both sides. In the meantime, I call on all parties to maintain the status quo at Jerusalem's holy sites, including the Temple Mount, also known as Haram al-Sharif. Above all, our greatest hope is for peace—the universal yearning in every human soul.

With today's action, I reaffirm my administration's longstanding commitment to a future of peace and security for the region. There will, of course, be disagreement and dissent regarding this announcement. But we are confident that ultimately, as we work through these disagreements, we will arrive at a peace and a place far greater in understanding and cooperation.

This sacred city should call forth the best in humanity—lifting our sights to what is possible, not pulling us back and down to the old fights that have become so totally predictable. Peace is never beyond the grasp of those willing to reach it. So today we call for calm, for moderation, and for the voices of tolerance to prevail over the purveyors of hate. Our children should inherit our love, not our conflicts.

I repeat the message I delivered at the historic and extraordinary summit in Saudi Arabia earlier this year: The Middle East is a region rich with culture, spirit, and history. Its people are brilliant, proud, and diverse, vibrant and strong. But the incredible future awaiting this region is held at bay by bloodshed, ignorance, and terror.

Vice President Pence will travel to the region in the coming days to reaffirm our commitment to work with partners throughout the Middle East to defeat radicalism that threatens the hopes and dreams of future generations.

It is time for the many who desire peace to expel the extremists from their midst. It is time for all civilized nations, and people, to respond to disagreement with reasoned debate, not violence. And it is time for young and moderate voices all across the Middle East to claim for themselves a bright and beautiful future.

So today, let us rededicate ourselves to a path of mutual understanding and respect. Let us rethink old assumptions and open our hearts and minds to possible and possibilities. And finally, I ask the leaders of the region—political and religious, Israeli and Palestinian, Jewish and Christian and Muslim—to join us in the noble quest for lasting peace.

Thank you. God bless you. God bless Israel. God bless the Palestinians. And God bless the United States. Thank you very much.

A New National Security Strategy

RONALD REAGAN BUILDING, WASHINGTON, DC

December 18, 2017

Thank you very much. Thank you. Please. I want to thank Vice President Pence, along with the many members of my Cabinet here with us today.

I also want to thank all of the dedicated professionals—military, civilian, and law enforcement—who devote their lives to serving our nation. In particular, I want to recognize General Dunford and the members of the Joint Chiefs of Staff. Thank you, thank you, thank you.

In addition, we are honored to be joined by House Majority Leader Kevin McCarthy, Homeland Security Chairman Mike McCaul, and Senate Majority Whip John Cornyn. Thank you very much. Thank you for being here. Thank you. Thank you.

Let me begin by expressing our deepest sympathies and most heartfelt prayers for the victims of the train derailment in Washington State. We are closely monitoring the situation, and coordinating with local authorities. It is all the more reason why we must start immediately fixing the infrastructure of the United States.

We're here today to discuss matters of vital importance to us all: America's security, prosperity, and standing in the world. I want to talk about where we've been, where we are now, and finally, our strategy for where we are going in the years ahead.

Over the past eleven months, I have traveled tens of thousands of miles to visit thirteen countries. I have met with more than a hundred world leaders. I have carried America's message to a grand hall in Saudi Arabia, a great square in Warsaw, to the General Assembly of the United Nations, and to the seat of democracy on the Korean Peninsula. Everywhere I traveled, it was my highest privilege and greatest honor to represent the American people.

Throughout our history, the American people have always been the true source of American greatness. Our people have promoted our culture and promoted our values. Americans have fought and sacrificed on the battlefields all over the world. We have liberated captive nations, transformed former enemies into the best of friends, and lifted entire regions of the planet from poverty to prosperity.

Because of our people, America has been among the greatest forces for peace and justice in the history of the world. The American people are generous. You are determined, you are brave, you are strong, and you are wise.

When the American people speak, all of us should listen. And just over one year ago, you spoke loud, and you spoke clear. On November 8th, 2016, you voted to make America great again. You embraced new leadership and very new strategies and also a glorious new hope. That is why we are here today.

But to seize the opportunities of the future, we must first understand the failures of the past. For many years, our citizens watched as Washington politicians presided over one disappointment after another. Too many of our leaders—so many who forgot whose voices they were to respect, and whose interests they were supposed to defend. Our leaders in Washington negotiated disastrous trade deals that brought massive profits to many foreign nations but sent thousands of American factories, and millions of American jobs, to those other countries.

Our leaders engaged in nation-building abroad, while they failed to build up and replenish our nation at home. They undercut and shortchanged our men and women in uniform, with inadequate resources, unstable funding, and unclear missions. They failed to insist that our often very wealthy allies pay their fair share for defense, putting a massive and unfair burden on the US taxpayer and our great US military.

They neglected a nuclear menace in North Korea; made a disastrous, weak, and incomprehensibly bad deal with Iran; and allowed terrorists, such as ISIS, to gain control of vast parts of territory all across the Middle East.

They put American energy under lock and key. They imposed punishing regulations and crippling taxes. They surrendered our sovereignty to foreign bureaucrats in faraway and distant capitals.

And over the profound objections of the American people, our politicians left our borders wide open. Millions of immigrants entered illegally. Millions more were admitted into our country without the proper vetting needed to protect our security and our economy. Leaders in Washington imposed on the country an immigration policy that Americans never voted for, never asked for, and never approved—a policy where the wrong people are allowed into our country, and the right people are rejected. American citizens, as usual, have been left to bear the cost and to pick up the tab.

On top of everything else, our leaders drifted from American principles. They lost sight of America's destiny. And they lost their belief in American greatness. As a result, our citizens lost something as well. The people lost confidence in their government, and eventually, even lost confidence in their future.

But last year, all of that began to change. The American people rejected the failures of the past. You rediscovered your voice and reclaimed ownership of this nation and its destiny.

On January 20th, 2017, I stood on the steps of the Capitol to herald the day the people became the rulers of their nation again. Thank you. Now, less than one year later, I am proud to report that the entire world has heard the news and has already seen the signs. America is coming back, and America is coming back strong.

Upon my inauguration, I announced that the United States would return to a simple principle: the first duty of our government is to serve its citizens, many of whom have been forgotten.

But they are not forgotten anymore. With every decision and every action, we are now putting America first.

We are rebuilding our nation, our confidence, and our standing in the world. We have moved swiftly to confront our challenges, and we have confronted them head-on.

We are once again investing in our defense. Almost seven hundred billion dollars—a record—this coming year. We are demanding extraordinary strength, which will hopefully lead to long and extraordinary peace. We are giving our courageous military men and women the support they need and so dearly deserve.

We have withdrawn the United States from job-killing deals such as the Trans-Pacific Partnership, and the very expensive and unfair Paris Climate Accord. And on our trip to Asia last month, I announced that we will no longer tolerate trading abuse.

We have established strict new vetting procedures to keep terrorists out of the United States, and our vetting is getting tougher each month.

To counter Iran and block its path to a nuclear weapon, I sanctioned the Islamic Revolutionary Guard Corps for its support of terrorism, and I declined to certify the Iran deal to Congress.

Following my trip to the Middle East, the Gulf states, and other Muslim-majority nations, joined together to fight radical Islamist ideology and terrorist financing, we have dealt ISIS one devastating defeat after another. The coalition to defeat ISIS has now recaptured almost one hundred percent of the land once held by these terrorists in Iraq and Syria. Great job. Great job. Really good. Really good. Thank you. Thank you. We have a great military. We're now chasing them wherever they flee, and we will not let them into the United States.

In Afghanistan, our troops are no longer undermined by artificial timelines, and we no longer tell our enemies of our plans. We are beginning to see results on the battlefield. And we have made clear to Pakistan that while we desire continued partnership, we must see decisive action against terrorist groups operating on their territory. And we make massive payments every year to Pakistan. They have to help.

Our efforts to strengthen the NATO Alliance set the stage for significant increases in member contributions, with tens of billions of dollars more pouring in because I would not allow member states to be delinquent in the payment while we guarantee their safety and are willing to fight wars for them. We have made clear that countries that are immensely wealthy should reimburse the United States for the cost of defending them. This is a major departure from the past, but a fair and necessary one—necessary for our country, necessary for our taxpayer, necessary for our own thought process.

Our campaign of maximum pressure on the North Korean regime has resulted in the toughest-ever sanctions. We have united our allies in an unprecedented effort to isolate North Korea. However, there is much more work to do. America and its allies will take all necessary steps to achieve a denuclearization and ensure that this regime cannot threaten the world. This situation should have been taken care of long before I got into office, when it was much easier to handle. But it will be taken care of. We have no choice.

At home, we are keeping our promises and liberating the American economy. We have created more than two million jobs since the election. Unemployment is at a seventeen-year low. The stock market is at an all-time high, and just a little while ago, hit yet another all-time high—the eighty-fifth time since my election.

We have cut twenty-two regulations for every one new regulation—the most in the history of our country. We have unlocked America's vast energy resources.

As the world watches—and the world is indeed watching—we are days away from passing historic tax cuts for American families and businesses. It will be the biggest tax cut and tax reform in the history of our country.

And we are seeing the response we fully expected. Economic growth has topped three percent for two quarters in a row. GDP growth—which is way ahead of schedule under my administration—will be one of America's truly greatest weapons.

Optimism has surged. Confidence has returned. With this new confidence, we are also bringing back clarity to our thinking. We are reasserting these fundamental truths:

A nation without borders is not a nation.

A nation that does not protect prosperity at home cannot protect its interests abroad.

A nation that is not prepared to win a war is a nation not capable of preventing a war.

A nation that is not proud of its history cannot be confident in its future.

And a nation that is not certain of its values cannot summon the will to defend them.

Today, grounded in these truths, we are presenting to the world our new National Security Strategy. Based on my direction, this document has been in development for over a year. It has the endorsement of my entire Cabinet.

Our new strategy is based on a principled realism, guided by our vital national interests, and rooted in our timeless values.

This strategy recognizes that, whether we like it or not, we are engaged in a new era of competition. We accept that vigorous military, economic, and political contests are now playing out all around the world.

We face rogue regimes that threaten the United States and our allies. We face terrorist organizations, transnational criminal networks, and others who spread violence and evil around the globe.

We also face rival powers—Russia and China—that seek to challenge American influence, values, and wealth. We will attempt to build a great partnership with those and other countries, but in a manner that always protects our national interest.

As an example, yesterday I received a call from President Putin of Russia, thanking our country for the intelligence that our CIA was able to provide them concerning a major terrorist attack planned in Saint Petersburg, where many people—perhaps in the thousands—could have been killed. They were able to apprehend these terrorists before the event, with no loss of life. And that's a great thing, and the way it's supposed to work. That is the way it's supposed to work.

But while we seek such opportunities of cooperation, we will stand up for ourselves, and we will stand up for our country like we have never stood up before.

We know that American success is not a forgone conclusion. It must be earned, and it must be won. Our rivals are tough, they're tenacious, and committed to the long term. But so are we.

To succeed, we must integrate every dimension of our national strength, and we must compete with every instrument of our national power.

Under the Trump administration, America is gaining wealth, leading to enhanced power—faster than anyone thought—with six trillion dollars more in the stock market alone since the election—six trillion dollars.

With the strategy I am announcing today, we are declaring that America is in the game, and America is going to win.

Our strategy advances four vital national interests. First, we must protect the American people, the homeland, and our great American way of life. This strategy recognizes that we cannot secure our nation if we do not secure our borders. So for the first time ever, American strategy now includes a serious plan to defend our homeland. It calls for the construction of a wall on our southern border; ending chain migration and the horrible visa and lottery programs; closing loopholes that undermine enforcement; and strongly supporting our Border Patrol agents, ICE officers, and Homeland Security personnel.

In addition, our strategy calls for us to confront, discredit, and defeat radical Islamic terrorism and ideology, and to prevent it from spreading into the United States. And we will develop new ways to counter those who use new domains, such as cyber and social media, to attack our nation or threaten our society.

The second pillar of our strategy is to promote American prosperity. For the first time, American strategy recognizes that economic security is national security. Economic vitality, growth, and prosperity at home is absolutely necessary for American power and influence abroad. Any nation that trades away its prosperity for security will end up losing both.

That is why this National Security Strategy emphasizes, more than any before, the critical steps we must take to ensure the prosperity of our nation for a long, long time to come.

It calls for cutting taxes and rolling back unnecessary regulations. It calls for trade based on the principles of fairness and reciprocity. It calls for firm action against unfair trade practices and intellectual property theft. And it calls for new steps to protect our national security industrial and innovation base.

The strategy proposes a complete rebuilding of American infrastructure—our roads, bridges, airports, waterways, and communications infrastructure. And it embraces a future of American energy dominance and self-sufficiency.

The third pillar of our strategy is to preserve peace through strength. We recognize that weakness is the surest path to conflict, and unrivaled power is the most certain means of defense. For this reason, our strategy breaks from the damaging defense sequester. We're going to get rid of that.

It calls for a total modernization of our military, and reversing previous decisions to shrink our armed forces—even as threats to national security grew. It calls for streamlining acquisition, eliminating bloated bureaucracy, and massively building up our military, which has the fundamental side benefit of creating millions and millions of jobs.

This strategy includes plans to counter modern threats, such as cyber and electromagnetic attacks. It recognizes space as a competitive domain, and calls for multi-layered missile defense. This strategy outlines important steps to address new forms of conflict such as economic and political aggression.

And our strategy emphasizes strengthening alliances to cope with these threats. It recognizes that our strength is magnified by allies who share principles—and our principles—and shoulder their fair share of responsibility for our common security.

Fourth and finally, our strategy is to advance American influence in the world, but this begins with building up our wealth and power at home.

America will lead again. We do not seek to impose our way of life on anyone, but we will champion the values without apology. We want strong alliances and partnerships based on cooperation and reciprocity. We will make new partnerships with those who share our goals, and make common interests into a common cause. We will not allow inflexible ideology to become an obsolete and obstacle to peace.

We will pursue the vision we have carried around the world over this past year—a vision of strong, sovereign, and independent nations that respect their citizens and respect their neighbors. Nations that thrive in commerce and cooperation, rooted in their histories, and branching out toward their destinies.

That is the future we wish for this world, and that is the future we seek in America.

With this strategy, we are calling for a great reawakening of America, a resurgence of confidence, and a rebirth of patriotism, prosperity, and pride.

And we are returning to the wisdom of our Founders. In America, the people govern, the people rule, and the people are sovereign. What we have built here in America is precious and unique. In all of history, never before has freedom reigned, the rule of law prevailed, and the people thrived as we have here for nearly two hundred fifty years.

We must love and defend it. We must guard it with vigilance and spirit—and if necessary, like so many before us, with our very lives. And we declare that our will is renewed, our future is regained, and our dreams are restored.

Every American has a role to play in this grand national effort. And today, I invite every citizen to take their part in our vital mission. Together, our task is to strengthen our families, to build up our communities, to serve our citizens, and to celebrate American greatness as a shining example to the world.

As long as we are proud—and very proud—of who we are, how we got here, and what we are fighting for to preserve, we will not fail.

If we do all of this, if we rediscover our resolve and commit ourselves to compete and win again, then together we will leave our children and our grandchildren a nation that is stronger, better, freer, prouder—and yes, an America that is greater than ever before.

God bless you. Thank you very much. Thank you.

America Is Open for Business

WORLD ECONOMIC FORUM, DAVOS, SWITZERLAND

January 26, 2018

It's a privilege to be here at this forum where leaders in business, science, art, diplomacy, and world affairs have gathered for many, many years to discuss how we can advance prosperity, security, and peace. I'm here today to represent the interests of the American people, and affirm America's friendship and partnership in building a better world.

Like all nations represented at this great forum, America hopes for a future in which everyone can prosper, and every child can grow up free from violence, poverty, and fear. Over the past year, we have made extraordinary strides in the US. We're lifting up forgotten communities, creating exciting new opportunities, and helping every American find their path to the American dream. The dream of a great job, a safe home, and a better life for their children.

After years of stagnation, the United States is once again experiencing strong economic growth. The stock market is smashing one record after another and has added more than seven trillion dollars in new wealth since my election. Consumer confidence, business confidence, and manufacturing confidence are the highest that they have been in many decades.

Since my election, we've created 2.4 million jobs, and that number is going up very, very substantially. Small business optimism is at an all-time high. New unemployment claims are near the lowest we've seen in almost half a century. African American unemployment has reached the lowest rate ever recorded in the United States, and so has unemployment among Hispanic Americans.

The world is witnessing the resurgence of a strong and prosperous America. I'm here to deliver a simple message. There has never been a better time to hire, to build, to invest, and to grow in the United States. America is open for business, and we are competitive once again. The American economy is by far the largest in the world, and we've just enacted the most significant tax cuts and reform in American history. We've massively cut taxes for the middle class and small businesses to let working families keep more of their hard-earned money.

We lowered our corporate tax rate from thirty-five percent all the way down to twenty-one percent. As a result, millions of workers have received tax-cut bonuses from their employers in amounts as large as three thousand dollars. The tax cut bill is expected to raise the average American's household income by more than four thousand dollars. The world's largest company, Apple, announced it plans to bring two hundred forty-five billion dollars in overseas profits home to America. Their total investment into the United States economy will be more than three hundred fifty billion dollars over the next five years. Now is the perfect time to bring your business, your jobs, and your investments to the United States.

This is especially true because we have undertaken the most extensively regulatory reduction ever conceived. Regulation is stealth taxation. The US, like many other countries' unelected bureaucrats, we have—believe me, we have them all over the place—and they have imposed crushing, and anti-business and anti-worker, regulations on our citizens, with no vote, no legislative debate, and no real accountability. In America, those days are over. I pledged to eliminate two unnecessary regulations for every one new regulation. We have succeeded beyond our highest expectations. Instead of two for one, we have cut twenty-two burdensome regulations for every one new rule. We are freeing our businesses and workers so they can thrive and flourish as never before. We are creating an environment that attracts capital, invites investment, and rewards production. America is the place to do business, so come to America where you can innovate, create, and build.

I believe in America. As President of the United States, I will always put America first—just like the leaders of other countries should put their country first also. But America first does not mean America alone. When the United States grows, so does the world. American prosperity has created countless jobs all around the globe, and the drive for excellence, creativity, and innovation in the US has led to important discoveries that help people everywhere live more prosperous and far healthier lives.

As the United States pursues domestic reforms to unleash jobs and growth, we are also working to reform the international trading system so that it promotes broadly shared prosperity and rewards to those who play by the rules. We cannot have free and open trade if some countries exploit the system at the expense of others. We support free trade, but it needs to be fair, and it needs to be reciprocal, because in the end, unfair trade undermines us all. The United States will no longer turn a blind eye to unfair economic practices, including massive intellectual property theft, industrial subsidies, and pervasive state-led economic planning.

These and other predatory behaviors are distorting the global markets and harming businesses and workers not just in the US, but around the globe. Just like we expect the leaders of other countries to protect their interests, as president of the United States, I will always protect the interests of our country, our companies, and our workers. We will enforce our trade laws and restore integrity to our trading system. Only by insisting on fair and reciprocal trade can we create a system that works not just for the US, but for all nations.

As I have said, the United States is prepared to negotiate mutually beneficial, bilateral trade agreements with all countries. This will include the countries in TPP, which are very important. We have agreements with several of them already. We would consider negotiating with the rest either individually, or perhaps as a group, if it is in the interests of all. My administration is also taking swift action in other ways to restore American confidence and independence. We are lifting self-imposed restrictions on energy production to provide affordable power to our citizens and businesses, and to promote energy security for our friends all around the world. No country should be held hostage to a single provider of energy. America is roaring back, and now is the time to invest in the future of America.

We have dramatically cut taxes to make America competitive. We are eliminating burdensome regulations at a record pace. We are reforming the bureaucracy to make it lean, responsive, and accountable. And we are insuring our laws are enforced fairly. We have the best colleges and universities in the world, and we have the best workers in the world. Energy is an abundant and affordable. There is never been a better time to do business in America. We are also making historic investments in the American military, because we cannot have prosperity without security. To make the world safer from rogue regimes, terrorism, and revisionist powers, we're asking our friends and allies to invest in their own defenses, and to meet their financial obligations. Our common security requires everyone to contribute their fair share.

My administration is proud to have led historic efforts at the United Nations Security Council, and all around the world, to unite all civilized nations in our campaign of maximum pressure to de-nuke the Korean peninsula. We continue to call on partners to confront Iran's support for terrorists, and block Iran's path to a nuclear weapon. We're also working with allies and partners to destroy jihadist terrorist organizations such as ISIS, and very successfully so. The United States is leading a very broad coalition to deny terrorists control of their territory and populations, to cut off their funding, and to discredit their wicked ideology. I am pleased to report that the coalition to defeat ISIS has retaken almost one hundred percent of the territory once held by these killers in Iraq and Syria. There is still more fighting and work to be done. And to consolidate our gains, we are committed to ensuring that Afghanistan never again becomes a safe haven for terrorists who want to commit mass murder on our civilian populations.

I want to thank those nations represented here today that have joined in these crucial efforts. You are not just securing your own citizens, but saving lives and restoring hope for millions and millions of people. When it comes to terrorism, we will do whatever is necessary to protect our nation. We will defend our citizens and our borders. We are also securing our immigration system as a matter of both national and economic security. America is a cutting-edge economy, but our immigration system is stuck in the past.

We must replace our current system of extended family chain migration, with a merit-based system of admissions that selects new arrivals based on their ability to contribute to our economy, to support themselves financially, and to strengthen our country.

In rebuilding America, we are also fully committed to developing our workforce. We are lifting people from dependence to independence, because we know the single best anti-poverty program is a very simple and very beautiful paycheck. To be successful, it is not enough to invest in our economy. We must invest in our people. When people are forgotten, the world becomes fractured. Only by hearing and responding to the voices of the forgotten can we create a bright future that is truly shared by all. The nation's greatness is more than the sum of its production. A nation's greatness is the sum of its citizens—the values, pride, love, devotion, and character of the people who call that nation home.

From my first international G7 Summit, to the G20, to the U.N. General Assembly, to APEC, to the World Trade Organization, and today at the World Economic Forum, my administration has not only been present, but has driven our message that we are all stronger when free, sovereign nations cooperate towards shared goals, and they cooperate toward shared dreams.

Represented in this room are some of the remarkable citizens from all over the world. You are national leaders, business titans, industry giants, and many of the brightest minds in many fields. Each of you has the power to change hearts, transform lives, and shape your countries' destinies. With this power comes an obligation, however—a duty of loyalty to the people, workers, and customers, who made you who you are.

So together, let us resolve to use our power, our resources, and our voices not just for ourselves, but for our people, to lift their burdens, to raise their hopes, and to empower their dreams. To protect their families, their communities, their histories, and their futures. That's what we're doing in America, and the results are totally unmistakable. It's why new businesses and investment are flooding in. It's why our unemployment rate is the lowest it's been in so many decades. It's why America's future has never been brighter.

Today, I am inviting all of you to become part of this incredible future we are building together. Thank you to our hosts. Thank you to the leaders and innovators in the audience. But most importantly, thank you to all of the hard-working men and women who do their duty each and every day, making this a better world for everyone. Together, let us send our love and our gratitude to them, because they really make our countries run. They make our countries great.

Thank you. And God bless you all. Thank you very much.

State of the Union Address: A New Tide of Optimism

US HOUSE OF REPRESENTATIVES, WASHINGTON, DC

January 30, 2018

Mister Speaker, Mister Vice President, Members of Congress, the First Lady of the United States, and my fellow Americans:

Less than one year has passed since I first stood at this podium, in this majestic chamber, to speak on behalf of the American people—and to address their concerns, their hopes, and their dreams. That night, our new administration had already taken very swift action. A new tide of optimism was already sweeping across our land.

Each day since, we have gone forward with a clear vision and a righteous mission—to make America great again for all Americans.

Over the last year, we have made incredible progress and achieved extraordinary success. We have faced challenges we expected, and others we could never have imagined. We have shared in the heights of victory and the pains of hardship. We have endured floods and fires and storms. But through it all, we have seen the beauty of America's soul and the steel in America's spine.

Each test has forged new American heroes to remind us who we are, and show us what we can be.

We saw the volunteers of the Cajun Navy, racing to the rescue with their fishing boats to save people in the aftermath of a totally devastating hurricane.

We saw strangers shielding strangers from a hail of gunfire on the Las Vegas Strip.

We heard tales of Americans like Coast Guard Petty Officer Ashlee Leppert, who is here tonight in the Gallery with Melania. Ashlee was aboard one of the first helicopters on the scene in Houston during Hurricane Harvey. Through eighteen hours of wind and rain, Ashlee braved live power lines and deep water to help save more than forty lives. Ashlee, we all thank you. Thank you very much.

We heard about Americans like firefighter David Dahlberg. He is here with us, too. David faced down walls of flame to rescue almost sixty children trapped at a California summer camp threatened by those devastating wildfires.

To everyone still recovering in Texas, Florida, Louisiana, Puerto Rico, and the Virgin Islands—everywhere—we are with you, we love you, and we always will pull through together. Always.

Thank you to David and the brave people of California. Thank you very much, David. Great job.

Some trials over the past year touched this chamber very personally. With us tonight is one of the toughest people ever to serve in this House—a guy who took a bullet, almost died, and was back to work three and a half months later. The legend from Louisiana, Congressman Steve Scalise. I think they like you, Steve.

We are incredibly grateful for the heroic efforts of the Capitol Police officers, the Alexandria Police, and the doctors, nurses, and paramedics who saved his life, and the lives of many others, some in this room.

In the aftermath of that terrible shooting, we came together, not as Republicans or Democrats, but as representatives of the people. But it is not enough to come together only in times of tragedy. Tonight, I call upon all of us to set aside our differences, to seek out common ground, and to summon the unity we need to deliver for the people. This is really the key: These are the people we were elected to serve.

Over the last year, the world has seen what we always knew: that no people on earth are so fearless, or daring, or determined as

Americans. If there is a mountain, we climb it. If there is a frontier, we cross it. If there is a challenge, we tame it. If there is an opportunity, we seize it.

So let us begin tonight by recognizing that the state of our Union is strong, because our people are strong. And together, we are building a safe, strong, and proud America.

Since the election, we have created 2.4 million new jobs, including two hundred thousand new jobs in manufacturing alone. Tremendous number. After years and years of wage stagnation, we are finally seeing rising wages.

Unemployment claims have hit a forty-five-year low. And something I'm very proud of: African American unemployment stands at the lowest rate ever recorded, and Hispanic American unemployment has also reached the lowest levels in history.

Small business confidence is at an all-time high. The stock market has smashed one record after another, gaining eight trillion dollars or more in value in just this short period of time. The great news for Americans: 401(k), retirement, pension, and college savings accounts have gone through the roof.

And just as I promised the American people from this podium eleven months ago, we enacted the biggest tax cuts and reforms in American history.

Our massive tax cuts provide tremendous relief for the middle class and small businesses.

To lower tax rates for hardworking Americans, we nearly doubled the standard deduction for everyone. Now, the first twenty-four thousand dollars earned by a married couple is completely tax-free. We also doubled the child tax credit.

A typical family of four making seventy-five thousand dollars will see their tax bill reduced by two thousand dollars—slashing their tax bill in half.

In April, this will be the last time you ever file under the old and very broken system—and millions of Americans will have more take-home pay starting next month—a lot more.

We eliminated an especially cruel tax that fell mostly on Americans making less than fifty thousand dollars a year—forcing them to pay tremendous penalties simply because they could not afford government-ordered health plans. We repealed the core of the disastrous Obamacare—the individual mandate is now gone. Thank heaven.

We slashed the business tax rate from thirty-five percent, all the way down to twenty-one percent, so American companies can compete and win against anyone else anywhere in the world. These changes alone are estimated to increase average family income by more than four thousand dollars—a lot of money.

Small businesses have also received a massive tax cut and can now deduct twenty percent of their business income.

Here tonight are Steve Staub and Sandy Keplinger of Staub Manufacturing—a small, beautiful business in Ohio. They have just finished the best year in their twenty-year history. Because of tax reform, they are handing out raises, hiring an additional fourteen people, and expanding into the building next door. Good feeling.

One of Staub's employees, Corey Adams, is also with us tonight. Corey is an all-American worker. He supported himself through high school, lost his job during the 2008 recession, and was later hired by Staub, where he trained to become a welder. Like many hardworking Americans, Corey plans to invest his taxcut raise into his new home and his two daughters' education. Corey, please stand. And he's a great welder. I was told that by the man that owns that company that's doing so well, so congratulations, Corey.

Since we passed tax cuts, roughly three million workers have already gotten tax-cut bonuses—many of them, thousands and thousands of dollars per worker, and it's getting more every month, every week. Apple has just announced it plans to invest a total of three hundred fifty billion dollars in America, and hire another twenty thousand workers.

And just a little while ago, Exxon Mobil announced a fifty billion-dollar investment in the United States. Just a little while ago.

This, in fact, is our new American moment. There has never been a better time to start living the American Dream.

So to every citizen watching at home tonight: no matter where you have been, or where you come from, this is your time. If you work hard, if you believe in yourself, if you believe in America, then you can dream anything, you can be anything, and together, we can achieve absolutely anything.

Tonight, I want to talk about what kind of future we are going to have and what kind of nation we are going to be. All of us, together, as one team, one people, and one American family can do anything.

We all share the same home, the same heart, the same destiny, and the same great American flag.

Together, we are rediscovering the American way.

In America, we know that faith and family, not government and bureaucracy, are the center of American life. The motto is "In God we trust."

And we celebrate our police, our military, and our amazing veterans as heroes who deserve our total and unwavering support.

Here tonight is Preston Sharp, a twelve-year-old boy from Redding, California, who noticed that veterans' graves were not marked with flags on Veterans Day. He decided, all by himself, to change that and started a movement that has now placed forty thousand flags at the graves of our great heroes. Preston: a job well-done.

Young patriots like Preston teach all of us about our civic duty as Americans. And I met Preston a little while ago, and he is something very special, that I can tell you. Great future. Thank you very much for all you've done, Preston. Thank you very much.

Preston's reverence for those who have served our nation reminds us why we salute our flag, why we put our hands on our hearts for the Pledge of Allegiance, and why we proudly stand for the national anthem.

Americans love their country. And they deserve a government that shows them the same love and loyalty in return.

For the last year, we have sought to restore the bonds of trust between our citizens and their government.

Working with the Senate, we are appointing judges who will interpret the Constitution as written, including a great new Supreme Court justice, and more circuit court judges than any new administration in the history of our country.

We are totally defending our Second Amendment and have taken historic actions to protect religious liberty.

And we are serving our brave veterans, including giving our veterans choice in their healthcare decisions. Last year, the Congress passed, and I signed, the landmark VA Accountability Act. Since its passage, my administration has already removed more than one thousand five hundred VA employees who failed to give our veterans the care they deserve—and we are hiring talented people who love our vets as much as we do.

And I will not stop until our veterans are properly taken care of, which has been my promise to them from the very beginning of this great journey.

All Americans deserve accountability and respect—and that is what we are giving to our wonderful heroes—our veterans. Thank you. So tonight, I call on the Congress to empower every cabinet secretary with the authority to reward good workers—and to remove federal employees who undermine the public trust or fail the American people.

In our drive to make Washington accountable, we have eliminated more regulations in our first year than any administration in the history of our country.

We have ended the war on American energy, and we have ended the war on beautiful clean coal. We are now very proudly an exporter of energy to the world.

In Detroit, I halted government mandates that crippled America's great, beautiful autoworkers so that we can get the Motor City revving its engines again, and that's what's happening.

Many car companies are now building and expanding plants in the United States—something we have not seen for decades. Chrysler is moving a major plant from Mexico to Michigan. Toyota and Mazda are opening up a plant in Alabama—a big one—and we haven't seen this in a long time. It's all coming back. Very soon, auto plants and other plants will be opening up all over our country. This is all news Americans are totally unaccustomed to hearing. For many years. companies and jobs wee only leaving us, but now they are roaring back. They're coming back. They want to be where the action is. They want to be in the United States of America. That's where they want to be.

Exciting progress is happening every single day.

To speed access to breakthrough cures and affordable generic drugs, last year the FDA approved more new and generic drugs and medical devices than ever before in our country's history.

We also believe that patients with terminal conditions and terminal illness should have access to experimental treatments that could potentially save their lives.

People who are terminally ill should not have to go from country to country to seek a cure—I want to give them a chance right here at home. It is time for Congress to give these wonderful, incredible Americans the right to try.

One of my greatest priorities is to reduce the price of prescription drugs. In many other countries, these drugs cost far less than what we pay in the United States, and it's very, very unfair. That is why I have directed my administration to make fixing the injustice of high drug prices one of my top priorities for the year. And prices will come down substantially. Watch.

America has also finally turned the page on decades of unfair trade deals that sacrificed our prosperity and shipped away our companies, our jobs, and our wealth. Our nation has lost its wealth, but we're getting it back so fast.

The era of economic surrender is over. From now on, we expect trading relationships to be fair and, very importantly, reciprocal.

We will work to fix bad trade deals and negotiate new ones, and they'll be good ones, and they'll be fair.

And we will protect American workers and American intellectual property through strong enforcement of our trade rules.

As we rebuild our industries, it is also time to rebuild our crumbling infrastructure.

America is a nation of builders. We built the Empire State Building in just one year—isn't it a disgrace that it can now take ten years just to get a minor permit approved for the building of a simple road?

I am asking both parties to come together to give us safe, fast, reliable, and modern infrastructure our economy needs, and our people deserve.

Tonight, I am calling on Congress to produce a bill that generates at least 1.5 trillion dollars for the new infrastructure investment that our country so desperately needs.

Every federal dollar should be leveraged by partnering with state and local governments, and where appropriate, tapping into private-sector investment—to permanently fix the infrastructure deficit—and we can do it.

Any bill must also streamline the permitting and approval process—getting it down to no more than two years, and perhaps even one.

Together, we can reclaim our great building heritage. We will build gleaming new roads, bridges, highways, railways, and waterways all across our land. And we will do it with American heart, American hands, and American grit.

We want every American to know the dignity of a hard day's work. We want every child to be safe in their home at night. And we want every citizen to be proud of this land that we all love so much.

We can lift our citizens from welfare to work, from dependence to independence, and from poverty to prosperity.

As tax cuts create new jobs, let's invest in workforce development, and et's invest in job training, which we need so badly. Let's open great vocational schools so our future workers can learn a craft and realize their full potential. And let's support working families by supporting paid family leave.

As America regains its strength, opportunity must be extended to all citizens. That is why, this year, we will embark on reforming our prisons to help former inmates, who have served their time, get a second chance at life.

Struggling communities, especially immigrant communities, will also be helped by immigration policies that focus on the best interests of American workers and American families.

For decades, open borders have allowed drugs and gangs to pour into our most vulnerable communities. They have allowed millions of low-wage workers to compete for jobs and wages against the poorest Americans. Most tragically, they have caused the loss of many innocent lives.

Here tonight are two fathers and two mothers: Evelyn Rodriguez, Freddy Cuevas, Elizabeth Alvarado, and Robert Mickens. Their two teenage daughters—Kayla Cuevas and Nisa Mickens—were close friends on Long Island. But in September 2016, on the eve of Nisa's sixteenth birthday—such a happy time it should have been—neither of them came home. These two precious girls were brutally murdered while walking together in their hometown. Six members of the savage MS-13 gang have been charged with Kayla and Nisa's murders. Many of these gang members took advantage of glaring loopholes in our laws to enter the country as illegal unaccompanied alien minors—and wound up in Kayla and Nisa's high school.

Evelyn, Elizabeth, Freddy, and Robert: Tonight, everyone in this chamber is praying for you. Everyone in America is grieving for you. Please stand. Thank you very much. I want you to know that, three hundred twenty million hearts are, right now, breaking for you. We love you. Thank you. While we cannot imagine the depth of that kind of sorrow, we can make sure that other families never have to endure this kind of pain.

Tonight, I am calling on Congress to finally close the deadly loopholes that have allowed MS-13 and other criminal gangs to break into our country. We have proposed new legislation that will fix our immigration laws and support our ICE and Border Patrol agents—these are great people, these are great, great people that work so hard in the midst of such danger—so that this cannot ever happen again.

The United States is a compassionate nation. We are proud that we do more than any other country, anywhere in the world, to help the needy, the struggling, and the underprivileged all over the world. But as president of the United States, my highest loyalty, my greatest compassion, my constant concern, is for America's children, America's struggling workers, and America's forgotten communities. I want our youth to grow up to achieve great things. I want our poor to have their chance to rise.

So tonight, I am extending an open hand to work with members of both parties—Democrats and Republicans—to protect our citizens of every background, color, religion, and creed. My duty, and the sacred duty of every elected official in this chamber, is to defend Americans—to protect their safety, their families, their communities, and their right to the American Dream. Because Americans are dreamers, too.

Here tonight is one leader in the effort to defend our country: Homeland Security Investigations Special Agent Celestino Martinez. He goes by DJ or CJ. He said, "call me either one," so we'll call you CJ." Served fifteen years in the Air Force before becoming an ICE agent and spending the last fifteen years fighting gang violence and getting dangerous criminals off of our streets—tough job. At one point, MS-13 leaders ordered CJ's murder, and they wanted it to happen quickly. But he did not cave to threats or fear. Last May, he commanded an operation to track down gang members on Long Island. His team has arrested nearly four hundred, including more than two hundred twenty MS-13 gang members.

And I have to tell you what the Border Patrol and ICE have done: We have sent thousands and thousands and thousands of MS-13 horrible people out of this country or into our prisons. So I just want to congratulate you, CJ. You're a brave guy. Thank you very much. And I asked CJ, "What's the secret?" He said, "We're just tougher than they are," and I like that answer.

Now let us get the Congress to send you and all of the people in this great chamber have to do it—we have no choice—CJ, we're going to send you reinforcements, and we're going to send them to you quickly. It's what you need. Over the next few weeks, the House and Senate will be voting on an immigration reform package.

In recent months, my administration has met extensively with both Democrats and Republicans to craft a bipartisan approach to immigration reform. Based on these discussions, we presented Congress with a detailed proposal that should be supported by both parties as a fair compromise—one where nobody gets everything they want, but where our country gets the critical reforms it needs and must have.

Here are the four pillars of our plan:

The first pillar of our framework generously offers a path to citizenship for 1.8 million illegal immigrants who were brought here by their parents at a young age—that covers almost three times more people than the previous administration covered. Under our plan, those who meet education and work requirements, and show good moral character, will be able to become full citizens of the United States over a twelve-year period.

The second pillar fully secures the border. That means building a great wall on the southern border, and it means hiring more heroes like CJ to keep our communities safe. Crucially, our plan closes the terrible loopholes exploited by criminals and terrorists to enter our country—and it finally ends the horrible and dangerous practice of catch and release.

The third pillar ends the visa lottery—a program that randomly hands out green cards without any regard for skill, merit, or the safety of American people. It is time to begin moving towards a merit-based immigration system—one that admits people who are skilled, who want to work, who will contribute to our society, and who will love and respect our country.

The fourth and final pillar protects the nuclear family by ending chain migration. Under the current broken system, a single immigrant can bring in virtually unlimited numbers of distant relatives. Under our plan, we focus on the immediate family by limiting sponsorships to spouses and minor children. This vital reform is necessary, not just for our economy, but for our security and or the future of America.

In recent weeks, two terrorist attacks in New York were made possible by the visa lottery and chain migration. In the age of terrorism, these programs present risks we can just no longer afford.

It is time to reform these outdated immigration rules and finally bring our immigration system into the twenty-first century.

These four pillars represent a down-the-middle compromise, and one that will create a safe, modern, and lawful immigration system.

For over thirty years, Washington has tried and failed to solve this problem. This Congress can be the one that finally makes it happen.

Most importantly, these four pillars will produce legislation that fulfills my ironclad pledge to sign a bill that puts America first. So let us come together, set politics aside, and finally get the job done.

These reforms will also support our response to the terrible crisis of opioid and drug addiction. Never before has it been like it is now. It is terrible. We have to do something about it.

In 2016, we lost sixty-four thousand Americans to drug overdoses: one hundred seventy-four deaths per day. Seven per hour. We must get much tougher on drug dealers and pushers if we are going to succeed in stopping this scourge.

My administration is committed to fighting the drug epidemic and helping get treatment for those in need—for those who have been so terribly hurt. The struggle will be long and it will be difficult—but, as Americans always do, we will succeed, we will prevail.

As we have seen tonight, the most difficult challenges bring out the best in America.

We see a vivid expression of this truth in the story of the Holets family of New Mexico. Ryan Holets is twenty-seven years old, an officer with the Albuquerque Police Department. He is here tonight with his wife, Rebecca. Last year, Ryan was on duty when he saw a pregnant, homeless woman preparing to inject heroin. When Ryan told her she was going to harm her unborn child, she began to weep. She told him she did not know where to turn, but badly wanted a safe home for her baby.

In that moment, Ryan said he felt God speak to him: "You will do it—because you can." He took out a picture of his wife and their four kids. Then he went home to tell his wife, Rebecca. In an instant, she agreed to adopt. The Holets named their new daughter Hope.

Ryan and Rebecca: You embody the goodness of our nation. Thank you. Thank you, Ryan and Rebecca.

As we rebuild America's strength and confidence at home, we are also restoring our strength and standing abroad.

Around the world, we face rogue regimes, terrorist groups, and rivals like China and Russia that challenge our interests, our economy, and our values. In confronting these horrible dangers, we know that weakness is the surest path to conflict, and unmatched power is the surest means to our true and great defense.

For this reason, I am asking the Congress to end the dangerous defense sequester and fully fund our great military.

As part of our defense, we must modernize and rebuild our nuclear arsenal—hopefully never having to use it, but making it so strong and so powerful that it will deter any acts of aggression by any other nation or anyone else. Perhaps someday in the future, there will be a magical moment when the countries of the world will get together to eliminate their nuclear weapons. Unfortunately, we are not there yet, sadly.

Last year, I also pledged that we would work with our allies to extinguish ISIS from the face of the earth. One year later, I am proud to report that the coalition to defeat ISIS has liberated very close to one hundred percent of the territory just recently held by these killers in Iraq and Syria and in other locations as well. But there is much more work to be done. We will continue our fight until ISIS is defeated.

Army Staff Sergeant Justin Peck is here tonight. Near Raqqa last November, Justin and his comrade, Chief Petty Officer Kenton Stacy, were on a mission to clear buildings that ISIS had rigged with explosives, so that civilians could return to that city, hopefully soon and hopefully safely.

Clearing the second floor of a vital hospital, Kenton Stacy was severely wounded by an explosion. Immediately, Justin bounded into the booby-trapped and unbelievably dangerous and unsafe building and found Kenton but in very, very bad shape. He applied pressure to the wound and inserted a tube to reopen an airway. He then performed CPR for twenty straight minutes during the ground transport and maintained artificial respiration through two and a half hours and through emergency surgery.

Kenton Stacy would have died if it were not for Justin's selfless love for his fellow warrior. Tonight, Kenton is recovering in Texas. Raqqa is liberated. And Justin is wearing his new Bronze Star, with a V for Valor. Staff Sergeant Peck: all of America salutes you.

Terrorists, who do things like place bombs in civilian hospitals, are evil. When possible, we have no choice but to annihilate them. When necessary, we must be able to detain and question them. But we must be clear: terrorists are not merely criminals; they are unlawful enemy combatants. And when captured overseas, they should be treated like the terrorists they are.

In the past, we have foolishly released hundreds and hundreds of dangerous terrorists, only to meet them again on the battlefield—including the ISIS leader, al-Baghdadi, who we captured, who we had, who we released.

So today, I am keeping another promise. I just signed, prior to walking in, an order directing Secretary Mattis, who is doing a great job, thank you, to re-examine our military detention policy, and to keep open the detention facilities in Guantánamo Bay.

I am asking Congress to ensure that, in the fight against ISIS and al-Qaeda, we continue to have all necessary power to detain terrorists—wherever we chase them down, wherever we find them, and in many cases, for them, it will now be Guantánamo Bay.

At the same time, as of a few months ago, our warriors in Afghanistan have new rules of engagement. Along with their heroic Afghan partners, our military is no longer undermined by artificial timelines, and we no longer tell our enemies our plans.

Last month, I also took an action endorsed unanimously by the US Senate just months before: I recognized Jerusalem as the capital of Israel.

Shortly afterwards, dozens of countries voted in the United Nations General Assembly, against America's sovereign right to make this decision. In 2016, American taxpayers generously sent those same countries more than twenty billion dollars in aid.

That is why, tonight, I am asking the Congress to pass legislation to help ensure American foreign-assistance dollars always serve American interests and only go to friends of America, not enemies of America.

As we strengthen friendships all around the world, we are also restoring clarity about our adversaries.

When the people of Iran rose up against the crimes of their corrupt dictatorship, I did not stay silent. America stands with the people of Iran in their courageous struggle for freedom.

I am asking Congress to address the fundamental flaws in the terrible Iran nuclear deal.

My administration has also imposed tough sanctions on the communist and socialist dictatorships in Cuba and Venezuela.

But no regime has oppressed its own citizens more totally or brutally than the cruel dictatorship in North Korea.

North Korea's reckless pursuit of nuclear missiles could very soon threaten our homeland. We are waging a campaign of maximum pressure to prevent that from ever happening.

Past experience has taught us that complacency and concessions only invite aggression and provocation. I will not repeat the mistakes of past administrations that got us into this very dangerous position.

We need only look at the depraved character of the North Korean regime to understand the nature of the nuclear threat it could pose to America and to our allies.

Otto Warmbier was a hard-working student at the University of Virginia, and a great student he was. On his way to study abroad in Asia, Otto joined a tour to North Korea. At its conclusion, this wonderful young man was arrested and charged with crimes against the state. After a shameful trial, the dictatorship sentenced Otto to fifteen years of hard labor, before returning him to America last June—horribly injured, and on the verge of death. He passed away just days after his return.

Otto's wonderful parents, Fred and Cindy Warmbier, are here with us tonight—along with Otto's brother and sister, Austin and Greta. Incredible people. You are powerful witnesses to a menace that threatens our world, and your strength truly inspires us all. Thank you very much. Thank you. Tonight, we pledge to honor Otto's memory with total American resolve. Thank you.

Finally, we are joined by one more witness to the ominous nature of this regime. His name is Mister Ji Seong-ho.

In 1996, Seong-ho was a starving boy in North Korea. One day, he tried to steal coal from a railroad car to barter for a few scraps of food, which were very hard to get. In the process, he passed out on the train tracks, exhausted from hunger. He woke up as a train ran over his limbs. He then endured multiple amputations without anything to dull the pain or the hurt. His brother and sister gave what little food they had to help him recover, and ate dirt themselves—permanently stunting their own growth. Later, he was tortured by North Korean authorities after returning from a brief visit to China. His tormentors wanted to know if he had met any Christians. He had—and he resolved to be free.

Seong-ho traveled thousands of miles on crutches across China and Southeast Asia to freedom. Most of his family followed. His father was caught trying to escape, and was tortured to death.

Today, he lives in Seoul, where he rescues other defectors, and broadcasts into North Korea what the regime fears most—the truth.

Today, he has a new leg, but Seong-ho, I understand you still keep those old crutches as a reminder of how far you have come. Your great sacrifice is an inspiration to us all.

Seong-ho's story is a testament to the yearning of every human soul to live in freedom.

It was that same yearning for freedom that, nearly two hundred fifty years ago, gave birth to a special place called America. It was a small cluster of colonies caught between a great ocean and a vast wilderness. It was home to an incredible people with a revolutionary idea: That they could rule themselves. That they could chart their own destiny. And that, together, they could light up the entire world.

That is what our country has always been about. That is what Americans have always stood for, always strived for, and always done.

Atop the dome of this Capitol stands the Statue of Freedom. She stands tall and dignified among the monuments to our ancestors who fought and lived and died to protect her.

Monuments to Washington and Jefferson and Lincoln and King. Memorials to the heroes of Yorktown and Saratoga. To young Americans who shed their blood on the shores of Normandy and the fields beyond. And others, who went down in the waters of the Pacific, and the skies all over Asia.

And freedom stands tall over one more monument: this one. This Capitol. This living monument. This is the monumen to the American people. We're a people whose heroes live not only in the past, but all around us—defending hope, pride, and defending the American way.

They work in every trade. They sacrifice to raise a family. They care for our children at home. They defend our flag abroad. They are strong moms and brave kids. They are firefighters, police officers, border agents, medics, and Marines. But above all else, they are Americans. And this Capitol, this city, and this nation, belongs entirely to them. Our task is to respect them, to listen to them, to serve them, to protect them, and to always be worthy of them.

Americans fill the world with art and music. They push the bounds of science and discovery. And they forever remind us of what we should never forget: The people dreamed this country. The people built this country. And it is the people who are making America great again.

As long as we are proud of who we are and what we are fighting for, there is nothing we cannot achieve.

As long as we have confidence in our values, faith in our citizens, and trust in our God, we will never fail. Our families will thrive. Our people will prosper.

And our nation will forever be safe, and strong, and proud, and mighty, and free.

Thank you. And God bless America. Good night.

The US Southern Border and the Government Shutdown

THE WHITE HOUSE, WASHINGTON, DC

January 19, 2019

Just a short time ago, I had the honor of presiding over the swearing in of five new great American citizens. It was a beautiful ceremony, and a moving reminder of our nation's proud history of welcoming legal immigrants from all over the world into our national family. I told them that the beauty and majesty of citizenship is that it draws no distinctions of race, or class, or faith, or gender, or background. All Americans, whether first generation or tenth generation, are bound together in love and loyalty, friendship and affection. We're all equal. We are one team and one people, proudly saluting one great American flag.

We believe in a safe and lawful system of immigration—one that upholds our laws, our traditions, and our most cherished values. Unfortunately, our immigration system has been badly broken for a very long time. Over the decades, many presidents and many lawmakers have come and gone, and no real progress has been made on immigration. We are now living with the consequences—and they are tragic—brought about by decades of political stalemate, partisan gridlock, and national neglect.

There is a humanitarian and security crisis on our southern border that requires urgent action. Thousands of children are being exploited by ruthless "coyotes" and vicious cartels and gangs. One in three women is sexually assaulted on the dangerous journey north. In fact, many loving mothers give their young daughters birth control pills for the long journey up to the United States, because they know they may be raped, or sexually accosted, or assaulted. Nearly fifty migrants a day are being referred for urgent medical care. Vast quantities of lethal narcotics are flooding through our border and into our communities, including meth, cocaine, heroin, and fentanyl.

Drugs kill seventy-eight thousand Americans a year and cost our society in excess of seven hundred billion dollars. Heroin alone kills three hundred Americans a week—ninety percent of which comes across our southern border.

We can stop heroin.

Illegal immigration reduces wages and strains public services. The lack of border control provides a gateway—and a very wide and open gateway—for criminals and gang members to enter the United States, including the criminal aliens who murdered a brave California police officer only a day after Christmas. I've gotten to know and love angel moms, dads, and family who lost loved ones to people illegally in our country.

I want this to end. It's got to end now. These are not talking points. These are the heartbreaking realities that are hurting innocent, precious human beings every single day on both sides of the border. As a candidate for president, I promised I would fix this crisis, and I intend to keep that promise, one way or the other. Our immigration system should be the subject of pride, not a source of shame, as it is all over the world.

Our immigration system should be the envy of the world, not a symbol of disunity and dysfunction. The good news is, these problems can all be solved, but only if we have the political courage to do what is just and what is right. Both sides in Washington must simply come together, listen to each other, put down their armor, build trust, reach across the aisle and find solutions.

It is time to reclaim our future from the extreme voices who fear compromise and demand open borders, which means drugs pouring in, human trafficking, and a lot of crime. That is why I am here today, to break the logjam and provide Congress with a path forward to end the government shutdown and solve the crisis on the southern border. If we are successful in this effort, we will then have the best chance in a very long time, at real bipartisan immigration reform. And it won't stop here. It will keep going until we do it all. The proposal I will outline today is based, first and foremost, on input from our border agents and Homeland Security professionals—and professionals they are. They know what they're doing.

It is a compassionate response to the ongoing tragedy on our southern border. In recent weeks, we have met with large numbers of Democrat lawmakers to hear their ideas and suggestions. By incorporating the priorities of rank-and-file Democrats in our plan, we hope they will offer their enthusiastic support. And I think many will.

This is a common-sense compromise both parties should embrace.

The radical Left can never control our borders. I will never let it happen. Walls are not immoral. In fact, they are the opposite of immoral, because they will save many lives and stop drugs from pouring into our country. Our plan includes the following: Eight hundred million dollars in urgent humanitarian assistance. Eight hundred five million dollars for drug-detection technology to help secure our ports of entry. An additional two thousand seven hundred fifty border agents and law enforcement professionals. Seventy-five new immigration judge teams to reduce the court backlog of—believe it or not—almost nine hundred thousand cases.

However, the whole concept of having lengthy trials for anyone who sets one foot in our country unlawfully, must be changed by Congress. It is unsustainable. It is ridiculous. Few places in the world would even consider such an impossible nightmare. Our plan includes critical measures to protect migrant children from exploitation and abuse.

This includes a new system to allow Central American minors to apply for asylum in their home countries, and reform to promote family reunification for unaccompanied children, thousands of whom wind up on our border doorstep. To physically secure our border, the plan includes 5.7 billion dollars for a strategic deployment of physical barriers, or a wall. This is not a two-thousand-mile concrete structure from sea to sea. These are steel barriers in high-priority locations.

Much of the border is already protected by natural barriers, such as mountains and water. We already have many miles of barrier, including one hundred fifteen miles that we are currently building, or under contract. It will be done quickly. Our request will add another two hundred thirty miles this year in the areas our border agents most urgently need. It will have an unbelievable impact.

If we build a powerful and fully designed see-through steel barrier on our southern border, the crime rate and drug problem in our country would be quickly and greatly reduced. Some say it could be cut in half. Because these criminals, drug smugglers, gangs, and traffickers do not stop at our border, they permeate throughout our country, and they end up in some places where you'd least expect them. They go all over our country.

A steel barrier will help us stop illegal immigration, while safely directing commerce to our lawful ports of entry. Many of these security ideas have been proposed by Democrats themselves, and all of them have been supported by Democrats in the past, including a physical barrier wall or fence.

Furthermore, in order to build the trust and goodwill necessary to begin real immigration reform, there are two more elements to my plan. Number one is three years of legislative relief for seven hundred thousand DACA recipients brought here unlawfully by their parents at a young age, many years ago. This extension will give them access to work permits, social security numbers, and protection from deportation, most importantly.

Secondly, our proposal provides a three-year extension of Temporary Protected Status, or TPS. This means that three hundred thousand immigrants whose protected status is facing expiration, will now have three more years of certainty, so that Congress can work on a larger immigration deal, which everybody wants—Republicans and Democrats. And our farms and vineyards won't be affected, because lawful and regulated entry into our country will be easy and consistent. That is our plan. Border security, DACA, TPS, and many other things—straightforward, fair, reasonable, and common sense, with lots of compromise.

Senate Majority Leader Mitch McConnell has pledged to bring this bill to a vote this week in the United States Senate. Our proposal is not intended to solve all of our immigration challenges. This plan solves the immediate crisis—and it is a horrible crisis. It is a humanitarian crisis like we rarely see in our country. And it provides humanitarian relief, delivers real border security, and immediately reopens our federal government.

If we are successful in this effort, then we can start the border project of remaking our immigration system for the twenty-first century. Once the government is open, and we have made a down payment on border security, and immigration reform starts to happen, I plan to convene weekly bipartisan meetings at the White House so we can do a finished product, a great product, a product that we can all be proud of, having to do with that elusive immigration problem.

Whatever we do, I can promise you this: I will never forget that my first duty and ultimate loyalty is to you, the American people. Any reforms we make to our immigration system will be designed to improve your lives, make your communities safer, and make our nation more prosperous and secure for generations to come.

Thank you. And God bless America. Thank you.

State of the Union Address: Courage Together

US HOUSE OF REPRESENTATIVES, WASHINGTON, DC

February 5, 2019

Madam Speaker, Mister Vice President, Members of Congress, the First Lady of the United States, and my fellow Americans:

We meet tonight in a moment of unlimited potential as we begin a new Congress. I stand here ready to work with you to achieve historic breakthroughs for all Americans. Millions of our fellow citizens are watching us now gathered in this great chamber, hoping that we will govern not as two parties, but as one nation.

The agenda I will lay out this evening is not a Republican agenda or a Democrat agenda. It's the agenda of the American people. Many of us have campaigned on the same core promises to defend American jobs and demand fair trade for American workers; to rebuild and revitalize our nation's infrastructure; to reduce the price of healthcare and prescription drugs; to create an immigration system that is safe, lawful, modern, and secure; and to pursue a foreign policy that puts America's interests first. There is a new opportunity in American politics, if only we have the courage together to seize it.

Victory is not winning for our party. Victory is winning for our country.

This year, America will recognize two important anniversaries that show us the majesty of America's mission, and the power of American pride. In June, we mark seventy-five years since the start of what General Dwight D. Eisenhower called the Great Crusade—the Allied liberation of Europe. On D-Day, June sixth, 1944, fifteen thousand young American men jumped from the sky, and sixty thousand more stormed in from the sea to save our civilization from tyranny. Here with us tonight are three of those incredible heroes: Private First Class Joseph Riley, Staff Sergeant Irving Locker, and Sergeant Herman Zeitchiek.

Gentlemen, we salute you. In 2019, we also celebrate fifty years since brave young pilots flew a quarter of a million miles through space to plant the American flag on the face of the moon. Half a century later, we are joined by one of the Apollo 11 astronauts who planted that flag—Buzz Aldrin.

Thank you, Buzz. This year, American astronauts will go back to space on American rockets.

In the twentieth century, America saved freedom, transformed science, redefined the middle class—and when you get down to it, there's nothing anywhere in the world that can compete with America.

Now, we must step boldly and bravely into the next chapter of this next great American adventure, and we must create a new standard of living for the twenty-first century. An amazing quality of life for all of our American citizens is within reach. We can make our communities safer, our families stronger, our culture richer, our faith deeper, and our middle class bigger and more prosperous than ever before.

But we must reject the politics of revenge, resistance, and retribution, and embrace the boundless potential of cooperation, compromise, and the common good.

Together, we can break decades of political stalemate, we can bridge old divisions, heal old wounds, build new coalitions, forge new solutions, and unlock the extraordinary promise of America's future. The decision is ours to make. We must choose between greatness or gridlock, results or resistance, vision or vengeance, incredible progress or pointless destruction. Tonight, I ask you to choose greatness.

Over the last two years, my administration has moved with urgency and historic speed to confront problems neglected by leaders of both parties, over many decades. In just over two years since the election, we have launched an unprecedented economic boom—a boom that has rarely been seen before. There's been nothing like it.

We have created 5.3 million new jobs, and importantly, added six hundred thousand new manufacturing jobs—something which almost everyone said was impossible to do. But the fact is, we are just getting started.

Wages are rising at the fastest pace in decades, and growing, for blue collar workers, who I promised to fight for. They're growing faster than anyone else thought possible. Nearly five million Americans have been lifted off food stamps.

The US economy is growing almost twice as fast today as when I took office, and we are considered, far and away, the hottest economy anywhere in the world. Not even close.

Unemployment has reached the lowest rate in over half a century.

African American, Hispanic American, and Asian American unemployment have all reached their lowest levels ever recorded.

Unemployment for Americans with disabilities has also reached an all-time low.

More people are working now than at any time in the history of our country. One hundred fifty-seven million people at work.

We passed a massive tax cut for working families and doubled the child tax credit.

We virtually ended the estate tax—or death tax, as it is often called—on small businesses, for ranches, and also for family farms.

We eliminated the very unpopular Obamacare individual mandate penalty. And to give critically ill patients access to life-saving cures, we passed—very importantly—Right to Try.

My administration has cut more regulations in a short period of time than any other administration during its entire tenure.

Companies are coming back to our country in large numbers, thanks to our historic reductions in taxes and regulations. And we have unleashed a revolution in American energy. The United States is now the number-one producer of oil and natural gas anywhere in the world.

And now, for the first time in sixty-five years, we are a net exporter of energy.

After twenty-four months of rapid progress, our economy is the envy of the world. Our military is the most powerful on earth, by far, and America is again winning each and every day.

Members of Congress, the state of our Union is strong. [USA! USA! USA!] That sounds so good. Our country is vibrant, and our economy is thriving like never before. On Friday, it was announced that we added another three hundred four thousand jobs last month alone—almost double the number expected.

An economic miracle is taking place in the United States, and the only thing that can stop it are foolish wars, politics, or ridiculous partisan investigations. If there is going to be peace and legislation, there cannot be war and investigation. It just doesn't work that way. We must be united at home to defeat our adversaries abroad. This new era of cooperation can start with finally confirming the more than three hundred highly qualified nominees who are still stuck in the Senate—in some cases, years and years waiting. Not right.

The Senate has failed to act on these nominations, which is unfair to the nominees, and very unfair to our country. Now is the time for a bipartisan action. Believe it or not, we have already proven that that's possible. In the last Congress, both parties came together to pass unprecedented legislation to confront the opioid crisis, a sweeping new farm bill, historic VA reforms, and after four decades of rejection, we passed VA Accountability so that we can finally terminate those who mistreat our wonderful veterans.

And just weeks ago, both parties united for groundbreaking criminal justice reform. They said it couldn't be done.

Last year, I heard, through friends, the story of Alice Johnson. I was deeply moved. In 1997, Alice was sentenced to life in prison as a first-time nonviolent drug offender. Over the next twenty-two years, she became a prison minister, inspiring others to choose a better path. She had a big impact on that prison population, and far beyond. Alice's story underscores the disparities and unfairness that can exist in criminal sentencing, and the need to remedy this total injustice. She served almost that twenty-two years, and had expected to be in prison for the remainder of her life.

In June, I commuted Alice's sentence. When I saw Alice's beautiful family greet her at the prison gates, hugging and kissing and crying and laughing, I knew I did something right. Alice is with us tonight, and she is a terrific woman.

Terrific. Alice, please.

Alice, thank you for reminding us that we always have the power to shape our own destiny. Thank you very much, Alice.

Inspired by stories like Alice's, my administration worked closely with members of both parties to sign the First Step Act into law. Big deal. It's a big deal.

This legislation reformed sentencing laws that have wrongly and disproportionately harmed the African American community. The First Step Act gives nonviolent offenders the chance to re-enter society as productive, law-abiding citizens. Now, states across the country are following our lead.

America is a nation that believes in redemption. We are also joined tonight by Matthew Charles from Tennessee. In 1996, at the age of thirty, Matthew was sentenced to thirty-five years for selling drugs, and related offenses. Over the next two decades, he completed more than thirty Bible studies, became a law clerk, and mentored many of his fellow inmates. Now, Matthew is the very first person to be released from prison under the First Step Act.

Matthew, please. Thank you, Matthew. Welcome home.

Now, Republicans and Democrats must join forces again to confront an urgent national crisis. Congress has ten days left to pass a bill that will fund our government, protect our homeland, and secure our very dangerous southern border. Now is the time for Congress to show the world that America is committed to ending illegal immigration, and putting the ruthless coyotes, cartels, drug dealers, and human traffickers out of business. As we speak, large, organized caravans are on the march to the United States.

We have just heard that Mexican cities, in order to remove the illegal immigrants from their communities, are getting trucks and buses to bring them up to our country, in areas where there is little border protection. I have ordered another three thousand seven hundred fifty troops to our southern border to prepare for this tremendous onslaught.

This is moral issue of the lawless state of our southern border is a threat to the safety, security, and financial well-being of all America. We have a moral duty to create an immigration system that protects the lives and jobs of our citizens. This includes our obligation to the millions of immigrants living here today, who follow the rules and respect our laws. Legal immigrants enrich our nation, and strengthen out society, in countless ways.

I want people to come into our country in the largest numbers ever, but they have to come in legally.

Tonight, I'm asking you to defend our very dangerous southern border, out of love and devotion to our fellow citizens, and to our country. No issue better illustrates the divide between America's working class and America's political class than illegal immigration.

Wealthy politicians and donors push for open borders while living their lives behind walls, and gates, and guards. Meanwhile, working-class Americans are left to pay the price for mass illegal immigration, reduced jobs, lower wages, overburdened schools, hospitals that are so crowded that you can't get in, increased crime, and a depleted social safety net. Tolerance for illegal immigration is not compassionate. It is actually very cruel.

One in three women is sexually assaulted on the long journey north. Smugglers use migrant children as human pawns to exploit our laws and gain access to our country. Human traffickers and sex traffickers take advantage of the wide-open areas between our ports of entry to smuggle thousands of young girls and women into the United States, and to sell them into prostitution and modern-day slavery.

Tens of thousands of innocent Americans are killed by lethal drugs that cross our border and flood into our cities, including meth, heroin, cocaine, and fentanyl. The savage gang, MS-13, now operates in at least twenty different American states, and they almost all come through our southern border.

Just yesterday, an MS-13 gang member was taken into custody for a fatal shooting on a subway platform in New York City. We are removing these gang members by the thousands. But until we secure our border, they are going to keep streaming right back in. Year after year, countless Americans are murdered by criminal illegal aliens.

I have gotten to know many wonderful angel moms, dads, and families. No one should have to suffer the horrible heartache that they have had to endure. Here tonight is Debra Bissell. Just three weeks ago, her parents, Gerald and Sharon, were burglarized and shot to death in their Reno, Nevada, home by an illegal alien. They were in their eighties, and are survived by four children, eleven grandchildren, and twenty great-grandchildren.

Also here tonight are Gerald and Sharon's granddaughter Heather and great-granddaughter Madison. Debra, Heather, Madison, please stand. Few can understand your pain. Thank you. And thank you for being here. Thank you very much.

I will never forget, and I will fight for the memory of Gerald and Sharon, that it should never happen again. Not one more American life should be lost because our nation failed to control its very dangerous border.

In the last two years, our brave ICE officers made two hundred sixty-six thousand arrests of criminal aliens, including those charged or convicted of nearly a hundred thousand assaults, thirty thousand sex crimes, and four thousand killings or murders. We are joined tonight by one of those law enforcement heroes, ICE Special Agent Elvin Hernandez.

When Elvin was a boy, he and his family immigrated to the United States from the Dominican Republic. At the age of eight, he told his dad he wanted to become a special agent. Today, Elvin leads investigations into the scourge of international sex trafficking.

Elvin says that, " If I could make sure these young girls get their justice, I've really done my job." Thanks to his work, and that of his incredible colleagues, more than three women and girls have been rescued from the horror of this terrible situation. And more than one thousand five hundred sadistic traffickers have been put behind bars.

We will always support the brave men and women of law enforcement. And I pledge to you tonight that I will never abolish our heroes from ICE. Thank you.

My administration has sent to Congress a commonsense proposal to end the crisis on the southern border. It includes humanitarian assistance, more law enforcement, drug detection at our ports, closing loopholes that enable child smuggling, and plans for a new physical barrier or wall to secure the vast areas between our ports of entry.

In the past, most of the people in this room voted for a wall. But the patrol wall never got built. I will get it built. This is a smart, strategic, see-through steel barrier, not just a simple concrete wall. It will be deployed in the areas identified by the border agents as having the greatest need. And these agents will tell you, where walls go up, illegal crossings go way, way down.

San Diego used to have the most illegal border crossings in our country. In response, a strong security wall was put in place. This powerful barrier almost completely ended illegal crossings. The border city of El Paso, Texas, used to have extremely high rates of violent crime—one of the highest in the entire country— and considered one of our nation's most dangerous cities. Now, immediately upon its building, with a powerful barrier in place, El Paso is one of the safest cities in our country. Simply put, walls work, and walls save lives.

So let's work together, compromise, and reach a deal that will truly make America safe. As we work to defend our people's safety, we must also ensure our economic resurgence continues at a rapid pace. No one has benefited more from our thriving economy than women who have filled fifty-eight percent of the newly created jobs last year.

All Americans can be proud that we have more women in the workforce than ever before.

Don't sit yet. You're going to like this.

And exactly one century after Congress passed the constitutional amendment giving women the right to vote, we also have more women serving in Congress than at any time before.

That's great. And congratulations. That's great. As part of our commitment to improving opportunity for women everywhere, this Thursday, we are launching the first ever government-wide initiative focused on economic empowerment for women in developing countries.

To build on our incredible economic success, one priority is paramount: reversing decades of calamitous trade policies. So bad. We are now making it clear to China that after years of targeting our industries and stealing our intellectual property, the theft of American jobs and wealth has come to an end.

Therefore, we recently imposed tariffs on two hundred fifty billion dollars of Chinese goods. And now our treasury is receiving billions and billions of dollars. But I don't blame China for taking advantage of us. I blame our leaders and representatives for allowing this travesty to happen.

I have great respect for President Xi, and we are now working on a new trade deal with China. But it must include real structural change to end unfair trade practices, reduce our chronic trade deficit, and protect American jobs.

Another historic trade blunder was the catastrophe known as NAFTA. I have met the men and women of Michigan, Ohio, Pennsylvania, Indiana, New Hampshire, and many other states whose dreams were shattered by the signing of NAFTA. For years, politicians promised them they would renegotiate for a better deal. But no one ever tried, until now.

Our new US–Mexico–Canada Agreement, the USMCA, will replace NAFTA and deliver for American workers like they haven't had delivered to for a long time. I hope you can pass the USMCA into law so that we can bring back our manufacturing jobs in even greater numbers, expand American agriculture, protect intellectual property, and ensure that more cars are proudly stamped with our four beautiful words—Made in the USA.

Tonight, I am also asking you to pass the United States Reciprocal Trade Act, so that if another country places an unfair tariff on an American product, we can charge them the exact same tariff on the exact same product that they sell to us. Both parties should be able to unite for a great rebuilding of America's crumbling infrastructure.

I know that Congress is eager to pass an infrastructure bill. And I am eager to work with you on legislation to deliver new and important infrastructure investment, including investments in the cutting-edge industries of the future. This is not an option; this is a necessity.

The next major priority for me, and for all of us, should be to lower the cost of healthcare and prescription drugs, and to protect patients with pre-existing conditions.

Already, as a result of my administration's efforts, in 2018, drug prices experienced their single largest decline in forty-six years.

But we must do more. It's unacceptable that Americans pay vastly more than people in other countries for the exact same drugs, often made in the exact same place. This is wrong, this is unfair, and together we will stop it, and we'll stop it fast.

I am asking Congress to pass legislation that finally takes on the problem of global freeloading and delivers fairness and price transparency for American patients, finally.

We should also require drug companies, insurance companies, and hospitals to disclose real prices to foster competition and bring costs way down. No force in history has done more to advance the human condition than American freedom. In recent years, we have made remarkable progress in the fight against HIV and AIDS. Scientific breakthroughs have brought a once distant dream within reach.

My budget will ask Democrats and Republicans to make the needed commitment to eliminate the HIV epidemic in the United States within ten years. We have made incredible strides. Incredible. Together, we will defeat AIDS in America and beyond.

Tonight, I am also asking you to join me in another fight that all Americans can get behind: the fight against childhood cancer.

Joining Melania in the Gallery this evening is a very brave ten-year-old girl, Grace Eline. Every birthday—hi, Grace. Every birthday since she was four, Grace asked her friends to donate to Saint Jude's Children's Hospital. She did not know that one day she might be a patient herself.

That's what happened. Last year, Grace was diagnosed with brain cancer. Immediately, she began radiation treatment. At the same time, she rallied her community and raised more than forty thousand dollars for the fight against cancer. When Grace completed treatment last fall, her doctors and nurses cheered—they loved her, they still love her—with tears in their eyes, and hung up a poster that read, "Last day of chemo."

Thank you very much, Grace. You are a great inspiration to everyone in this room. Thank you very much.

Many childhood cancers have not seen new therapies in decades. My budget will ask Congress for five hundred million dollars over the next ten years to fund this critical life-saving research. To help support working parents, the time has come to pass school choice for America's children.

I'm also proud to be the first president to include in my budget a plan for a nationwide paid family leave so that every new parent has the chance to bond with their newborn child.

There could be no greater contrast to the beautiful image of a mother holding her infant child, than the chilling displays our nation saw in recent days.

Lawmakers in New York cheered with delight upon the passage of legislation that would allow a baby to be ripped from the mother's womb moments from birth. These are living, feeling, beautiful babies who will never get the chance to share their love and dreams with the world. And then we had the case of the governor of Virginia, where he stated he would execute a baby after birth. To defend the dignity of every person, I am asking Congress to pass legislation to prohibit the late-term abortion of children who can feel pain in a mother's womb.

Let us work together to build a culture that cherishes innocent life. And let us reaffirm a fundamental truth: All children, born and unborn, are made in the holy image of God.

The final part of my agenda is to protect American security.

Over the last two years, we have begun to fully rebuild the United States military, with seven hundred billion dollars last year, and seven hundred sixteen billion dollars this year. We are also getting other nations to pay their fair share. Finally.

For years, the United States was being treated very unfairly by friends of ours—members of NATO. But now, we have secured, over the last couple of years, more than one hundred billion dollars of increase in defense spending from our NATO allies. They said it couldn't be done.

As part of our military buildup, the United States is developing a state-of-the-art missile defense. And under my administration, we will never apologize for advancing America's interests.

For example, decades ago, the United States entered into a treaty with Russia, in which we agreed to limit and reduce our missile capability. While we followed the agreement and the rules to the letter, Russia repeatedly violated its terms. It's been going on for many years. That is why I announced that the United States is officially withdrawing from the Intermediate-Range Nuclear Forces Treaty, or INF Treaty. We really have no choice. Perhaps we can negotiate a different agreement, adding China and others. Or perhaps we can't—in which case, we will outspend and out-innovate all others, by far.

As part of a bold new diplomacy, we continue our historic push for peace on the Korean Peninsula. Our hostages have come home. Nuclear testing has stopped, and there has not been a missile launch in more than fifteen months. If I had not been elected president of the United States, we would right now, in my opinion, be in a major war with North Korea.

Much work remains to be done, but my relationship with Kim Jong-un is a good one. Chairman Kim and I will meet again on February twenty-seventh and twenty-eighth, in Vietnam.

Two weeks ago, the United States officially recognized the legitimate government of Venezuela and its new President, Juan Guaido.

We stand with the Venezuelan people and their noble quest for freedom. And we condemn the brutality of the Maduro regime, whose socialist policies have turned that nation from being the wealthiest in South America, into a state of abject poverty and despair.

Here in the United States, we are alarmed by the new calls to adopt socialism in our country.

America was founded on liberty and independence, and not government coercion, domination, and control. We are born free, and we will stay free.

Tonight, we renew our resolve that America will never be a socialist country.

One of the most complex set of challenges we face, and have for many years, is in the Middle East. Our approach is based on principle, realism, not discredited theories that have failed for decades to yield progress. For this reason, my administration recognized the true capital of Israel and proudly opened the American Embassy in Jerusalem.

Our brave troops have now been fighting in the Middle East for almost nineteen years—in Afghanistan and Iraq. Nearly seven thousand American heroes have given their lives. More than fifty-two thousand Americans have been badly wounded. We have spent more than seven trillion dollars in fighting wars in the Middle East. As a candidate for president, I loudly pledged a new approach.

Great nations do not fight endless wars. When I took office, ISIS controlled more than twenty thousand square miles in Iraq and Syria, just two years ago. Today, we have liberated virtually all of the territory from the grip of these blood-thirsty monsters. Now, as we work with our allies to destroy the remnants of ISIS, it is time to give our brave warriors in Syria a warm welcome home.

I have also accelerated our negotiations to reach, if possible, a political settlement in Afghanistan. The opposing side is also very happy to be negotiating. Our troops have fought with unmatched valor. And thanks to their bravery, we are now able to pursue a possible political solution to this long and bloody conflict.

In Afghanistan, my administration is holding constructive talks with a number of Afghan groups, including the Taliban. As we make progress in these negotiations, we will be able to reduce our troops' presence, and focus on counterterrorism. And we will, indeed, focus on counterterrorism. We don't know whether we will achieve an agreement, but we do know tht after two decades of war, the hour has come to at least try for peace. And the other side would like to do the same thing. It's time.

Above all, friend and foe alike must never doubt this nation's power and will to defend our people. Eighteen years ago, violent terrorists attacked the USS *Cole*. And last month, American forces killed one of the leaders of that attack.

We are honored to be joined tonight by Tom Wibberley, whose son, Navy Seaman Craig Wibberley, was one of the seventeen sailors we tragically lost. Tom, we vow to always remember the heroes of the USS *Cole*. Thank you, Tom.

My administration has acted decisively to confront the world's leading state sponsor of terror—the radical regime in Iran. It is a radical regime. They do bad, bad things. To ensure this corrupt dictatorship never acquires nuclear weapons, I withdrew the United States from the disastrous Iran nuclear deal.

And last fall, we put in place the toughest sanctions ever imposed by us on a country. We will not avert our eyes from a regime that chants, "Death to America" and threatens genocide against the Jewish people. We must never ignore the vial poison of antisemitism, or those who spread its venomous creed.

With one voice, we must confront this hatred anywhere and everywhere it occurs. Just months ago, eleven Jewish Americans were viciously murdered in an antisemitic attack on the Tree of Life Synagogue in Pittsburgh. SWAT Officer Timothy Matson raced into the gunfire and was shot seven times, chasing down the killer. And he was very successful. Timothy has just had his twelfth surgery, and he's going in for many more. But he made the trip to be here with us tonight.

Officer Matson, please. Thank you. We are forever grateful. Thank you very much.

Tonight, we are also joined by Pittsburgh survivor Judah Samet. He arrived at the synagogue as the massacre began. But not only did he escape death last fall, more than seven decades ago, he narrowly survived the Nazi concentration camps. Today is Judah's eighty-first birthday.

They wouldn't do that for me, Judah. [Audience sings Happy Birthday.]

Judah says he can still remember the exact moment, nearly seventy-five years ago, after ten months in a concentration camp, when he and his family were put on a train and told they were going to another camp. Suddenly, the train screeched to a very strong halt. A soldier appeared. Judah's family braced for the absolute worst. Then his father cried out with joy: "It's the Americans! It's the Americans!"

Thank you. A second Holocaust survivor, who is here tonight, Joshua Kaufman, was a prisoner at Dachau. He remembers watching through a hole in the wall of a cattle car, as American soldiers rolled in with tanks. "For me," Joshua recalls, "the American soldiers were proof that God exists." And they came down from the sky. They came down from heaven.

I began this evening by honoring three soldiers who fought on D-Day in the Second World War. One of them was Herman Zeitchiek. But there is more to Herman's story. A year after he stormed the beaches of Normandy, Herman was one of the American soldiers who helped liberate Dachau. He was one of the Americans who helped rescue Joshua from that hell on earth. Almost seventy-five years later, Herman and Joshua are both together in the Gallery tonight, seated side by side, here in the home of American freedom. Herman and Joshua, your presence this evening is very much appreciated. Thank you very much. Thank you.

When American soldiers set out beneath the dark skies over the English Channel in the early hours of D-Day, 1944, they were just young men of eighteen and nineteen, hurtling on fragile landing craft, toward the most momentous battle in the history of war. They did not know if they would survive the hour. They did not know if they would grow old. But they knew that America had to prevail. Their cause was this nation, and generations yet unborn.

Why did they do it? They did it for America. They did it for us.

Everything that has come since—our triumph over communism, our giant leaps of science and discovery, our unrivaled progress towards equality and justice—all of it is possible, thanks to the blood and tears and courage and vision of the Americans who came before.

Think of this Capitol. Think of this very chamber, where lawmakers before you voted to end slavery, to build the railroads and the highways, and defeat fascism, to secure civil rights, and to face down evil empires.

Here tonight, we have legislators from across this magnificent republic. You have come from the rocky shores of Maine, and the volcanic peaks of Hawaii, from the snowy woods of Wisconsin, and the red deserts of Arizona, from the green farms of Kentucky, and the golden beaches of California.

Together, we represent the most extraordinary nation in all of history. What will we do with this moment? How will we be remembered? I ask the men and women of this Congress, look at the opportunities before us. Our most thrilling achievements are still ahead. Our most exciting journeys still await.

Our biggest victories are still to come. We have not yet begun to dream. We must choose whether we are defined by our differences or whether we dare to transcend them. We must choose whether we squander our great inheritance, or whether we proudly declare that we are Americans. We do the incredible. We defy the impossible. We conquer the unknown.

This is the time to reignite the American imagination. This is the time to search for the tallest summit and set our sights on the brightest star. This is the time to rekindle the bonds of love and loyalty and memory that link us together as citizens, as neighbors, as patriots. This is our future, our fate, and our choice to make. I am asking you to choose greatness. No matter the trials we face, no matter the challenges to come, we must go forward together. We must keep America first in our hearts. We must keep freedom alive in our souls. And we must always keep faith in America's destiny. That one nation under God must be the hope, and the promise, and the light, and the glory among all the nations of the world.

Thank you. God bless you. And God bless America. Thank you very much.

Toast at a State Dinner with Queen Elizabeth

BUCKINGHAM PALACE, LONDON, ENGLAND

June 3, 2019

Your Majesty, Melania and I are profoundly honored to be your guests for this historic state visit. Thank you for your warm welcome, for this beautiful weather—your gracious hospitality, and Your Majesty's nearly seven decades of treasured friendship with the United States of America.

This week, we commemorate a mighty endeavor of righteous nations, and one of the greatest undertakings in all of history. Seventy-five years ago, more than one hundred fifty thousand Allied troops were preparing on this island to parachute into France, storm the beaches of Normandy, and win back our civilization. As Her Majesty remembers, the British people had hoped and prayed and fought for this day for nearly five years.

When Britain stood alone during the Blitz of 1940 and 1941, the Nazi war machine dropped thousands of bombs on this country, and right on this magnificent city. Buckingham Palace alone was bombed on sixteen separate occasions. In that dark hour, the people of this nation showed the world what it means to be British.

They cleared wreckage from the streets, displayed the Union Jack from their shattered homes, and kept fighting on to victory. They only wanted victory. The courage of the United Kingdom's sons and daughters ensured that your destiny would always remain in your own hands. Through it all, the Royal Family was the resolute face of the Commonwealth's unwavering solidarity.

In April of 1945, newspapers featured a picture of The Queen Mother visiting the women's branch of the Army, watching a young woman repair a military truck engine. That young mechanic was the future Queen—that great, great woman. Her Majesty inspired her compatriots in that fight to support the troops, defend her homeland, and defeat the enemy at all cost.

We also pay tribute to Prince Philip's distinguished and valiant service in the Royal Navy during the Second World War. On D-Day, the Queen's beloved father, King George the Sixth, delivered a stirring national address. That day, he said: "After nearly five years of toil and suffering, we must renew that crusading impulse on which we entered the war and met its darkest hour . . . . Our fight is against evil and for a world in which goodness and honor may be the foundation of the life of men in every land."

This evening, we thank God for the brave sons of the United Kingdom and the United States, who defeated the Nazis and the Nazi regime, and liberated millions from tyranny.

The bond between our nations was forever sealed in that Great Crusade. As we honor our shared victory and heritage, we affirm the common values that will unite us long into the future: freedom, sovereignty, self-determination, the rule of law, and reverence for the rights given to us by Almighty God. From the Second World War to today, Her Majesty has stood as a constant symbol of these priceless traditions. She has embodied the spirit of dignity, duty, and patriotism that beats proudly in every British heart.

On behalf of all Americans, I offer a toast to the eternal friendship of our people, the vitality of our nations, and to the long, cherished, and truly remarkable reign of Her Majesty, the Queen. Thank you.

Establishment of US Space Command

THE WHITE HOUSE, WASHINGTON, DC

August 29, 2019

Thank you very much. It's a great honor. What a beautiful day in the Rose Garden. Please sit. Thank you.

To ensure that all resources of the federal government are focused on the arriving storm, I have decided to send our vice president, Mike Pence, to Poland this weekend, in my place. It's something very important for me to be here.

The storm looks like it could be a very, very big one indeed. And Mike will be going.

I've just spoken to President Duda of Poland and expressed to him my warmest wishes, and the wishes of the American people. Our highest priority is the safety and security of the people in the path of the hurricane. And I will be rescheduling my trip to Poland in the near future.

We're gathered here in the Rose Garden to establish the United States Space Command. It's a big deal. As the newest combatant command, SPACECOM will defend America's vital interests in space—the next warfighting domain. And I think that's pretty obvious to everybody. It's all about space. We're joined by Vice President Mike Pence; Secretary of Defense, Doctor Mark Esper; Acting Director of National Intelligence, Joe Maguire; Acting Secretary of the Army, Ryan McCarthy; Acting Secretary of the Air Force, Matt Donovan; Chairman of the Joint Chiefs of Staff, General Joseph Dunford; and Congressman Mike Turner.

We're especially grateful to welcome the new leader of SPACECOM, General Jay Raymond—a highly respected man within the military—joined this afternoon by his wife, Mollie. Thank you. Thank you, Mollie. Congratulations, Mollie. It's great. Their wonderful family, and several of their friends. General Raymond, congratulations.

So important. I know he's going to do a fantastic job. Thank you very much. The United States combatant commands were developed to join branches of our armed forces in common cause across diverse fields of battle. Each of the United States military's combatant commands has an area of responsibility, from CENTCOM, which oversees our mission in the Middle East, to our most recent, CYBERCOM, which we established just last year to protect Americans from the most advanced cyber threats and also to create very, very severe and powerful offensive threats, should we need them.

The dangers to our country constantly evolve, and so must we. Now, those who wish to harm the United States seek to challenge us in the ultimate high ground of space. It's going to be a whole different ballgame. Our adversaries are weaponizing Earth's orbits with new technology targeting American satellites that are critical to both battlefield operations and our way of life at home.

Our freedom to operate in space is also essential to detecting and destroying any missile launched against the United States. So just as we have recognized land, air, sea, and cyber as vital warfighting domains, we will now treat space as an independent region overseen by a new unified geographic combatant command.

The establishment of the eleventh combatant command is a landmark moment. This is a landmark day—one that recognizes the centrality of space to America's national security and defense. Under General Raymond's leadership, SPACECOM will boldly deter aggression and outpace America's rivals, by far. For thirty-five years, General Raymond has led and commanded space operations at every level in the US Air Force.

Mollie, I hope you're very proud of him. I'll bet you are. I am, too. He's a warrior who has integrated space capabilities to make our military even stronger, and to pave the way for a new era of national defense. He's respected by everybody sitting in front of us, everybody in the military, and everybody that knows him.

SPACECOM will soon be followed, very importantly, by the establishment of the United States Space Force, as the sixth branch of the United States Armed Forces. And that's really something, when you think about it. The Space Force will organize, train, and equip warriors to support SPACECOM's mission. With today's action, we open another great chapter in the extraordinary history of the United States military.

SPACECOM will ensure that America's dominance in space is never questioned and never threatened, because we know the best way to prevent conflict is to prepare for victory.

From our nation's first days, America's military blazed the trails and crossed the frontiers that secured our nation's future. No adversary on earth will ever match the awesome courage, skill, and might of American Armed Forces.

Today, we salute the heroic men and women who will serve in SPACECOM and keep America's horizons forever bright and forever free. We have budgets, since we came into the administration, since the election of 2016—since January twentieth of 2017, we have done things with the military that few people would have thought possible.

Budgets of seven hundred dollars, seven hundred sixteen dollars, and now seven hundred thirty-eight billion dollars. Nobody would have thought that that was possible, but we had them approved by Republicans and Democrats. And that money is now building the most advanced equipment anywhere one earth—equipment that nobody even could have conceived of, even two years ago.

It's very necessary. And hopefully we'll never have to use it.

I would now like to ask Secretary Esper to sign documents formally establishing the United States Space Command. Thank you. Mister Secretary? [The documents are signed.]

JOHN W. RAYMOND: Good afternoon. Mister President, thank you for hosting us today. In doing so, you honor the airmen, sailors, soldiers, and Marines that secure our high ground for our nation. On behalf of those men and women, we'd like to present you with a small memento that reads, "United States Space Command Establishment: 29 August 2019." On behalf of the space warfighters, thank you for your leadership.

PRESIDENT TRUMP: That's a big one. Thank you very much. I'd now like to invite Chief Master Sergeant Roger Towberman to the stage to unfurl the flag of the United States Space Command. Thank you very much. [The flag is unfurled.]

Great Contests, High Stakes, and Clear Choices

U.N. GENERAL ASSEMBLY, NEW YORK, NEW YORK

September 24, 2019

Thank you very much. Mister President, Mister Secretary-General, distinguished delegates, ambassadors, and world leaders:

Seven decades of history have passed through this hall, in all of their richness and drama. Where I stand, the world has heard from presidents and premiers at the height of the Cold War. We have seen the foundation of nations. We have seen the ringleaders of revolution. We have beheld saints who inspired us with hope, rebels who stirred us with passion, and heroes who emboldened us with courage—all here to share plans, proposals, visions, and ideas on the world's biggest stage.

Like those who met us before, our time is one of great contests, high stakes, and clear choices. The essential divide that runs all around the world and throughout history is once again thrown into stark relief. It is the divide between those whose thirst for control deludes them into thinking they are destined to rule over others, and those people and nations who want only to rule themselves.

I have the immense privilege of addressing you today as the elected leader of a nation that prizes liberty, independence, and self-government above all. The United States, after having spent over two and a half trillion dollars since my election to completely rebuild our great military, is also, by far, the world's most powerful nation. Hopefully, it will never have to use this power.

Americans know that, in a world where others seek conquest and domination, our nation must be strong in wealth, in might, and in spirit. That is why the United States vigorously defends the traditions and customs that have made us who we are.

Like my beloved country, each nation represented in this hall has a cherished history, culture, and heritage that is worth defending and celebrating, and which gives us our singular potential and strength.

The free world must embrace its national foundations. It must not attempt to erase them or replace them.

Looking around, and all over this large, magnificent planet, the truth is plain to see: If you want freedom, take pride in your country. If you want democracy, hold on to your sovereignty. And if you want peace, love your nation. Wise leaders always put the good of their own people and their own country first.

The future does not belong to globalists. The future belongs to patriots. The future belongs to sovereign and independent nations who protect their citizens, respect their neighbors, and honor the differences that make each country special and unique.

It is why we in the United States have embarked on an exciting program of national renewal. In everything we do, we are focused on empowering the dreams and aspirations of our citizens.

Thanks to our pro-growth economic policies, our domestic unemployment rate reached its lowest level in over half a century. Fueled by massive tax cuts and regulations cuts, jobs are being produced at a historic rate. Six million Americans have been added to the employment rolls in under three years.

Last month, African American, Hispanic American, and Asian American unemployment reached their lowest rates ever recorded. We are marshaling our nation's vast energy abundance, and the United States is now the number one producer of oil and natural gas anywhere in the world. Wages are rising, incomes are soaring, and 2.5 million Americans have been lifted out of poverty in less than three years.

As we rebuild the unrivaled might of the American military, we are also revitalizing our alliances by making it very clear that all of our partners are expected to pay their fair share of the tremendous defense burden, which the United States has borne in the past.

At the center of our vision for national renewal is an ambitious campaign to reform international trade. For decades, the international trading system has been easily exploited by nations acting in very bad faith. As jobs were outsourced, a small handful grew wealthy at the expense of the middle class.

In America, the result was 4.2 million lost manufacturing jobs, and fifteen trillion dollars in trade deficits over the last quarter-century. The United States is now taking that decisive action to end this grave economic injustice. Our goal is simple: We want balanced trade that is both fair and reciprocal.

We have worked closely with our partners in Mexico and Canada to replace NAFTA with the brand-new, and hopefully bipartisan, US–Mexico–Canada Agreement.

Tomorrow, I will join Prime Minister Abe of Japan to continue our progress in finalizing a terrific new trade deal.

As the United Kingdom makes preparations to exit the European Union, I have made clear that we stand ready to complete an exceptional new trade agreement with the UK that will bring tremendous benefits to both of our countries. We are working closely with Prime Minister Boris Johnson on a magnificent new trade deal.

The most important difference in America's new approach on trade concerns our relationship with China. In 2001, China was admitted to the World Trade Organization. Our leaders then argued that this decision would compel China to liberalize its economy and strengthen protections to provide things that were unacceptable to us, and for private property, and for the rule of law. Two decades later, this theory has been tested and proven completely wrong.

Not only has China declined to adopt promised reforms, it has embraced an economic model dependent on massive market barriers, heavy state subsidies, currency manipulation, product dumping, forced technology transfers, and the theft of intellectual property, and also trade secrets, on a grand scale.

As just one example, I recently met the CEO of a terrific American company, Micron Technology, at the White House. Micron produces memory chips used in countless electronics. To advance the Chinese government's five-year economic plan, a company owned by the Chinese state allegedly stole Micron's designs, valued at up to 8.7 billion dollars. Soon, the Chinese company obtains patents for nearly an identical product, and Micron was banned from selling its own goods in China. But we are seeking justice.

The United States lost sixty thousand factories after China entered the WTO. This is happening to other countries all over the globe.

The World Trade Organization needs drastic change. The second-largest economy in the world should not be permitted to declare itself a "developing country" in order to game the system at others' expense.

For years, these abuses were tolerated, ignored, or even encouraged. Globalism exerted a religious pull over past leaders, causing them to ignore their own national interests.

But as far as America is concerned, those days are over. To confront these unfair practices, I placed massive tariffs on more than five hundred billion dollars' worth of Chinese-made goods. Already, as a result of these tariffs, supply chains are relocating back to America and to other nations, and billions of dollars are being paid to our Treasury.

The American people are absolutely committed to restoring balance to our relationship with China. Hopefully, we can reach an agreement that would be beneficial for both countries. But as I have made very clear, I will not accept a bad deal for the American people.

As we endeavor to stabilize our relationship, we're also carefully monitoring the situation in Hong Kong. The world fully expects that the Chinese government will honor its binding treaty—made with the British, and registered with the United Nations—in which China commits to protect Hong Kong's freedom, legal system, and democratic ways of life. How China chooses to handle the situation will say a great deal about its role in the world in the future. We are all counting on President Xi as a great leader.

The United States does not seek conflict with any other nation. We desire peace, cooperation, and mutual gain with all. But I will never fail to defend America's interests.

One of the greatest security threats facing peace-loving nations today is the repressive regime in Iran. The regime's record of death and destruction is well-known to us all. Not only is Iran the world's number-one state sponsor of terrorism, but Iran's leaders are fueling the tragic wars in both Syria and Yemen. At the same time, the regime is squandering the nation's wealth and future in a fanatical quest for nuclear weapons and the means to deliver them. We must never allow this to happen.

To stop Iran's path to nuclear weapons and missiles, I withdrew the United States from the terrible Iran nuclear deal, which has very little time remaining, did not allow inspection of important sites, and did not cover ballistic missiles.

Following our withdrawal, we have implemented severe economic sanctions on the country. Hoping to free itself from sanctions, the regime has escalated its violent and unprovoked aggression. In response to Iran's recent attack on Saudi Arabian oil facilities, we just imposed the highest level of sanctions on Iran's central bank and sovereign wealth fund.

All nations have a duty to act. No responsible government should subsidize Iran's bloodlust. As long as Iran's menacing behavior continues, sanctions will not be lifted; they will be tightened. Iran's leaders will have turned a proud nation into just another cautionary tale of what happens when a ruling class abandons its people and embarks on a crusade for personal power and riches.

For forty years, the world has listened to Iran's rulers as they lash out at everyone else for the problems they alone have created. They conduct ritual chants of "Death to America" and traffic in monstrous anti-Semitism. Last year, the country's Supreme Leader stated: "Israel is a malignant cancerous tumor . . . that has to be removed and eradicated. It is possible, and it will happen." America will never tolerate such anti-Semitic hate.

Fanatics have long used hatred of Israel to distract from their own failures. Thankfully, there is a growing recognition in the wider Middle East that the countries of the region share common interests in battling extremism and unleashing economic opportunity. That is why it is so important to have full, normalized relations between Israel and its neighbors. Only a relationship built on common interests, mutual respect, and religious tolerance can forge a better future.

Iran's citizens deserve a government that cares about reducing poverty, ending corruption, and increasing jobs—not stealing their money to fund a massacre abroad and at home.

After four decades of failure, it is time for Iran's leaders to step forward and to stop threatening other countries, and focus on building up their own country. It is time for Iran's leaders to finally put the Iranian people first.

America is ready to embrace friendship with all who genuinely seek peace and respect.

Many of America's closest friends today were once our gravest foes. The United States has never believed in permanent enemies. We want partners, not adversaries. America knows that while anyone can make war, only the most courageous can choose peace.

For this same reason, we have pursued bold diplomacy on the Korean Peninsula. I have told Kim Jong-un what I truly believe—that, like Iran, his country is full of tremendous untapped potential, but that to realize that promise, North Korea must denuclearize.

Around the world, our message is clear: America's goal is lasting. America's goal is harmony. And America's goal is not to go with these endless wars—wars that never end.

With that goal in mind, my administration is also pursuing the hope of a brighter future in Afghanistan. Unfortunately, the Taliban has chosen to continue their savage attacks. We will continue to work with our coalition of Afghan partners to stamp out terrorism. And we will never stop working to make peace a reality.

Here in the Western Hemisphere, we are joining with our partners to ensure stability and opportunity all across the region. In that mission, one of our most critical challenges is illegal immigration, which undermines prosperity, rips apart societies, and empowers ruthless criminal cartels.

Mass illegal migration is unfair, unsafe, and unsustainable for everyone involved—the sending countries, and the depleted countries. And they become depleted very fast, but their youth is not taken care of, and human capital goes to waste.

The receiving countries are overburdened with more migrants than they can responsibly accept. And the migrants themselves are exploited, assaulted, and abused by vicious coyotes. Nearly one-third of women who make the journey north to our border are sexually assaulted along the way. Yet, here in the United States and around the world, there is a growing cottage industry of radical activists and non-governmental organizations that promote human smuggling. These groups encourage illegal migration and demand erasure of national borders.

Today, I have a message for those open-border activists who cloak themselves in the rhetoric of social justice: Your policies are not just. Your policies are cruel and evil. You are empowering criminal organizations that prey on innocent men, women, and children. You put your own false sense of virtue before the lives, well-being, [of] countless innocent people. When you undermine border security, you are undermining human rights and human dignity.

Many of the countries here today are coping with the challenges of uncontrolled migration. Each of you has the absolute right to protect your borders. And so, of course, does our country. Today, we must resolve to work together to end human smuggling, end human trafficking, and put these criminal networks out of business for good.

To our country, I can tell you sincerely: we are working closely with our friends in the region—including Mexico, Canada, Guatemala, Honduras, El Salvador, and Panama—to uphold the integrity of borders and ensure safety and prosperity for our people.

I would like to thank President López Obrador of Mexico for the great cooperation we are receiving, and for right now putting twenty-seven thousand troops on our southern border. Mexico is showing us great respect, and I respect them in return.

The US, we have taken very unprecedented action to stop the flow of illegal immigration. To anyone considering crossings of our border illegally, please hear these words: Do not pay the smugglers. Do not pay the coyotes. Do not put yourself in danger. Do not put your children in danger. Because if you make it here, you will not be allowed in; you will be promptly returned home. You will not be released into our country. As long as I am president of the United States, we will enforce our laws and protect our borders.

For all of the countries of the Western Hemisphere, our goal is to help people invest in the bright futures of their own nation. Our region is full of such incredible promise—dreams waiting to be built, and national destinies for all. And they are waiting also to be pursued.

Throughout the hemisphere, there are millions of hardworking, patriotic young people eager to build, innovate, and achieve. But these nations cannot reach their potential if a generation of youth abandon their homes in search of a life elsewhere. We want every nation in our region to flourish, and its people to thrive in freedom and peace.

In that mission, we are also committed to supporting those people in the Western Hemisphere who live under brutal oppression—such as those in Cuba, Nicaragua, and Venezuela.

According to a recent report from the U.N. Human Rights Council, women in Venezuela stand in line for ten hours a day, waiting for food. Over fifteen thousand people have been detained as political prisoners. Modern-day death squads are carrying out thousands of extrajudicial killings.

The dictator Maduro is a Cuban puppet, protected by Cuban bodyguards, hiding from his own people while Cuba plunders Venezuela's oil wealth to sustain its own corrupt communist rule.

Since I last spoke in this hall, the United States and our partners have built a historic coalition of fifty-five countries that recognize the legitimate government of Venezuela.

To the Venezuelans trapped in this nightmare: please know that all of America is united behind you. The United States has vast quantities of humanitarian aid ready and waiting to be delivered. We are watching the Venezuela situation very closely. We await the day when democracy will be restored, when Venezuela will be free, and when liberty will prevail throughout this hemisphere.

One of the most serious challenges our countries face is the specter of socialism. It's the wrecker of nations and destroyer of societies.

Events in Venezuela remind us all that socialism and communism are not about justice. They are not about equality. They are not about lifting up the poor. And they are certainly not about the good of the nation. Socialism and communism are about one thing only: power for the ruling class.

Today, I repeat a message for the world that I have delivered at home: America will never be a socialist country.

In the last century, socialism and communism killed one hundred million people. Sadly, as we see in Venezuela, the death toll continues in this country. These totalitarian ideologies, combined with modern technology, have the power to [exercise] new and disturbing forms of suppression and domination.

For this reason, the United States is taking steps to better screen foreign technology and investments, and to protect our data and our security. We urge every nation present to do the same.

Freedom and democracy must be constantly guarded and protected, both abroad and from within. We must always be skeptical of those who want conformity and control. Even in free nations, we see alarming signs and new challenges to liberty.

A small number of social media platforms are acquiring immense power over what we can see, and over what we are allowed to say. A permanent political class is openly disdainful, dismissive, and defiant of the will of the people. A faceless bureaucracy operates in secret and weakens democratic rule. Media and academic institutions push flat-out assaults on our histories, traditions, and values.

In the United States, my administration has made clear to social media companies that we will uphold the right of free speech. A free society cannot allow social media giants to silence the voices of the people. And a free people must never, ever be enlisted in the cause of silencing, coercing, canceling, or blacklisting their own neighbors.

As we defend American values, we affirm the right of all people to live in dignity. For this reason, my administration is working with other nations to stop criminalizing of homosexuality, and we stand in solidarity with LGBTQ people who live in countries that punish, jail, or execute individuals based upon sexual orientation.

We are also championing the role of women in our societies. Nations that empower women are much wealthier, safer, and much more politically stable. It is therefore vital not only to a nation's prosperity, but also is vital to its national security, to pursue women's economic development.

Guided by these principles, my administration launched the Women's Global Development and Prosperity Initiatives. The W-GDP is first-ever government-wide approach to women's economic empowerment, working to ensure that women all over the planet have the legal right to own and inherit property, work in the same industries as men, travel freely, and access credit and institutions.

Yesterday, I was also pleased to host leaders for a discussion about an ironclad American commitment: protecting religious leaders and also protecting religious freedom. This fundamental right is under growing threat around the world. Hard to believe, but eighty percent of the world's population lives in countries where religious liberty is in significant danger or even completely outlawed. Americans will never tire in our effort to defend and promote freedom of worship and religion. We want and support religious liberty for all.

Americans will also never tire of defending innocent life. We are aware that many United Nations projects have attempted to assert a global right to taxpayer-funded abortion on demand, right up until the moment of delivery. Global bureaucrats have absolutely no business attacking the sovereignty of nations that wish to protect innocent life. Like many nations here today, we in America believe that every child—born and unborn—is a sacred gift from God.

There is no circumstance under which the United States will allow international [entities] to trample on the rights of our citizens, including the right to self-defense. That is why, this year, I announced that we will never ratify the U.N. Arms Trade Treaty, which would threaten the liberties of law-abiding American citizens. The United States will always uphold our constitutional right to keep and bear arms. We will always uphold our Second Amendment.

The core rights and values America defends today were inscribed in America's founding documents. Our nation's Founders understood that there will always be those who believe they are entitled to wield power and control over others. Tyranny advances under many names and many theories, but it always comes down to the desire for domination. It protects not the interests of many, but the privilege of few.

Our Founders gave us a system designed to restrain this dangerous impulse. They chose to entrust American power to those most invested in the fate of our nation—a proud and fiercely independent people.

The true good of a nation can only be pursued by those who love it—by citizens who are rooted in its history, who are nourished by its culture, committed to its values, attached to its people, and who know that its future is theirs to build or theirs to lose. Patriots see a nation and its destiny in ways no one else can.

Liberty is only preserved, sovereignty is only secured, democracy is only sustained, greatness is only realized, by the will and devotion of patriots. In their spirit is found the strength to resist oppression, the inspiration to forge legacy, the goodwill to seek friendship, and the bravery to reach for peace. Love of our nations makes the world better for all nations.

So to all the leaders here today, join us in the most fulfilling mission a person could have, the most profound contribution anyone can make: Lift up your nations. Cherish your culture. Honor your histories. Treasure your citizens. Make your countries strong, and prosperous, and righteous. Honor the dignity of your people, and nothing will be outside of your reach.

When our nations are greater, the future will be brighter, our people will be happier, and our partnerships will be stronger.

With God's help, together we will cast off the enemies of liberty and overcome the oppressors of dignity. We will set new standards of living, and reach new heights of human achievement. We will rediscover old truths, unravel old mysteries, and make thrilling new breakthroughs. And we will find more beautiful friendship and more harmony among nations than ever before.

My fellow leaders, the path to peace and progress, and freedom and justice, and a better world for all humanity, begins at home.

Thank you. God bless you. God bless the nations of the world. And God bless America. Thank you very much.

State of the Union Address: Incredible Results

US HOUSE OF REPRESENTATIVES, WASHINGTON, DC

February 4, 2020

Thank you much. Thank you. Thank you very much.

Madam Speaker, Mister Vice President, Members of Congress, the First Lady of the United States, and my fellow citizens:

Three years ago, we launched the great American comeback. Tonight, I stand before you to share the incredible results. Jobs are booming, incomes are soaring, poverty is plummeting, crime is falling, confidence is surging, and our country is thriving and highly respected again. America's enemies are on the run. America's fortunes are on the rise. And America's future is blazing bright.

The years of economic decay are over. The days of our country being used, taken advantage of, and even scorned by other nations, are long behind us. Gone, too, are the broken promises, jobless recoveries, tired platitudes, and constant excuses for the depletion of American wealth, power, and prestige.

In just three short years, we have shattered the mentality of American decline, and we have rejected the downsizing of America's destiny. We have totally rejected the downsizing. We are moving forward at a pace that was unimaginable just a short time ago, and we are never, ever going back.

I am thrilled to report to you tonight that our economy is the best it has ever been. Our military is completely rebuilt, with its power being unmatched anywhere in the world—and it's not even close. Our borders are secure. Our families are flourishing. Our values are renewed. Our pride is restored. And for all of these reasons, I say to the people of our great country, and to the members of Congress: The state of our Union is stronger than ever before.

The vision I will lay out this evening demonstrates how we are building the world's most prosperous and inclusive society—one where every citizen can join in America's unparalleled success, and where every community can take part in America's extraordinary rise.

From the instant I took office, I moved rapidly to revive the US economy—slashing a record number of job-killing regulations, enacting historic and record-setting tax cuts, and fighting for fair and reciprocal trade agreements. Our agenda is relentlessly pro-worker, pro-family, pro-growth, and most of all, pro-American. Thank you. We are advancing with unbridled optimism and lifting our citizens of every race, color, religion, and creed very, very high.

Since my election, we have created seven million new jobs—five million more than government experts projected during the previous administration.

The unemployment rate is the lowest in over half a century. And very incredibly, the average unemployment rate under my administration is lower than any administration in the history of our country. True. If we hadn't reversed the failed economic policies of the previous administration, the world would not now be witnessing this great economic success.

The unemployment rate for African Americans, Hispanic Americans, and Asian Americans has reached the lowest levels in history. African American youth unemployment has reached an all-time low. African American poverty has declined to the lowest rate ever recorded.

The unemployment rate for women reached the lowest level in almost seventy years. And last year, women filled seventy two percent of all new jobs added.

The veterans unemployment rate dropped to a record low. The unemployment rate for disabled Americans has reached an all-time low.

Workers without a high-school diploma have achieved the lowest unemployment rate recorded in US history. A record number of young Americans are now employed.

Under the last administration, more than ten million people were added to the food stamp rolls. Under my administration, seven million Americans have come off food stamps, and ten million people have been lifted off of welfare.

In eight years under the last administration, over three hundred thousand working-age people dropped out of the workforce. In just three years of my administration, 3.5 million people—working-age people—have joined the workforce.

Since my election, the net worth of the bottom half of wage earners has increased by forty-seven percent—three times faster than the increase for the top one percent. After decades of flat and falling incomes, wages are rising fast—and wonderfully, they are rising fastest for low-income workers, who have seen a sixteen percent pay increase since my election. This is a blue-collar boom.

Real median household income is now at the highest level ever recorded.

Since my election, US stock markets have soared seventy percent, adding more than twelve trillion dollars to our nation's wealth, transcending anything anyone believed was possible. This is a record. It is something that every country in the world is looking up to. They admire. Consumer confidence has just reached amazing new highs.

All of those millions of people with 401(k)s and pensions are doing far better than they have ever done before, with increases of sixty, seventy, eighty, ninety, and one hundred percent, and even more.

Jobs and investments are pouring into nine thousand previously neglected neighborhoods, thanks to Opportunity Zones, a plan spearheaded by Senator Tim Scott, as part of our great

Republican tax cuts. In other words, wealthy people and companies are pouring money into poor neighborhoods or areas that haven't seen investment in many decades—creating jobs, energy, and excitement. This is the first time that these deserving communities have seen anything like this. It's all working.

Opportunity Zones are helping Americans like Army veteran Tony Rankins from Cincinnati, Ohio. After struggling with drug addiction, Tony lost his job, his house, and his family. He was homeless. But then Tony found a construction company that invests in Opportunity Zones. He is now a top tradesman, drug-free, reunited with his family, and he is here tonight. Tony, keep up the great work. Tony. Thank you, Tony.

Our roaring economy has, for the first time ever, given many former prisoners the ability to get a great job and a fresh start. This second chance at life is made possible because we passed landmark criminal justice reform into law. Everybody said that criminal justice reform couldn't be done, but I got it done, and the people in this room got it done.

Thanks to our bold regulatory reduction campaign, the United States has become the number one producer of oil and natural gas anywhere in the world, by far. With the tremendous progress we have made over the past three years, America is now energy independent, and energy jobs, like so many other elements of our country, are at a record high. We are doing numbers that no one would have thought possible just three years ago.

Likewise, we are restoring our nation's manufacturing might—even though predictions were, as you all know, that this could never, ever be done. After losing sixty thousand factories under the previous two administrations, America has now gained twelve thousand new factories under my administration, with thousands upon thousands of plants and factories being planned or being built. Companies are not leaving; they are coming back to the USA. The fact is that everybody wants to be where the action is, and the United States of America is indeed the place where the action is.

One of the biggest promises I made to the American people was to replace the disastrous NAFTA trade deal. In fact, unfair trade is perhaps the single biggest reason that I decided to run for president. Following NAFTA's adoption, our nation lost one in four manufacturing jobs. Many politicians came and went, pledging to change or replace NAFTA, only to do so, and then absolutely nothing happened. But unlike so many who came before me, I keep my promises. We did our job.

Six days ago, I replaced NAFTA and signed the brand-new US–Mexico–Canada Agreement into law. The USMCA will create nearly one hundred thousand new high-paying American auto jobs, and massively boost exports for our farmers, ranchers, and factory workers. It will also bring trade with Mexico and Canada to a much higher level, but also to be a much greater degree of fairness and reciprocity. We will have that—fairness and reciprocity. And I say that, finally, because it's been many, many years [since] we were treated fairly on trade.

This is the first major trade deal in many years to earn the strong backing of America's labor unions.

I also promised our citizens that I would impose tariffs to confront China's massive theft of America's jobs. Our strategy has worked. Days ago, we signed the groundbreaking new agreement with China that will defend our workers, protect our intellectual property, bring billions and billions of dollars into our treasury, and open vast new markets for products made and grown right here in the USA.

For decades, China has taken advantage of the United States. Now we have changed that, but at the same time, we have perhaps the best relationship we've ever had with China, including with President Xi. They respect what we've done because, quite frankly, they could never really believe that they were able to get away with what they were doing year after year, decade after decade, without someone in our country stepping up and saying, "That's enough." Now we want to rebuild our country, and that's exactly what we're doing. We are rebuilding our country.

As we restore American leadership throughout the world, we are once again standing up for freedom in our hemisphere. That's why my administration reversed the failing policies of the previous administration on Cuba.

We are supporting the hopes of Cubans, Nicaraguans, and Venezuelans to restore democracy. The United States is leading a fifty-nine-nation diplomatic coalition against the socialist dictator of Venezuela, Nicolás Maduro. Maduro is an illegitimate ruler, a tyrant who brutalizes his people. But Maduro's grip on tyranny will be smashed and broken.

Here this evening is a very brave man who carries with him the hopes, dreams, and aspirations of all Venezuelans. Joining us in the Gallery is the true and legitimate president of Venezuela, Juan Guaidó. Mister President, please take this message back to your homeland. Thank you, Mister President. Great honor. Thank you very much.

Please take this message back that all Americans are united with the Venezuelan people in their righteous struggle for freedom. Thank you very much, Mister President. Thank you very much.

Socialism destroys nations. But always remember—freedom unifies the soul.

To safeguard American liberty, we have invested a record-breaking 2.2 trillion dollars in the United States military. We have purchased the finest planes, missiles, rockets, ships and every other form of military equipment, and it's all made right here in the USA.

We are also getting our allies, finally, to help pay their fair share. I have raised contributions from the other NATO members by more than four hundred billion dollars, and the number of Allies meeting their minimum obligations has more than doubled.

And just weeks ago, for the first time since President Truman established the Air Force more than seventy years earlier, we created a brand-new branch of the United States Armed Forces. It's called the Space Force. Very important.

In the Gallery tonight, we have a young gentleman. And what he wants so badly—thirteen years old—Iain Lanphier. He's an eighth grader from Arizona. Iain, please stand up.

Iain has always dreamed of going to space. He was the first in his class, and among the youngest at an aviation academy. He aspires to go to the Air Force Academy, and then he has his eye on the Space Force. As Iain says, "Most people look up at space. I want to look down on the world."

But sitting behind Iain tonight is his greatest hero of them all. Charles McGee was born in Cleveland, Ohio, one century ago. Charles is one of the last surviving Tuskegee Airmen—the first black fighter pilots—and he also happens to be Iain's great-grand-father. Incredible story.

After more than one hundred thirty combat missions in World War Two, he came back home to a country still struggling for civil rights, and went on to serve America in Korea and Vietnam. On December seventh, Charles celebrated his one hundredth birth-day. A few weeks ago, I signed a bill promoting Charles McGee to brigadier general. And earlier today, I pinned the stars on his shoulders in the Oval Office. General McGee, our nation salutes you. Thank you, sir.

From the Pilgrims to the Founders, from the soldiers at Valley Forge to the marchers at Selma, and from President Lincoln to the Reverend Martin Luther King, Americans have always rejected limits on our children's future.

Members of Congress, we must never forget that the only vic-tories that matter in Washington are victories that deliver for the American people. The people are the heart of our country, their dreams are the soul of our country, and their love is what powers and sustains our country. We must always remember that our job is to put America first.

The next step forward in building an inclusive society is mak-ing sure that every young American gets a great education and the opportunity to achieve the American Dream. Yet, for too long, countless American children have been trapped in failing gov-ernment schools. To rescue these students, eighteen states have created school choice in the form of Opportunity Scholarships. The programs are so popular that tens of thousands of students remain on a waiting list.

One of those students is Janiyah Davis, a fourth grader from Philadelphia. Janiyah. Janiyah's mom, Stephanie, is a single parent. She would do anything to give her daughter a better future. But last year, that future was put further out of reach when Pennsylvania's governor vetoed legislation to expand school choice to fifty thousand children.

Janiyah and Stephanie are in the Gallery. Stephanie, thank you so much for being here with your beautiful daughter. Thank you very much.

But Janiyah, I have some good news for you, because I am pleased to inform you that your long wait is over. I can proudly announce tonight that an Opportunity Scholarship has become available, it's going to you, and you will soon be heading to the school of your choice.

Now I call on Congress to give one million American children the same opportunity Janiyah has just received. Pass the Education Freedom Scholarships and Opportunities Act—because no parent should be forced to send their child to a failing government school.

Every young person should have a safe and secure environment in which to learn and to grow. For this reason, our magnificent First Lady has launched the Be Best initiative to advance a safe, healthy, supportive, and drug-free life for the next generation—online, in school, and in our communities. Thank you, Melania, for your extraordinary love and profound care for America's children. Thank you very much.

My administration is determined to give our citizens the opportunities they need, regardless of age or background. Through our Pledge to American Workers, over four hundred companies will also provide new jobs and education opportunities to almost fifteen million Americans.

My budget also contains an exciting vision for our nation's high schools. Tonight, I ask Congress to support our students and back my plan to offer vocational and technical education in every single high school in America.

To expand equal opportunity, I am also proud that we achieved record and permanent funding for our nation's historically black colleges and universities.

A good life for American families also requires the most affordable, innovative, and high-quality healthcare system on earth. Before I took office, health insurance premiums had more than doubled in just five years. I moved quickly to provide affordable alternatives. Our new plans are up to sixty percent less expensive—and better.

I've also made an ironclad pledge to American families: We will always protect patients with pre-existing conditions. And we will always protect your Medicare. And we will always protect your Social Security. Always.

The American patient should never be blindsided by medical bills. That is why I signed an executive order requiring price transparency. Many experts believe that transparency—which will go into full effect at the beginning of next year—will be even bigger than healthcare reform. It will save families massive amounts of money for substantially better care.

But as we work to improve Americans' healthcare, there are those who want to take away your healthcare, take away your doctor, and abolish private insurance entirely.

One hundred thirty-two lawmakers in this room have endorsed legislation to impose a socialist takeover of our healthcare system, wiping out the private health insurance plans of one hundred eighty million very happy Americans. To those watching at home tonight, I want you to know: We will never let socialism destroy American healthcare.

Over one hundred thirty legislators in this chamber have endorsed legislation that would bankrupt our nation by providing free taxpayer-funded healthcare to millions of illegal aliens, forcing taxpayers to subsidize free care for anyone in the world who unlawfully crosses our borders. These proposals would raid the Medicare benefits of our seniors, and that our seniors depend on, while acting as a powerful lure for illegal immigration. That is what is happening in California and other states. Their systems are totally out of control, costing taxpayers vast and unaffordable amounts of money.

If forcing American taxpayers to provide unlimited free healthcare to illegal aliens sounds fair to you, then stand with the radical Left. But if you believe that we should defend American patients and American seniors, then stand with me and pass legislation to prohibit free government healthcare for illegal aliens.

This will be a tremendous boon to our already very strongly guarded southern border, where, as we speak, a long, tall, and very powerful wall is being built. We have now completed over one hundred miles, and have over five hundred miles fully completed in a very short period of time. Early next year, we will have substantially more than five hundred miles completed.

My administration is also taking on the big pharmaceutical companies. We have approved a record number of affordable generic drugs, and medicines are being approved by the FDA at a faster clip than ever before. And I was pleased to announce last year that, for the first time in fifty-one years, the cost of prescription drugs actually went down.

And working together, Congress can reduce drug prices substantially from current levels. I've been speaking to Senator Chuck Grassley of Iowa, and others in Congress, in order to get something on drug pricing done—and done quickly and properly. I'm calling for bipartisan legislation that achieves the goal of dramatically lowering prescription drug prices. Get a bill on my desk, and I will sign it into law immediately.

With unyielding commitment, we are curbing the opioid epidemic. Drug overdose deaths declined for the first time in nearly thirty years. Among the states hardest hit, Ohio is down twenty-two percent, Pennsylvania is down eighteen percent, Wisconsin is down ten percent—and we will not quit until we have beaten the opioid epidemic, once and for all.

Protecting Americans' health also means fighting infectious diseases. We are coordinating with the Chinese government and working closely together on the coronavirus outbreak in China.

My administration will take all necessary steps to safeguard our citizens from this threat.

We have launched ambitious new initiatives to substantially improve care for Americans with kidney disease, Alzheimer's, and those struggling with mental health. And because Congress was so good as to fund my request, new cures for childhood cancer, and we will eradicate the AIDS epidemic in America by the end of this decade.

Almost every American family knows the pain when a loved one is diagnosed with a serious illness. Here tonight is a special man, beloved by millions of Americans who just received a stage-four advanced cancer diagnosis. This is not good news. But what is good news is that he is the greatest fighter and winner that you will ever meet. Rush Limbaugh, thank you for your decades of tireless devotion to our country.

And Rush, in recognition of all that you have done for our nation—the millions of people a day that you speak to and that you inspire, and all of the incredible work that you have done for charity—I am proud to announce tonight that you will be receiving our country's highest civilian honor, the Presidential Medal of Freedom. [The *Medal of Freedom is presented.*]

Rush and Kathryn, congratulations. Thank you, Kathryn.

As we pray for all who are sick, we know that America is constantly achieving new medical breakthroughs. In 2017, doctors at Saint Luke's Hospital in Kansas City delivered one of the earliest premature babies ever to survive. Born at just twenty-one weeks and six days, and weighing less than a pound, Ellie Schneider was a born fighter. Through the skill of her doctors and the prayers of her parents, little Ellie kept on winning the battle of life. Today, Ellie is a strong, healthy two-year-old girl sitting with her amazing mother, Robin, in the Gallery. Ellie and Robin, we are glad to have you with us tonight.

Ellie reminds us that every child is a miracle of life. And thanks to modern medical wonders, fifty percent of very premature babies delivered at the hospital where Ellie was born now survive. It's an incredible thing. Thank you very much.

Our goal should be to ensure that every baby has the best chance to thrive and grow, just like Ellie. That is why I'm asking Congress to provide an additional fifty million dollars to fund neonatal research for America's youngest patients.

That is why I'm also calling upon members of Congress here tonight to pass legislation finally banning the late-term abortion of babies. Whether we are Republican, Democrat, or Independent, surely we must all agree that every human life is a sacred gift from God.

As we support America's moms and dads, I was recently proud to sign the law providing new parents in the federal workforce paid family leave, serving as a model for the rest of the country.

Now I call on the Congress to pass the bipartisan Advancing Support for Working Families Act, extending family leave to mothers and fathers all across our nation.

Forty million American families have an average twenty-two hundred dollars extra, thanks to our child tax credit. I've also overseen historic funding increases for high-quality child care, enabling seventeen states to help more children, many of which have reduced or eliminated their waitlists altogether. And I sent Congress a plan with a vision to further expand access to high-quality child care, and urge you to act immediately.

To protect the environment, days ago I announced that the United States will join the One Trillion Trees Initiative—an ambitious effort to bring together government and private sector to plant new trees in America and all around the world.

We must also rebuild America's infrastructure. I ask you to pass Senator John Barrasso's highway bill to invest in new roads, bridges, and tunnels all across our land.

I'm also committed to ensuring that every citizen can have access to high-speed Internet, including, and especially in, rural America.

A better tomorrow for all Americans also requires us to keep America safe. That means supporting the men and women of law enforcement at every level, including our nation's heroic ICE officers.

Last year, our brave ICE officers arrested more than one hundred twenty thousand criminal aliens charged with nearly ten thousand burglaries, five thousand sexual assaults, forty-five thousand violent assaults, and two thousand murders.

Tragically, there are many cities in America where radical politicians have chosen to provide sanctuary for these criminal illegal aliens.

In sanctuary cities, local officials order police to release dangerous criminal aliens to prey upon the public, instead of handing them over to ICE to be safely removed.

Just twenty-nine days ago, a criminal alien freed by the sanctuary city of New York was charged with the brutal rape and murder of a ninety-two-year-old woman. The killer had been previously arrested for assault, but under New York's sanctuary policies, he was set free. If the city had honored ICE's detainer request, his victim would still be alive today.

The state of California passed an outrageous law declaring their whole state to be a sanctuary for criminal illegal immigrants—a very terrible sanctuary, with catastrophic results.

Here is just one tragic example. In December 2018, California police detained an illegal alien with five prior arrests, including convictions for robbery and assault. But as required by California's Sanctuary Law, local authorities released him.

Days later, the criminal alien went on a gruesome spree of deadly violence. He viciously shot one man going about his daily work. He approached a woman sitting in her car, and shot her in the arm and in the chest. He walked into a convenience store and wildly fired his weapon. He hijacked a truck and smashed into vehicles, critically injuring innocent victims. One of the victims is—a terrible, terrible situation . . . died—fifty-one-year-old American named Rocky Jones.

Rocky was at a gas station when this vile criminal fired eight bullets at him from close range, murdering him in cold blood. Rocky left behind a devoted family, including his brothers, who loved him more than anything else in the world. One of his grieving brothers is here with us tonight. Jody, would you please stand?

Jody, thank you. Jody, our hearts weep for your loss, and we will not rest until you have justice.

Senator Thom Tillis has introduced legislation to allow Americans like Jody to sue sanctuary cities and states when a loved one is hurt or killed as a result of these deadly practices.

I ask Congress to pass the Justice for Victims of Sanctuary Cities Act immediately. The United States of America should be a sanctuary for law-abiding Americans, not criminal aliens.

In the last three years, ICE has arrested over five thousand wicked human traffickers. And I have signed nine pieces of legislation to stamp out the menace of human trafficking, domestically and all around the globe. My administration has undertaken an unprecedented effort to secure the southern border of the United States.

Before I came into office, if you showed up illegally on our southern border and were arrested, you were simply released and allowed into our country, never to be seen again. My administration has ended catch and release. If you come illegally, you will now be promptly removed from our country.

Very importantly, we entered into historic cooperation agreements with the governments of Mexico, Honduras, El Salvador, and Guatemala. As a result of our unprecedented efforts, illegal crossings are down seventy-five percent since May, dropping eight straight months in a row. And as the wall rapidly goes up, drug seizures rise, and the border crossings are down—and going down very rapidly.

Last year, I traveled to the border in Texas and met Chief Patrol Agent Raul Ortiz. Over the last twenty-four months, Agent Ortiz and his team have seized more than two hundred thousand pounds of poisonous narcotics, arrested more than three thousand human smugglers, and rescued more than two thousand migrants. Days ago, Agent Ortiz was promoted to deputy chief of Border Patrol. And he joins us tonight. Chief Ortiz, please stand. A grateful nation thanks you and all of the heroes of Border Patrol and ICE. Thank you very much. Thank you.

To build on these historic gains, we are working on legislation to replace our outdated and randomized immigration system with one based on merit, welcoming those who follow the rules, contribute to our economy, support themselves financially, and uphold our values.

With every action, my administration is restoring the rule of law and reasserting the culture of American freedom. Working with Senate Majority Leader Mitch McConnell—thank you, Mitch—and his colleagues in the Senate, we have confirmed a record number of one hundred eighty-seven new federal judges to uphold our Constitution as written. This includes two brilliant new Supreme Court justices, Neil Gorsuch and Brett Kavanaugh. Thank you. And we have many in the pipeline.

My administration is also defending religious liberty, and that includes the constitutional right to pray in public schools. In America, we don't punish prayer. We don't tear down crosses. We don't ban symbols of faith. We don't muzzle preachers and pastors. In America, we celebrate faith, we cherish religion, we lift our voices in prayer, and we raise our sights to the glory of God.

Just as we believe in the First Amendment, we also believe in another constitutional right that is under siege all across our country. So long as I am president, I will always protect your Second Amendment right to keep and bear arms.

In reaffirming our heritage as a free nation, we must remember that America has always been a frontier nation. Now we must embrace the next frontier—America's manifest destiny in the stars. I am asking Congress to fully fund the Artemis program to ensure that the next man and the first woman on the moon will be American astronauts, using this as a launching pad to ensure that America is the first nation to plant its flag on Mars.

My administration is also strongly defending our national security and combating radical Islamic terrorism.

Last week, I announced a groundbreaking plan for peace between Israel and the Palestinians. Recognizing that all past attempts have failed, we must be determined and creative in order to stabilize the region and give millions of young people the chance to realize a better future.

Three years ago, the barbarians of ISIS held over twenty thousand square miles of territory in Iraq and Syria. Today, the ISIS territorial caliphate has been one hundred percent destroyed, and the founder and leader of ISIS—the bloodthirsty killer known as al-Baghdadi—is dead.

We are joined this evening by Carl and Marsha Mueller. After graduating from college, their beautiful daughter, Kayla, became a humanitarian aid worker. She once wrote: "Some people find God in church. Some people find God in nature. Some people find God in love. I find God in suffering. I've known for some time what my life's work is—using my hands as tools to relieve suffering."

In 2013, while caring for suffering civilians in Syria, Kayla was kidnapped, tortured, and enslaved by ISIS, and kept as a prisoner of al-Baghdadi himself. After more than five hundred horrifying days of captivity, al-Baghdadi murdered young, beautiful Kayla. She was just twenty-six years old.

On the night that US Special Forces Operations ended al-Baghdadi's miserable life, the Chairman of the Joint Chiefs of Staff, General Mark Milley, received a call in the Situation Room. He was told that the brave men of the elite Special Forces team that so perfectly carried out the operation had given their mission a name: Task Force 8-14. It was a reference to a special day: August fourteenth—Kayla's birthday. Carl and Marsha, America's warriors never forgot Kayla—and neither will we. Thank you.

Every day, America's men and women in uniform demonstrate the infinite depth of love that dwells in the human heart.

One of these American heroes was Army Staff Sergeant Christopher Hake. On his second deployment to Iraq in 2008, Sergeant Hake wrote a letter to his one-year-old son, Gage: "I will be with you again," he wrote to Gage. "I will teach you to ride your first bike, build your first sandbox, watch you play sports, and see you have kids also. I love you, son. Take care of your mother. I am always with you. Daddy."

On Easter Sunday of 2008, Chris was out on patrol in Baghdad when his Bradley Fighting Vehicle was hit by a roadside bomb. That night, he made the ultimate sacrifice for our country. Sergeant Hake now rests in eternal glory in Arlington. And his wife, Kelli, is in the Gallery tonight, joined by their son, who is now a thirteen-year-old and doing very, very well. To Kelli and Gage: Chris will live in our hearts forever. He is looking down on you now. Thank you. Thank you very much. Thank you both very much.

The terrorist responsible for killing Sergeant Hake was Qassim Suleimani, who provided the deadly roadside bomb that took Chris's life. Suleimani was the Iranian regime's most ruthless butcher—a monster who murdered or wounded thousands of American service members in Iraq. As the world's top terrorist, Suleimani orchestrated the deaths of countless men, women, and children. He directed the December assault, and went on to assault US forces in Iraq. Was actively planning new attacks when we hit him very hard. And that's why, last month, at my direction, the US military executed a flawless precision strike that killed Suleimani and terminated his evil reign of terror forever.

Our message to the terrorists is clear: You will never escape American justice. If you attack our citizens, you forfeit your life.

In recent months, we have seen proud Iranians raise their voices against their oppressive rulers. The Iranian regime must abandon its pursuit of nuclear weapons; stop spreading terror, death, and destruction; and start working for the good of its own people.

Because of our powerful sanctions, the Iranian economy is doing very, very poorly. We can help them make a very good and short-time recovery. It can all go very quickly, but perhaps they are too proud or too foolish to ask for that help. We are here. Let's see which road they choose. It is totally up to them.

As we defend American lives, we are working to end America's wars in the Middle East.

In Afghanistan, the determination and valor of our warfighters has allowed us to make tremendous progress, and peace talks are now underway. I am not looking to kill hundreds of thousands of people in Afghanistan—many of them totally innocent. It is also not our function to serve other nations as law enforcement agencies. These are warfighters that we have—the best in the world—and they either want to fight to win, or not fight at all. We are working to finally end America's longest war, and bring our troops back home.

War places a heavy burden on our nation's extraordinary military families, especially spouses like Amy Williams from Fort Bragg, North Carolina, and her two children—six-year-old Elliana and three-year-old Rowan. Amy works full-time and volunteers countless hours, helping other military families. For the past seven months, she has done it all while her husband, Sergeant First Class Townsend Williams, is in Afghanistan on his fourth deployment in the Middle East. Amy's kids haven't seen their father's face in many months. Amy, your family's sacrifice makes it possible for all of our families to live in safety and in peace, and we want to thank you. Thank you, Amy.

But Amy, there is one more thing. Tonight, we have a very special surprise. I am thrilled to inform you that your husband is back from deployment. He is here with us tonight, and we couldn't keep him waiting any longer.

Welcome home, Sergeant Williams. Thank you very much.

As the world bears witness tonight, America is a land of heroes. This is a place where greatness is born, where destinies are forged, and where legends come to life. This is the home of Thomas Edison and Teddy Roosevelt, of many great generals, including Washington, Pershing, Patton, and MacArthur. This is the home of Abraham Lincoln, Frederick Douglass, Amelia Earhart, Harriet Tubman, the Wright Brothers, Neil Armstrong, and so many more. This is the country where children learn names like Wyatt Earp, Davy Crockett, and Annie Oakley. This is the place where the pilgrims landed at Plymouth, and where Texas patriots made their last stand at the Alamo—the beautiful, beautiful Alamo.

The American nation was carved out of the vast frontier by the toughest, strongest, fiercest, and most determined men and women ever to walk on the face of the earth. Our ancestors braved the unknown; tamed the wilderness; settled the Wild West; lifted millions from poverty, disease, and hunger; vanquished tyranny and fascism; ushered the world to new heights of science and medicine; laid down the railroads, dug out the canals, raised up the skyscrapers. And ladies and gentlemen, our ancestors built the most exceptional republic ever to exist in all of human history. And we are making it greater than ever before.

This is our glorious and magnificent inheritance. We are Americans. We are pioneers. We are the pathfinders. We settled the New World. We built the modern world. And we changed history forever by embracing the eternal truth that everyone is made equal by the hand of Almighty God.

America is the place where anything can happen. America is the place where anyone can rise. And here, on this land, on this soil, on this continent, the most incredible dreams come true.

This nation is our canvas, and this country is our masterpiece. We look at tomorrow and see unlimited frontiers just waiting to be explored. Our brightest discoveries are not yet known. Our most thrilling stories are not yet told. Our grandest journeys are not yet made. The American Age, the American Epic, the American Adventure, has only just begun.

Our spirit is still young. The sun is still rising. God's grace is still shining. And my fellow Americans, the best is yet to come.

Thank you. God bless you. And God bless America. Thank you very much.

United States Military Academy Graduation

WEST POINT, NEW YORK

June 13, 2020

Thank you, General. And hello, cadets. On behalf of our entire nation, let me say congratulations to the incredible West Point Class of 2020. Congratulations. Everyone, have a good time, enjoy yourselves, because we are here to celebrate your achievements— and great achievements they are.

Let us also recognize your remarkable superintendent, General Darryl Williams, for his outstanding stewardship. General, thank you very much. Great job. Thank you.

Few words in the English language, and few places in history have commanded as much awe and admiration as West Point. This premier military academy produces only the best of the best, the strongest of the strong, and the bravest of the brave. West Point is a universal symbol of American gallantry, loyalty, devotion, discipline, and great skill. There is no place on earth I would rather be than right here with all of you. It's a great honor.

Across this hallowed plain have passed many of the greatest and most fearsome soldiers that ever lived. They were heroes who drove thundering columns of Sherman tanks into the heart of a wicked empire. They were legends who unleashed the fury of American artillery upon our enemies on remote islands and distant shores. They were titans who strode through cannon blast and cavalry charge, and stared down our foes through gray clouds of smoke and shrapnel. They were the Army Rangers who led the way up jagged cliffs, the Airborne soldiers who rained down justice in the dark of night, the infantry whose very sight meant liberation was near, and the mighty forces who sent tyrants, terrorists, and sadistic monsters running scared through the gates of hell. No evil force on earth can match the noble power and righteous glory of the American warrior.

I have no doubt that the young men and women before me today will add your names to this eternal chronicle of American heroes. You will go forth from this place, adored by your countrymen, dreaded by your enemies, and respected by all throughout the world. Someday, generations of future West Point cadets will study your legacy. They will know your deeds, they will celebrate your triumphs, and they will proudly follow your example.

To the eleven hundred and seven cadets, who today become the newest officers in the most exceptional Army ever to take the field of battle, I am here to offer America's salute. Thank you for answering your nation's call.

On this special occasion, we are delighted to be joined by Congressman Steve Womack; Secretary of the Army, Ryan McCarthy; Assistant Secretary Casey Wardynski; and Army Chief of Staff, General James McConville, an old grad from the class of 1981.

Let's also express our appreciation to General Curtis Buzzard, General Cindy Jebb, and all of the wonderful instructors, coaches, and faculty members who are continuing West Point's two-century tradition of unrivaled excellence.

To all of the parents, grandparents, and family members watching this ceremony from your beautiful home: Even though you could not be here today, we know this day could never have happened without you. Your love and sacrifice have given America these phenomenal men and women. Cadets, please join me in sending your parents and families the heartfelt thanks that they so richly deserved. They're all watching right now. Please. Thank you very much.

The depth and breadth of the US military's contributions to our society are an everlasting inspiration to us all. I want to take this opportunity to thank all members of America's Armed Forces, in every branch—active duty, National Guard, and reserve—who stepped forward to help battle the invisible enemy: the new virus that came to our shores from a distant land called China. We will vanquish the virus. We will extinguish this plague.

I also want to thank the men and women of our National Guard, who respond with precision to so many recent challenges—from hurricanes and natural disasters, to ensuring peace, safety, and the constitutional rule of law on our streets. We thank every citizen who wears a uniform in selfless service to our nation.

The members of this class have come from every state in our Union. You have come from the farms and the cities, from states big and small, and from every race, religion, color, and creed. But when you entered these grounds, you became part of one team, one family, proudly serving one great American nation. You became brothers and sisters pledging allegiance to the same timeless principles, joined together in a common mission to protect our country, to defend our people, and to carry on the traditions of freedom, equality, and liberty that so many gave their lives to secure. You exemplify the power of shared national purpose to transcend all differences and achieve true unity. Today, you graduate as one class, and you embody one noble creed: Duty, Honor, Country.

Every graduate on this field could have gone to virtually any top-ranked university that you wanted. You chose to devote your life to the defense of America. You came to West Point because you know the truth: America is the greatest country in human history, and the United States military is the greatest force for peace and justice the world has ever known.

The survival of America, and the endurance of civilization itself, depends on the men and women just like each of you. It depends on people who love their country with all their heart and energy and soul. It depends on citizens who build, sustain, nurture, and defend institutions like this one. That is how societies are made, and how progress is advanced. What has historically made America unique is the durability of its institutions against the passions and prejudices of the moment. When times are turbulent, when the road is rough, what matters most is that which is permanent, timeless, enduring, and eternal.

It was on this soil that American patriots held the most vital fortress in our war for independence. It was this school that gave us the men who fought and won a bloody war to extinguish the evil of slavery within one lifetime of our founding. It was the graduates of West Point—towering figures like McArthur, Patton, Eisenhower, and Bradley—who led America to victory over the sinister Nazis and imperial fascists, seventy-five years ago. It was under the leadership of West Point graduates like the legendary General Matthew Ridgway that the Army was at the forefront of ending the terrible injustice of segregation. It was Army strength that held the line against the brutal opposition and oppression from Communism. And it has been thanks to patriots like you, that America has climbed to new heights of human achievement and national endeavor.

This is your history. This is the legacy that each of you inherits. It is the legacy purchased with American blood at the crest of Little Round Top, on the crimson beaches of Normandy, in the freezing mud of Bastogne, and the dense jungles of Vietnam. It is the legacy of courageous, selfless, faithful patriots who fought for every inch of dirt, with every ounce of strength, and every last scrap of heart and drive and grit they had.

And they did it because they believed in the undying principles of our founding. They did it because they cherished their homes, their faith, their family, and their flag. And they did it because, when they came to this school, they were taught to hold fast to their love of our country—to cherish our heritage, learn from it, and build upon it. That is what young Americans are taught here at West Point. That is the legacy that you carry forward as second lieutenants in the United States Army, and you must never forget it.

Through four long years, you have honed your skills, trained your mind and body, overcome every obstacle, and earned your place of pride in the Long Gray Line. You made it through the rigors of R-Day and Beast, and intensity of CLDT, and weeks of training in the blistering heat. You have pushed yourselves far beyond every limit imaginable.

Some of you have even pushed the limits a bit too much. So for any cadets who have not finished walking off their hours, as commander-in-chief, I hereby absolve all cadets on restriction for minor conduct offenses, and that is effective immediately. Congratulations. That's a nice one, isn't it? Don't you feel better now?

Surviving the forty-seven-month experience is never easy, but only the class of 2020 can say it survived forty-eight months. And when it comes to bragging rights, no one can boast louder than the class that brought Navy's fourteen-year football winning streak to a screeching halt. You did that. I happened to be there. I happened to be there. That's right. That was a big day. I was there. You beat Navy and brought the Commander-in-Chief's Trophy back to West Point for two straight years. So we say, "Go, Army, go."

This graduating class secured more than a thousand victories for the Black Knights, including three bowl victories, thirteen NCAA team appearances, and a Women's Rugby Championship, with the help of somebody that I just met: 2019 MVP, Sam Sullivan. Fantastic job. Thank you. A fantastic job. Five cadets won national boxing championships, and Adaya Queen brought home two. Brendan Brown earned the title of Powerlifting National Champion.

In academics, thirty-eight cadets have earned fellowships to continue their studies, including First Captain Dane Van de Wall, who received one of the most prestigious awards in academia: the Rhodes Scholarship. Congratulations, Dane. It's a great achievement. Thank you. Congratulations. Great achievement.

But no one modeled the values of the soldier-scholar quite like Lindy Mooradian. Lindy earned both the highest overall class standing and the highest physical program score. She has published scientific research in a prominent journal, and set five new records on the athletic track. Lindy, incredible job. Where is Lindy? Where is Lindy? For somebody that did so well, they didn't give you a very good seat, Lindy. We have to talk about that. Congratulations.

Right now, America needs a class of cadets that lives by your motto: "With Vision, We Lead." We need you to carry on the spirit of the great General Ulysses S. Grant. Soon after assuming overall command, following three years of Union setbacks, General Grant encountered someone heading north to Washington during the Battle of the Wilderness: "If you see the President," Grant said, "tell him from me that whatever happens, there will never be no turning back."

We need you to be as visionary as Patton, who as a young man in 1917 became the first soldier assigned to the Army Tank Corps. One month into the job, he saw the future, writing: "If resistance is broken, and the line is pierced, the tank must and will assume the role of pursuit cavalry and ride the enemy to death." Under Patton's leadership, that's exactly what they did.

We need you to be as bold and determined as the immortal General Douglas MacArthur, who knew that the American soldier never, ever quits. After leaving the Philippines for Australia, at a low point of the Pacific War in 1942, MacArthur famously vowed: "I shall return." For two years, he then took great strategic risks and placed himself often in personal danger. On October twentieth, 1944, McArthur stepped off a landing boat, strode through knee-high water, and proclaimed: "People of the Philippines: I have returned. By the grace of Almighty God, our forces stand again on Philippine soil." He then called upon the islands' brave people to rise up and join the fight. America's momentum was unstoppable.

These great leaders were not afraid of what others might say about them. They didn't care. They knew their duty was to protect their country. They knew the Army exists to preserve the republic, and the strong foundations upon which it stands: family, God, country, liberty, and justice. They were true, tough American patriots. That is what our country needs, especially in these times. And that is what you are.

Each of you begins your career in the Army at a crucial moment in American history. We are restoring the fundamental principles that the job of the American soldier is not to rebuild foreign nations, but defend—and defend strongly—our nation from foreign enemies. We are ending the era of endless wars. In its place is a renewed, clear-eyed focus on defending America's vital interests. It is not the duty of US troops to solve ancient conflicts in faraway lands that many people have never even heard of. We are not the policemen of the world.

But let our enemies be on notice: If our people are threatened, we will never, ever hesitate to act. And when we fight, from now on, we will fight only to win. As MacArthur said: "In war, there is no substitute for victory."

To ensure you have the very best equipment and technology available, my administration has embarked on a colossal rebuilding of the American Armed Forces—a record like no other. After years of devastating budget cuts and a military that was totally depleted from these endless wars, we have invested over two trillion—trillion . . . that's with a T—dollars in the most powerful fighting force, by far, on the planet Earth. We are building new ships, bombers, jet fighters, and helicopters by the hundreds; new tanks, military satellites, rockets, and missiles; even a hypersonic missile that goes seventeen times faster than the fastest missile currently available in the world, and can hit a target one thousand miles away, within fourteen inches from center point.

For the first time in seventy years, we established a new branch of the United States military—the Space Force. It's a big deal.

In recent years, America's warriors have made clear to all, the high cost of threatening the American people. The savage ISIS caliphate has been one hundred percent destroyed under the Trump administration. And its barbaric leader, al-Baghdadi, is gone—killed, over. And the world's number-one terrorist, Qasem Soleimani, is likewise dead.

As commander-in-chief, I never forget, for one instant, the immense sacrifices we ask of those who wear this nation's uniform. Already, you have known the crushing pain of losing a brother in arms. Today, we remember an extraordinary cadet who made the supreme sacrifice in an accident last year—CJ Morgan. We are deeply moved to be joined by his father, Christopher Morgan. And CJ was something very special. Christopher is a

Secret Service agent. A tough guy. Great guy. Great son, who is looking down right now. Christopher, I want you to know that we will carry CJ's blessed memory in our hearts forever. Thank you very much. Thank you.

Tomorrow, America will celebrate a very important anniversary: the two hundred forty-fifth birthday of the United States Army. Unrelated, going to be my birthday also. I don't know if that happened by accident. Did that happen by accident, please? But it's a great day because of that Army birthday.

And as you know, the Army's first commander-in-chief, General George Washington, called the fort that stood on this majestic point, "the most important post in America." Its strategic location on the Hudson River was vital to our war for independence. If British ships gained control of this river, they would have divided our young nation in two. So American soldiers stretched a massive metal chain across the waters of the Hudson, from West Point all the way to Constitution Island. I saw a piece of that chain. It's incredible. No enemy ship even dared try to cross. Every link in that great chain was formed from over a hundred pounds of pure American iron, mined from American soil, and made with American pride. Together, those links formed an unbreakable line of defense.

Standing here before you, more than two centuries later, it is clearer than ever that General Washington's words still hold true. West Point is still the indispensable post for America, the vital ground that must not lose. And the survival of our nation still depends on the great chain reaching out from this place—one made not of iron, but of flesh and blood, of memory and spirit, of sheer faith and unyielding courage.

Today, each of you becomes another link in that unbroken chain, forged in the crucible known as the United States Military Academy—the greatest on earth. It has given you soldiers that you can rely on to your right and to your left. And now we are entrusting you with the most noble task any warrior has ever had the privilege to carry out—the task of preserving American liberty.

As long as you remain loyal, faithful, and true, then our enemies don't even stand a chance. Our rights will never be stolen, our freedoms will never be trampled, our destiny will never be denied, and the United States of America will never be defeated. With the grace of God, and the heroes of West Point, America will always prevail. Nothing will stand in your way. Nothing will slow you down. And nothing will stop the West Point Class of 2020 from achieving a true and lasting victory.

God bless you. God bless the United States Army. And God bless America. Congratulations. Thank you very much. Thank you.

Campaign Rally

TULSA, OKLAHOMA

June 20, 2020

Thank you, thank you. So we begin, Oklahoma. We begin. Thank you, Oklahoma. And thank you to Vice President Mike Pence. We begin—we begin our campaign. Thank you. We begin our campaign, and I just want to thank all of you. You are warriors.

I've been watching the fake news for weeks now, and everything is negative. Don't go, don't come, don't do anything. Today it was like—I've never seen anything like it. I've never seen anything like it. You are warriors. Thank you.

We had some very bad people outside. We had some very bad people outside. They were doing bad things. But I really do—I appreciate it. We have just a tremendous group of people in Oklahoma. And I hear—I hear from your two great senators and your governor—that we're doing very well in Oklahoma. That's the word. That's the word.

I stand before you today to declare the silent majority is stronger than ever before. Five months from now, we're going to defeat sleepy Joe Biden. Boy, does he get a pass from these people, huh? We're going to stop the radical Left. We're going to build a future of safety and opportunity for Americans of every race, color, religion, and creed.

Republicans are the party of liberty, equality, and justice for all. We are the party of Abraham Lincoln, and we are the party of law and order. Think of what we've done. We will have close to three hundred federal judges appointed and approved by the end of my first time. That's an all-time record. That's an all-time record. I've always heard how important judges are. Now we know how important they are. Think of that, over three hundred—around three hundred—by the end of the term. And when we have another four years, we're going to have a big, big percentage of the total number. Very important, November third.

And two great Supreme Court judges. So we have two justices of the Supreme Court—Justice Gorsuch, Justice Kavanaugh. They're great. They're great. They are. They're great. We have two. And we could get a few more. Yeah, we can get a few more.

We've spent over two trillion dollars to completely rebuild the unmatched strength and power of the United States military. And all of that incredible equipment—whether it's submarines, or missiles, or rockets, or jet fighters, bombers—it's all built in the USA. We passed VA Choice. Thank you very much, Jim. Where's my senator? Jim Inhofe, you better vote for him. He's running. He's great.

But we'll get to him and James Lankford in a second—two great senators. You have two great senators. So we passed VA Choice. So if you're a veteran—for years and years, they've wanted to do it for almost fifty years. We got it done. We get a lot of things done. And so if you're a veteran, and you have to wait on line for one week, two weeks, three weeks, five weeks, seven weeks, two months—what happens is you go outside, you get a private doctor, you get fixed up, and they pay your bill. We take care of the bill. We take care of the bill, and you get immediate service. It's never happened before. And our approval rating at the VA is now ninety-one percent. That's how good it is. Never been anywhere near that number. Never been anywhere near that number.

And VA accountability—we had a lot of bad people in the VA. People that didn't love our vets. People that were sadistic. People that stole. A lot of bad people. You couldn't get rid of them, because they were—let's say it could be unions. It could be civil service, right. Let's say. Let's just say. And so you couldn't get it done. That was another one for decades and decades, they wanted to get it changed. And I got it done with those people and your congressman. Your congressman, who I'm going to introduce. VA accountability—and now somebody treats our veterans badly, and we look at them, and what do we say? We say, "You're fired. Get out, right? Get out."

They got rid of a lot of bad people that were there for a long time. Sort of like me in Washington, draining the swamp. I never knew it was so deep. But it's happening. It's happening. I never knew it was so deep. It's deep and thick, and a lot of bad characters. Thank you.

We're lowering the price of prescription drugs, making our allies pay their fair share. They get a big bargain on drug prices. And enacting fair trade deals that finally, finally, after all these years, put America first. I've been saying it for a long time.

We passed the largest tax cuts in the history of our country. The Democrats want to raise your taxes. Tell me about that. Tell me about that. I guess I'm old fashioned y'know, all my life, all my life, I heard politicians want to lower taxes, not raise them. If you could lower them, you couldn't lose. The Democrats want to substantially raise your taxes. How do you figure that? How do you figure that? And regulation cuts—we passed more regulation cuts than any administration in the history of our country. And with the help of our great energy workers, many of them come from the great state of Oklahoma.

Do you ever notice that Biden—no, do you ever notice that Biden oftentimes gets the state wrong? He's in Iowa, and he says it's good to be in Idaho. No, no, you're in Iowa. He's in New Hampshire, and he says it's great to be in Ohio. No, no, no, you're in New Hampshire. That happens to him all the time. Hasn't happened to me yet. Y'know, when that happens, there's nothing you can do to make up for it. You might as well just walk off the stage, because the speech is a disaster. Right, right.

But we just turned the United States into the dominant energy superpower of the world. Of the world. And because of the Chinese virus, what happened about three months ago? It looked like we were in big trouble, and we were. And I got it back together. I called Russia. Right, I called Russia.

I called Saudi Arabia, and believe it or not, I called Mexico. Mexico was a little bit tough. That's called OPEC Plus. Did you ever hear of OPEC Plus? That's OPEC Plus-Plus. And we got them to do the right thing, and we have our energy back to almost forty dollars a barrel, meaning you have an energy business again. Almost forty dollars a barrel. Couple of months ago, it was zero, and we were going to lose ten million energy jobs. Ten million jobs. So Texas and Oklahoma and North Dakota, and many other states, would have been hurt. Now you think you're going to be hurt there. You try putting AOC in charge of your energy. That will make the pandemic look like child's play to the people in energy. She has one problem—it's called petroleum. No president or administration has done more in the first three and a half years than the Trump administration. Not even close. Nobody.

Our incredible success in rebuilding America stands in stark contrast to the extremism and destruction and violence of the radical Left. We just saw it outside. We just saw it outside. You saw these thugs that came along. These people—call them protesters. Isn't it beautiful. It's so beautiful. No, they're so wonderful. They call them the Boston Tea Party. They're so wonderful. Yeah, they call them—you ever watch fake news, CNN? You ever watch?

How about the CNN anchor? How about the CNN anchor? You know, did a little shave job in the head. Which is fine. And he's standing in front of a building, saying, "Things are very peaceful here." And the building is—it looks like the biggest fire I've ever seen. The whole town is burning. It's like the biggest fire. And he said, "Things are very good here, Anderson. I think it's great. These are wonderful people, Anderson." Did you ever see that? It looked like the world was coming to an end. And we did something in Minneapolis after watching for three or four days. I called, I said, "You got to get . . . you can't protect yourselves." I got them to take eight thousand National Guardsmen. And in one hour, it all ended. And they rode through the next three weeks with no problem.

And we did the same thing in other cities. But how about Seattle? Isn't that great? So they take over a big chunk of a city called Seattle. I mean, we're not talking about some little place. We're talking about Seattle. Have you ever been to Seattle? They took over a big chunk, and the governor, who's radical Left—all of these places I talk about are Democrat. You know that. Every one of them. Every one of them. And I'd have an offer out—I said, "Anytime you want, we'll come in, we'll straighten it out in one hour or less." Now I may be wrong, but it's probably better for us to just watch that disaster.

I flew in with some of our great congressmen, who we're going to introduce in a second. And I said to them, "Congressmen, what do you think? I can straighten it out fast. Should we just go in? No, sir. Let it simmer for a little while. Let people see what radical Left Democrats will do to our country." But Americans have watched left-wing radicals burn down buildings, loot businesses, destroy private property, injure hundreds of dedicated police officers. These police officers, they get injured, they don't complain. They're incredible. And injure thousands upon thousands of people, only to hear the radical fake news say what a beautiful rally it was.

And they never talk about COVID. They don't talk about. When you see twenty-five thousand people walking down Fifth Avenue or walking down a street of a Democrat-run city, you never hear them saying, "They're not wearing their mask." You don't hear them say—as they're breaking windows and running in. And then when I say the looters, the anarchists, the agitators, they say, "What a terrible thing for our president to say. What a terrible thing."

But you don't hear them talking about COVID. COVID—to be specific, COVID-19. That name gets further and further away from China, as opposed to calling it the Chinese virus. And despite the fact that we—I—have done a phenomenal job with it. I shut down the United States to very heavily infected, but all people from China, in late January, which is months earlier than other people would have done it, if they would have done it at all. I saved hundreds of thousands of lives. We don't ever get even a mention. Then I closed it down to Europe early. Closed it down because I saw what was happening. And by the way, most people said, "Don't do it. Don't do it." We saved hundreds of thousands of lives, and all we do is get hit on like we're terrible. And what we've done with the ventilators and with the medical equipment. And with testing—you know, testing is a double-edged sword. We've tested now twenty-five million people. It's probably twenty million people more than anybody else. Germany's done a lot. South Korea has done a lot.

They called me, they said, "The job you're doing—here's the bad part. When you do testing to that extent, you're going to find more people, you're going to find more cases." So I said to my people, "Slow the testing down, please." They test and they test. We had tests, and people don't know what's going on. We got tests. We got another one over here. The young man's ten years old. He's got the sniffles. He'll recover in about fifteen minutes. That's a case—add him to it. That's OK. That's a case. I was actually with a very nice man, very good man, even though he's very liberal—the governor of New Jersey, right? We know him? Now listen, he said to me something that's amazing. New Jersey was very heavily hit. Very hard hit. Thousands of people. He said, with thousands of people that died—thousands of people—there was only one person that died under the age of eighteen. Would you believe that? Which tells me one thing: that kids are much stronger than us.

When you see a little kid running around, say, "Boy, oh boy, do you have a great immune system! How about a piece of your immune system?" They don't even know about this.

Let's open the schools, please. Open the schools. Open the schools. We got to get them open. In the fall, we got to get them open.

The unhinged left-wing mob is trying to vandalize our history, desecrate our monuments. Our beautiful monuments. Tear down our statues and punish, cancel, and persecute anyone who does not conform to their demands for absolute and total control. We're not conforming. That's why we're here, actually. This cruel campaign of censorship and exclusion violates everything we hold dear as Americans. They want to demolish our heritage so they can impose their new oppressive regime in its place. They want to defund and dissolve our police departments. Think of that.

And I heard it for the first time, two weeks ago. I said, "Well, that one . . . I mean, they're only kidding." I said, "They're only— they're not." Minneapolis, you see what's going on. They're not kidding. They got a lot of problems. They'll have a lot of problems. Hey, it's one o'clock in the morning, and a very tough—I've used the word on occasion—*hombre*. A very tough *hombre* is breaking into the window of a young woman whose husband is away as a traveling salesman or whatever he may do. And you call 911, and they say, "I'm sorry, this number's no longer working." By the way, you have many cases like that. Many, many, many. Whether it's a young woman, an old woman, a young man, or an old man, and you're sleeping. So what are you going to do, right? So they want to defund. They really do. This as a serious movement. And in Minneapolis, the council's already passed it. In Seattle, you see what's going on there. It's even worse, OK. These people are stone-cold crazy. They're crazy.

So if you want to save your heritage—you want to save that beautiful heritage of ours. We have a great heritage. We're a great country. You are so lucky I'm president. That's all I can tell you. [USA! USA! USA!]

People have come up to me, say, "How do you take it?" I say, "Do I have a choice? Do I have a choice?" We deal with a lot of bad people, but we're winning. And every once in a while, I'll have one of these days where I'm hit left and right, left and right—like even this great event. If you could have seen outside, or if you could have heard the reports. The reports, "Oh, it's COVID. It's this again." By the way, it's a disease, without question, has more names than any disease in history. I can name—Kung Flu. I can name, nineteen different versions of names. Many call it a virus, which it is. Many call it a flu. What difference? I think we have nineteen or twenty versions of the name. But they say to me, "Where do you get the energy?" I say, "I don't have a choice. I don't have a choice."

Y'know, it was interesting to show you how fake they are. You might've seen it. So last week they called me and they say, "Sir, West Point, West Point. We're ready." I said, "Oh, that's right. I have to make the commencement speech at West Point."

You know, they delayed it for six weeks because of COVID. So they delayed it, and I went there. One thousand one hundred six cadets were graduated—and beautiful. Beautiful cadets. Just to show you how bad the fake news is, so they say to me, "Sir, we're ready to go." I say, "Let's go." This is after saying hello to a lot of cadets, inspecting little areas of a building. That was very exciting. Actually, it's beautiful. Very old. Studied a lot of our great generals, some of our presidents that went there. West Point is beautiful—right on the Hudson River.

But after an hour—the general that runs it is a fantastic guy. After an hour, we land, we do some more inspections, and they say, "Sir, are you ready?"

"Yes, I am."

So we walked, like, the equivalent of about three blocks, which is fine. We go onstage, which is fine. They make speeches. Then I make a speech that lasted a long time. I don't know, maybe forty-five minutes. Maybe longer. I don't know, but a long time. The sun is pouring down on me, OK.

But they said to me before the speech, "Sir, would you like to salute each cadet. Each single cadet? Or maybe there'll be in groups of two. Would you like to salute?"

"Like this? Yes."

Like this, almost six hundred times. You know what that is? Six hundred times. Thank God they were in twos, because let me tell you—you do that six hundred times, you go home and you say it's like a workout without a weight, right? Six hundred times. So I did that. Then the incredible helicopters—brand-new gorgeous helicopters—the Apaches, and the other new ones that we just bought. Helicopters—the Apaches, and the other new ones that we just bought. So they fly over, and the kids throw the hats in the air. It's beautiful. It really is. It was a beautiful day, and we're all finished. I was on the stage for hours. Hours. Sun.

I came home, I had a nice tan—meaning, I had a nice sun-burn. The sun's gone right like that, but I make this speech. I salute for probably an hour and a half. Maybe more. But around that. Watch—if I'm off by two minutes, they'll say, "He exaggerated. It was only an hour and twenty-five minutes. He exaggerated. He lied, he lied. He's a liar." These people are sick, the fake news.

So then I finish saluting my final salute, I said, "Thank goodness. Thank you very much." Think of it. So essentially, almost six hundred times. Now the general says, "Sir, are you ready?" I said, "I'm ready, General. Where are we going now?"

You have to understand, I left early in the morning to get there. Now it's sort of late in the afternoon. A lot of these fakers were with us. So they know.

He said, "Sir, we can now leave the stage." I said, "Great, General. Let's go. I'll follow you." And he goes like this. "Right here, sir," and I walked off. The stage was higher than this one, and the ramp was probably ten yards long. I say, "General." Now you got to understand, I have the whole corps of cadets looking at me, and I want them to love their president. I did this big thing. I love them. I love them. They're incredible—and they do.

I said, "General, I've got myself a problem, General." Because I'm wearing leather-bottom shoes, which is good if you're walking on flat surfaces. It's not good for ramps. And if I fall down—look at all those press back there. Look at them. This was a steel ramp. You all saw it, because everybody saw it. This was a steel ramp. It had no handrail. It was like an ice skating rink. And I said, "General, I have a problem," and he didn't understand that at first. I said, "There's no way." He understood, I just saluted almost six hundred times. I just made a big speech. I sat for other speeches. I'm being baked. I'm being baked like a cake. I said, "General, there's no way I can make it down that ramp without falling on my ass, General. I have no railing."

It's true. So I said, "Is there, like, something else around?"

"Sir, the ramp is ready to go. Grab me, sir. Grab me."

I didn't really want to grab him. You know why? Because I said, "That will be a story, too."

So now I have a choice. I can stay up there for another couple of hours and wait till I'm rescued. Or I can go down this really steep—really, really, really . . . it's an ice skating rink. It's brutal. So I said, "General, get ready because I may grab you so fast." Because I can't fall with the fake news watching. If I fall . . . if I fall—I remember when President Ford fell out of the plane. Do you remember? I remember when another president—nice man—threw up in Japan, and they did slow-motion replays. It's true, right?

"I don't want that, General."

Now he's standing there—big, strong guy—and he's got these shoes, but they're loaded with rubber on the bottom—because I looked. The first thing I did, I looked at his shoes. Then I looked at mine. Very, very slippery.

So I end up saying, "OK, General, let's go. I will only grab you if I need you."

That's not a good story. Falling would be a disaster. It turned out to be worse than anything. I would have been better off if I fell and slid down the damn ramp. Right?

So what happens is, I start the journey, inch by inch, right? I was really bent over, too. I didn't like that. I didn't like this picture. This picture, I'm sure will be an ad by the fakers. So I was bent over, right? Bent over like this. Then we finally reached almost the end, and the fake news—the most dishonest human beings—they cut it off. You know why? Because when I was ten feet short, I said, "General, I'm sorry," and I ran down the rest, right? I looked very handsome. That was the only good. I wouldn't want to run down the whole thing, because the fall there would be definitely bad. So I took these little steps. I ran down the last ten. And by the way, their tape—take a look. In almost every instance, it ends just before I run. And they said, "Here was the number one trending story."

I call my wife, I said, "How good was that speech? I thought it was a . . ." Hey, look, I will tell you when I make good ones and bad ones. Like, so far tonight, I'm average. But we're having fun. We're having fun. So far tonight—but I call my wife, and I said, "How good was it, darling?"

She said, "You're trending number one."

I said to our great First Lady—I said, "Let me ask you a question. Was it that good of a speech that I'm trending number one? Because I felt it was really good."

"No, no, they don't even mention the speech. They mention the fact that you may have Parkinson's disease."

It's true. It's true. It's true.

They say there is something wrong with our president. I'll let you know if there's something wrong, OK? I'll let you know if there's something. I'll tell you what, there's something wrong with Biden. That, I could tell you.

So then my wife said, "Well, it wasn't only the ramp. Did you have water?"

I said, "Yeah. I was speaking for a long time. I didn't want to drink it, but I wanted to wet my lips a little bit." You're drinking, you're working hard up there, with the sun pouring down on you. I love this location—the sun's like this. This way, they save on lighting, right? That's why they did it, probably.

So what happens is, I said, "What does it have to do with water?"

"They said you couldn't lift your hand up to your mouth with water."

I said, "I just saluted six hundred times, like this. And this was before I saluted, so what's the problem?"

She said, "Well, I know what you did. You had on a very good red tie that's sort of expensive."

It's silk, because they look better. They have a better sheen to them. And I don't want to get water on the tie, and I don't want to drink much, so I lift it up, the water. I see we have a little glass of water. Where the hell did this water come from? Where did it come from? I look down at my tie, because I've done it. I've taken water, and it spills down onto your tie. Doesn't look good for a long time. And frankly, the tie is never the same. So I put it up to my lip, and then I say—and they gave me another disease. They gave me another disease. Anyway, that's a long story.

But here's the story. I have lived with more the ramp than the water. But I have lived with the ramp and the water since I left West Point. Not one media group said I made a good speech, or I made a great speech. But the kids loved it, because they broke their barrier, which wasn't good in terms of COVID. But they broke their barrier, and they wanted to shake hands. They wanted to—I don't want to tell anybody, but there were a couple of kids, they put out their hand . . . I actually shook their hand, OK. I actually shook them. Because they were excited. They were excited. They were with their president. They were excited. The most beautiful young people. Men, women—the most beautiful young people you've ever seen.

So think of how you feel if you're me. I go there: "How did I do?"

"Sir, that was a great speech." You know all my people: "Sir, that was one of your best. That was great."

I said, "That's great. I agree, it was a good speech. I like that speech."

They don't mention the speech, but they have been going down this ramp at an inch at a time. It's so unfair. It really is. So unfair. They are among the most dishonest people anywhere on earth. They're bad people. Bad people.

OK, that's enough of that. I wanted to tell that story. Does everybody understand that story? The left-wing anarchists tore down a statue of Thomas Jefferson. Now we're getting into the real stuff. They decapitated a statue of Christopher Columbus—except in New York, when the Italians surrounded it. They didn't have too much of a chance. Those Italians—I love the Italians. They heard they were going to rip down their beautiful Christopher Columbus, and all of a sudden, they circled that thing. They didn't do too well in hurting Christopher, did they? Thank you to our Italian population. We're very proud of you, right?

Two days ago, leftist radicals in Portland, Oregon, ripped down a statue of George Washington and wrapped it in an American flag, and set the American flag on fire. Democrat. All Democrat. Everything I tell you is Democrat. And you know, we ought to do something, Mister Senators. We have two great senators. We ought to come up with legislation that if you burn the American flag, you go to jail for one year. One year. Jim and James. Jim and James. We ought to do it.

You know they talk about freedom of speech—and I'm a big believer in freedom of speech—but that's desecration. That's a terrible thing they do. We used to have things. We don't have them anymore because we want to be so open, so everything. And look what happens. We should have legislation that if somebody wants to burn the American flag and stomp on it, or just burn it, they go to jail for one year, OK?

In Seattle, the Democrat mayor and the Democrat city council have surrendered control of six city blocks to an anarchist. Now these are anarchists; these are not protestors. You listen to the fake news, they say, "Oh, the protesters were lovely." Could you imagine if people just even slightly to the right tried to take over Seattle? They'd have machine guns out to get them. But these people can take over the city. Look at what they've done to businesspeople that have spent years and years building their business, and now they're wiped out. Take it away. Governor Inslee ought to get his act together. Get in there. I'll help you. I'll do whatever you want. I'm waiting for a call, I would love to do it. I would love to do it. It'll take less than an hour, and it'll all be over with. And you'll have your city back.

Yet, Biden remains silent in his basement, in the face of this brutal assault on our nation and the values of our nation. Joe Biden has surrendered to his party, and to the left-wing mob. He has no control. Does anybody honestly think he controls these radical maniacs? You know what he says to his wife when he's not confusing her with his sister? "Get me the hell out of there. These people are crazy." That's what he says. He has absolutely no control.

You know, a lot of times I'll make like a speech, and I'll have this beautiful paragraph come out criticizing every little aspect of the speech. Beautiful, brilliant. But Joe didn't. It'll say, "A comment from Joe Biden," but he didn't say it. Professional people, great students in English lit, people that are very smart say it. Joe Biden said, and they'll go into this highly complex paragraph, beautifully worded. And I say, "Joe didn't say that. Joe doesn't even understand it."

If Biden is elected, he will surrender your country to these mobsters, one hundred percent. Your 401(k)s—by the way, look at how we're doing in the stock market. Just set another record with NASDAQ. NASDAQ. Your 401(k)s, and money itself, will be worthless. Your 401(k)s are doing very well unless—I don't want to say. If you were stupid, I'd say, "Don't sell. Don't sell. It went down." But we got it back up, and now NASDAQ—think of it—NASDAQ just set a record. And I think you're going to see a lot of records. And next year, if we don't do anything stupid on November third, you are going to have the greatest economic year we've ever had. That will be next year. If the Democrats gain power, then the rioters will be in charge, and no one will be safe, and no one will have control.

Joe Biden is not the leader of his party. Joe Biden is a helpless puppet of the radical Left, and he's not radical Left. I don't think he knows what he is anymore. But he was never radical Left, but he's controlled by the radical Left. And now he's really controlled. His campaign staff even donated a lot of money to bail out rioters, looters, and arsonists who ravaged Minneapolis. They bailed them out. They put up a lot of money to bail them out—the rioters, the looters—and they were . . . they were the arsonists. They'll say, "Oh, it's terrible what he says about the people of our nation." Maybe some of them aren't even from our nation.

The leftists try to do everything they can to stop us. Every hour of every day—including even violence and mayhem—they'll do anything they can to stop us. Look what happened tonight. Look at what happened tonight. Law enforcement said, "Sir, they can't be outside. It's too dangerous." We had a bunch of maniacs come and sort of attack our city. The mayor and the governor did a great job, but they were very violent people. Our people are not nearly as violent. But if they ever were, it would be a terrible, terrible day for the other side. Because I know our people. I know our people. But we will never submit to their threats, and we will never let them destroy our nation.

What they did tonight, I saw it on television, coming in on Air Force One. One thing about Air Force One, we got plenty of televisions. We have televisions in closets. You open up the closet, got a television. We got a lot of televisions. It's a great plane. Great everything.

By the way, we ordered new ones. No president wanted to do it. They thought it was luxurious—so wait a minute, Air Force One is thirty-one years old. People don't realize that. So I said—they gave me a charge, very early in my administration. Like, how about the first week? "Sir, would you sign for this plane?" Now, it's actually two planes. "Would you sign for this plane? Air Force One?"

I said, "How old is the original, or the one we have now?"

"Sir, it's thirty-one, thirty-two years."

I'd see people coming in from foreign lands that can't compete with us. Rich countries, but they can't compete with the—hey, have a brand-new beautiful 747-8. And I say, "Wait a minute. That country has new, and we have a thirty-one-year. So somebody had to do it. "

So the deal was made, and it was made for a lot of money. I think it was 5.7 or 5.6 billion dollars. Now in all fairness, it's two planes, and there's a lot of stuff in those planes I won't talk to you about.

So I told Boeing, the head of Boeing—they said, "Sir, please, we'd like to get started on the planes."

I said, "I do, too, but I'm not paying 5.6 billion, and I'm not paying 4.6 billion." I said, "It has to have a three on the front of it." That's a hell of a lot of money, too, but it is a rather complex situation.

They said, "No way. No way."

This was before Boeing had problems, by the way. But Boeing is coming back. They're coming back. Greatest company in the world, and—they had some big problems—that's their big problem. It had a couple of problems that didn't work out. That was terrible. But the greatest—I think before that, it was the greatest company in the world. It made up a quarter—one-quarter of a point, of our GDP. Think how big that is—one company. It was an unbelievable machine, and then they made a plane, and they did some foolish things, and a terrible thing happened, and all of a sudden they've gone through hell. But you know what? They're coming back. We're ready to help them if they need it, but they're coming back.

This was the Boeing before that, and they were riding high, like I was before this thing came in. But we're still riding high, because you know what? On November third, we're going to win. We're going to win. So they came in—and they came in and they said, "No, no, no. We want 5.6 billion." Whatever it was. Whatever it was. If I'm a little bit off, they'll go crazy. Whatever, but it was a lot.

5.6 billion. Nope. Got to have a three. Got to have a three—call me up. Nope, cancel the contract. I said, "Cancel the contract. I want it canceled." I said, "General, can you cancel the contract?"

He said, "Yes, sir. I'm very proud of it."

"Oh, good. Cancel it."

"OK, sir."

"By the way, to cancel it, do you have to pay anything?"

"Yes, sir. We have a cancellation fee, sir."

"How much is it, General?"

"Two hundred fifty million dollars."

I said, "What?"

"Sir, we made a good deal. Two hundred fifty million dollars to kill."

"You mean, if we don't buy the plane, we have to hand them two hundred fifty million dollars." That's not good, right? Look at these two guys—they're looking.

By the way, that's like a good story compared to some I could tell you—like with aircraft carriers.

So they said, "Two hundred fifty million dollars?" Or I always say this, or around that number, because if I'm off by a little bit, they say, "Oh, he exaggerates." I look at numbers all day long. That's what I look at for years now. For my whole life, when you think of it.

Two-hundred-fifty-million cancellation fee, sir. He was very proud of himself. What a great . . . I say, "General. Don't cancel.

Don't cancel. Just tell them I don't want the planes. Don't put anything in writing. Don't put it in writing, General."

"Why, sir?"

"Because I don't want to pay two-fifty." True. You hear that Jim? Jim Inhofe, he's great. You hear that Jim? You know that story. He does a great job.

So here's what happened—the bottom line. Boeing says, "No way, no way, no way." The next week, they say, "No way we're doing it." The next week they said, "How about five billion?"

I said, "No way. No way." The next week they said, "4.8."

I said, "Nope. It's got to have a three at the front of it. Don't you understand, you dumb son of a bitch? Don't you understand?"

I turned out to be right. Turned out to be right. Nobody gets that. Nope. Got to have a three.

Next day, they come back, "4.5 is our best offer."

"Nope. I'm not doing it. I'm not doing it. Come back when you're ready."

A month goes by. Another month. They never heard about it. They never heard from me. They thought I was serious. I was. And they came back at four billion.

That's a lot of money, but I save like a billion six or a billion seven. Nobody wants to talk about it. Nobody wants to talk about it. When I get foreign nations to pay us billions and billions of dollars, nobody wants to talk about that. When I take soldiers out of countries because they're not treating us properly—Germany is an example. I mean, I have a German heritage, like some of you.

I said, "Let's get it down from fifty thousand to twenty-five thousand, because they're delinquent. For many years, they're delinquent. They haven't been paying what they're supposed to be paying. They're paying one percent instead of two percent, and two percent is a very low number."

And they say, "Yes, we think by 2030, maybe 2032, we could get current.

I said, "No, Angela, Angela, please. Don't say that, Angela. It's true. You know who I'm talking about. By the way, very nice woman. Very good negotiator. I said, "Angela, that's a long time."

This was in 2019. She said 2032. I said, "No, Angela, that's not working." But I said, because now they want to get current—but I said, "Well, what about the last twenty-five years? All the money you owe us?" Everybody forgot about that. They forget about all the money that wasn't paid. I said, "What about the trillion dollars that you really owe?" So we're negotiating. Let's see . . . but in the meantime, we're reducing our troops.

Remember this, remember this, we're supposed to protect Germany from Russia. But Germany is paying Russia billions of dollars for energy coming from a pipeline—brand-new pipeline. So they pay the country we're supposed to protect them from. They pay billions of dollars to that country. We're supposed to protect them. Excuse me, how does that work? How does that work?

And the great thing is, with Jim Inhofe, and with James Lankford, likewise—they just said they love you, James. When they hear it, they get it. A lot of people don't get it. They get it. We cannot continue to be ripped off. We're ripped off by so many countries, and we're stopping it. And that means that a lot of people don't want me here. They don't want me. There are a lot of people that don't want me. They don't sell a lot of bombs when we're not dropping bombs on people. You know that, right? It's called the military–industrial complex.

When rioting and looting broke out in our nation's capital, I very quickly deployed the National Guard. I said, "Get them in." After watching for an evening or two, we stopped the violence and restored peace and order to the streets.

And last night, that had a little breakout again. They ripped down a statue that was a hundred and ten years old—beautiful piece of art—in front of the police precinct, with our radical Left mayor watching on television. We're not happy. That's going to be very expensive for DC. They're always looking for money. "We need more money. We always need more money." And then they don't do the proper job. So it's not going to be good for Mayor Bowser—Mayor Bowser.

They were heading over to the Jefferson Memorial recently, and they wanted to do damage to our great, beautiful Jefferson

Memorial. Not going to happen. Don't worry about it. We have it surrounded with very strong people.

The choice in 2020 is very simple. Do you want to bow before the left-wing mob? Or do you want to stand up tall and proud as Americans.

And explain this to the NFL. I like the NFL. I like Roger Goodell. But I didn't like what he said a week ago. I said, "Where did that come from in the middle of the summer? Nobody's even asking?" We will never kneel to our national anthem, or our great American flag. We will stand proud, and we will stand tall. I thought we won that battle with the NFL. The stadiums were emptying out. Did you see those stadiums? It took them a long time to get you back. A lot of people didn't like that. A lot of people that you wouldn't even think would care that much. I've had people that I said, "These are super-left liberals, and they didn't like it."

Joe Biden and the Democrats want to prosecute Americans for going to church, but not for burning a church. They believe you can riot, vandalize, and destroy, but you cannot attend a peaceful pro-America rally. They want to punish your thought, but not their violent crimes. They want to abolish bail, abolish and open up your borders. They want open borders, let everyone—and by the way, we're doing so well. We have a record this month on the borders. Nobody's coming in. Very few people. And they want to abolish ICE—our great people from ICE, who send the roughest, toughest, meanest people that you've ever seen or ever heard.

Generally speaking, when they have lots of tattoos on their face, they're not looking to do you much help. ICE, they're rough guys. They're rough. They're great Americans, but they'll walk in a pack. They'll walk into a pack of tough MS-13 gang members. And you know, we shouldn't say this; it's not nice. They want us to negotiate. They start swinging. And the others start—everybody's swinging. At the end, they carry them back, and they throw them into the paddy wagon, right? They're great. And these people want to get rid of ICE. They get rid of murderers. They get rid of rapists. They get rid of the worst scum on earth.

And when I called them animals, I said, "They're animals." And Nancy Pelosi—they cut up a young woman. They cut up a young woman and her friend. Cut them up with a knife because it was more painful. Dead. Cut them up with a knife because it's more painful. It takes longer than shooting a gun. They cut them up. I said, "These are animals." And Nancy Pelosi said, "These are human beings. They're not animals." If I lose an election over that, you know what? This country is in big trouble. Big trouble. They want to disarm law-abiding citizens and dismantle our police forces while freeing vicious MS-13 gang members. In Joe Biden's America, rioters, looters, and criminal aliens have more rights than law-abiding citizens. And that's true. In my administration, we defend American citizens, and we deport MS-13 members, or put them in jail if we have to. The chaos you're seeing in our Democratic-run cities—these are all run by the Democrats—is what will happen in every city and community in America. And much, much worse if we don't keep them out.

We have to do this. We have to go to the polls on November third, and the rest you know what to do. You know what to do. Got to keep the White House. Joe Biden's record can be summed up as four decades of betrayal, calamity, and failure. He never did anything. He was a senator. He was a vice president. He was, before that, something. You know what's great? President Trump was tough on this, or he was tough. They complained, never did anything about it. He's been there for forty-three years or forty-seven years. He never did anything about it. Biden's supported every globalist attack on the American worker. Let's make every country of the world rich but ourselves, including NAFTA—the disaster of NAFTA. He wanted to go, and TPP would have ruined our automobile industry.

Korea, I renegotiated the deal. I took a horrible deal. That was a Hillary Clinton special. That was a Hillary Clinton special. She said, "We have to make this deal with South Korea. It's going to mean two hundred fifty thousand jobs." And she was right—for South Korea. Two hundred fifty thousand jobs. And China's entry into the World Trade Organization was supported by sleepy Joe

Biden. That was one of the worst deals economically in the history of our country. When China joined the World Trade Organization, they became—they were flat line for decades—they became like a rocket ship. He voted for the war in Iraq. He voted for mass amnesty for illegal aliens. He supports sanctuary cities. And now Biden wants to end immigration enforcement, and he wants to require you to provide free healthcare for millions and millions of illegal aliens, OK.

When I took early and decisive action to ban travel from China and protect Americans from the virus—and as I said, Joe Biden opposed my decision and called it hysteria, xenophobia. He doesn't know what the word means—xenophobia and fear-mongering. And then he apologized a month later. He said he was wrong, but he didn't say it. And they didn't cover it. They didn't cover it. On one of the single most important policy decisions of our lifetime, Joe Biden sided with China over America—that's closing the border. He thought it was a terrible thing. Remember, this was in January. That's early. Real early. The end of January. He thought it was a terrible thing when we closed the border to many people that were badly infected with COVID.

When the chips are down, Biden will always cave to the radical Left. He'll always bow to the angry mob, and he will never protect you or your family, and you know that. Joe Biden will always let you down. That's been his history. At my direction early this year, the heroes of the US military took out the world's top terrorist—the savage killer and leader of ISIS, al-Baghdadi, and the number-one terrorist anywhere in the world, Qasem Soleimani. We took them out. Joe Biden opposed killing Soleimani. He was vehemently—we killed this number-one terrorist. He didn't like it. You know why he didn't like it? Because he thought it would be good politically. That didn't work out too well. Just as he opposed the raid that killed Osama bin Laden. He opposed it, you know that. Biden is always on the wrong side of history, as said by people that are with him and worked with him. He never made a correct foreign-policy decision. Biden is a puppet for China. Son walked out with 1.5 billion. I think it's a little bit. . . .

Allowing them to rip off America for many years. Now they're paying us billions and billions of dollars. We give a lot of it to our farmers. We have plenty left-over. China is not exactly happy with me. Billions. They pay us billions and billions of dollars. And they targeted our great farmers. And I took the money that they targeted—I took that money, and I gave it to the farmers. So they were even. So they're OK.

[Trump shares praises with the crowd as some attendees find their seats.]

He never did anything against China, Joe Biden. And that's why they desperately want him to win. They want him to win so badly. Iran wants him to win so badly. Let me tell you, I'm going to make a very fast deal. The best deal you've ever seen. I've already made one with China, but I can make even more. They want me to lose, because they will own the United States if I lose.

Iran—President Obama gave them a hundred fifty billion dollars for nothing. And almost more incredible, he gave them 1.8 billion in green cash. Beautiful cash. And now they're not doing so well, are they? They're not doing so well. Someday, we're going to get credit for this someday, but they are waiting. Iran wants to make a deal so badly. But they're told by Kerry and all these other—they shouldn't, the Logan Act. But they're told, Kerry and all these people: "Wait, because if Trump loses, you'll own America. You're going to own it." They'll say you own it. So I don't mind. I told them we can wait, but when I win, you're going to pay a much higher price than if you made a deal now. It's true. I told them.

And look what happened to Biden in Ukraine, where his son's paid eighty-three thousand a month. And he was jobless. Give me a break. Eighty-three thousand a month. More than anybody.

If Joe Biden were to become president, an emboldened Left will launch a full-scale assault on American life. You know that. They'll expel anyone who disagrees with them. Look what happens when you disagree. You use a term that's perfect, and they're not happy with it. They call you a racist. They call you a horrible person. They want to crush religious liberty. They don't want religion. Silence religious believers, indoctrinate your children with hateful and vicious lies about our country, subsidize late-term abortion and after-birth execution.

They want to take away your guns through the repeal of your Second Amendment, as sure as you're sitting there. In fact, he even put the big gun-grabber, Beto O'Rourke, who made a fool out of himself when he ran for president. They put him in charge of guns. Lots of luck on your Second Amendment. Just remember I said—and hopefully you won't have to think back about it too much, because it won't matter. Hopefully it won't matter. No, Beto O'Rourke, who wants to give up guns, is in charge of the Second Amendment.

The Dems will also eliminate private health insurance, ban fracking—that's not good—and American energy will be in a position of weakness like it's never been before. And that's after we built the greatest energy country anywhere in the world, by far.

And they want to appoint Supreme Court justices who will utterly obliterate your Constitution. And you now see how important the Supreme Court is. Think if we didn't have two justices—that I think have been very, very, very good. But think how important it is. Think how important it is. And we still—I guess it's a—I don't know if it's an equal court. It's almost like we're a minority court, right? It's almost like we're a minority court. The recent Supreme Court cases prove that if Joe Biden is elected, he will stack the court with extremists.

The forgotten men and women—together with everyone else—we'll lose everything. The forgotten men and women—I campaigned on the forgotten. These are great people. These are substantial people. These are the elite. By the way, you're the elite. They're not the elite. You're the elite.

Somebody, two days ago, said, "Sir, the elite are really working hard on trying to destroy you." I said, "Yeah? Why do you call them the elite," I said, "Why?" Well, they're not elite. I look better than them. Much more handsome. Got better hair than they do. I got nicer properties. I got nicer houses. I got nicer apartments. I got nicer everything. I ran for politics once—just once in my life—and I became president of the United States. Once. And hopefully, if you get out and vote, we'll do it one more time. We won't even toy with them about three or four more times. We won't. We'll do it one more time. We'll be two for two. And our country will never, ever be stronger.

But I'll be soon announcing a new list of exceptional candidates for the United States Supreme Court. And I'll choose only from that list. A hundred percent. Probably twenty-five incredible people, any one of which could be a great justice. Any one of which. And I did it last time, and people loved when I did it. And I'll only pick from that list. Biden can't release his list, because the names would be too extreme, too radical. They wouldn't be acceptable, but they will be very radical people.

People don't understand, but we actually won on DACA yesterday. We actually won, because they basically said, "You won, but you have to come back and redo it." It's almost like, "Gee, come on back, your paperwork was no good." But we're going to be refiling, but don't let it get you. Everything's going to work out really good. Everything's going to work out good.

It was a great—it was great. I mean, would have been nice if we won. And everybody said, "Oh, you're going to win DACA. You're going to win DACA. That's easy. You're going to win DACA. That's easy." They all said it. And they came back and they said, "We don't like what you did with your paperwork," essentially. So we're refiling it. Most people would say we lost. We didn't lose. We're going to refile it. And everything is going to work out for the young people. Most of whom aren't so young anymore, by the way. But we're going to work it out for everybody.

Biden is fully controlled by the fringe of his party. He is their pawn. He doesn't even know where the hell he is. Let's face it. He installed socialist Alexandria Ocasio-Cortez to be in charge of his environmental policy and his energy. Energy—you can forget petroleum. How does Oklahoma feel about being petroleum-free? Not good, right? Our country will have no energy. Our country will have nothing. Oklahoma, Texas, North Dakota, and many others will all be out of business. I don't think that's going to work out too well. But she's actually in charge of environmental policy. And you know what that means. She doesn't even want to win. She doesn't want those bird-killing machines that go round and round. You want to see a lot of birds that are dead? Go under a windmill sometime. She wants us to go back to the stone ages, because she's got no sense, no credentials. She's got a little charisma, not much. But she doesn't have a clue. You know it. But she's in charge of the environment. No airplanes. We can forget Boeing, I guess, come to think of it. We talked about Boeing. We could forget Boeing. Let's cancel those brand-new Air Force Ones, right?

Likewise, Representative Ilhan Omar is going to be very much involved in a Biden government. They will put this hate-filled, America-bashing socialist front and center in deciding the fate of your family, and deciding the fate of your country. I don't think so. She would like to make the government of our country just like the country from where she came—Somalia. No government, no safety, no police, no nothing. Just anarchy. And now she's telling us how to run our country. No thank you. And I think we're going to have a big victory in the state of Minnesota, because they've had it. They've had it.

Biden is a very willing Trojan horse for socialism. When Biden first ran for president over thirty-three years ago, remember I used to call him One Percent Joe. He never got more than one percent until Obama took him off the trash heap. But he blatantly copied the speech of a British politician, even ripping off the man's personal biography and family history, and claiming it was his own. He forgot to say he was born in America.

Joe Biden is a shameless hypocrite. Since 2003, he has delivered fawning eulogies to the funeral, and at those funerals of three leading supporters of segregation, including a former member of the KKK—and yet Biden is now smearing as racist, tens of millions of people like yourselves. Decent, hardworking Americans who he's never met. And he frankly probably doesn't want to meet. America should not take lectures on racial justice from Joe Biden. Sleepy Joe. A man who praised and partnered with segregationists, shifted millions of black American jobs overseas—and everyone else's jobs, too, by the way. If I didn't come along—we're building auto plants. We're building everything. And there's never been a comeback like we're making right now. Never been.

He hollowed out our middle class—including our black middle class—with open borders. Trapped young children in failing government schools. Built cages. Those cages were built by Obama and Biden. Look it up, 2014. And the fake news doesn't wanted to—remember the picture of the cage? A cage for children. Remember the picture of the cage? And they said "President Trump." And then they realized that was at a newspaper, 2014. The same—built by Obama and Biden, the cages.

And they don't want to report the way it is. They know the way it is. They're not stupid. They sent young boys to fight in Iraq while the inner cities crumble. Helped the big banks while hammering community leaders. And made our cities less safe and secure for all. They've done a terrible job, and they shouldn't be awarded. They should not get rewarded with an election victory on November third. That shouldn't happen. It'll destroy this country. Our country will be destroyed. We've all worked too hard. They don't know what the hell they're doing. Some do, actually, but in a very sinister way. Virtually every policy that has hurt black Americans for half a century, Joe Biden has supported or enacted. I've done more for the black community in four years than Joe Biden has done in forty-seven years.

Racial justice begins with Joe Biden's retirement from public life. We are joined tonight by many outstanding Republican leaders. These are great people. We have two of our most distinguished, hardworking, wonderful friends, senators. They do a great job. Senator Jim Inhofe and James Lankford, please stand up. Two very respected—I will tell you, two very respected people in Washington. They're respected by everybody. They do some job. And I'd have you come up, but you can relax. I will say this. Jim is running on November third. Jim Inhofe. He's running on November third. I don't even know. Does he . . . hey, James? Does he have any competition? Is somebody actually running against . . . there's no competition that he's got. I know he's got James's support. He's got my support. I give him one hundred percent endorsement. Jim Inhofe. I'd give it to James, too, but he's not running this time. Thank you. Jim, great job. Thank you very much. What a great senator he is.

Also here is a man who's respected by so many. He's a little bit right of the people we've been talking about tonight. Senator Tom Cotton of the great state of Arkansas. Thank you, Tom. They like you people.

Thank you, Tom. Great job you're doing.

We're glad to be joined as well by a man that I've gotten to know. He's done an incredible job with COVID, and with everything else he touches—Governor Kevin Stitt. Thank you both. Thank you both for being here. Thank you. Lieutenant Governor Matt Pinnell. Thanks, Matt. Thanks, Matt. And Representatives Frank Lucas, Tom Cole. He's been here for a little while. He's done an incredible job.

Markwayne Mullin. You don't want to fight with him. I want to put him and Jim Jordan in a match together. I want to.

Kevin Hern. Great job today, Kevin. The great Jim Jordan. Jim Jordan. Elise Stefanik. Lee Zeldin. Tom Emmer. Tom, thank you. These are warriors, folks. These are great warriors. During the fake impeachment trial, I'll tell you what. There was nobody that could have done the job they've done. That includes the Senate and the House. These people are incredible.

David Kustoff. David. A great friend of mine. Debbie Lesko, Arizona. Great job, Debbie. Great job. And a man who's got very good genes, Greg Pence. Thank you all. Great job. They're great. They are. They're warriors. I'll tell you what. Not every person is, but this group is, and we have a lot of them in Washington. And we'll send Jim Inhofe back, and we'll send all of them. You'll send every one of them. They have to come back, because they have been fighting for us, and they've been fighting for you. And they are just incredible, talented, tough, strong people that love your state a lot. So thank you very much.

So we built the greatest single economy in the world. And then we say not only the world, but actually in the history of the world, and they never even challenged me. So I guess I'm right. We did it. We had the best numbers anybody's ever had. We have the best employment numbers—African American, Hispanic American, Asian American—the best employment numbers in history. The best stock market numbers in history. We were the envy of the world. Everybody would come in to see me—presidents, prime ministers, kings, queens, and dictators. Dictators would even come in to say congratulations on the economy. And then the plague came in, and now what we're doing is, we're doing it again. And it's going fast. We have to have a lot of it done, because people don't quite get it. We're doing record business. It's happening at a level and a speed that nobody can believe.

Two weeks ago, job numbers came in—the single biggest number in the history of our country. Last week, retail sales numbers came in. Retail sales—the single greatest number in the history of our country. So here's what's going to happen. Here's what's going to happen. They blame a president for anything. When you see looters, even though we put them down—if we didn't stop them, nobody would. Because the other side will never stop them. But they always blame a president.

Here's what's happening. We're going up. We're going up. We're going up. We're going to go up. Then we're going to hit October. We're going to be up. We're going to be way up. We're not going to be where we were. But in many ways—other than all of the horrible, horrible death that was so needlessly caused by a virus that should have been stopped where it originated, which was China.

But we're going to go up, up, up, up—August, September, October—and people are going to say, "Man, this guy is doing a good job. He knows what he's doing. I don't believe the fake news anymore." And you're not going to want to lose your 401(k)s. And you're not going to want to lose all of that wealth that you've accumulated, whether it's real estate wealth or any wealth you can think. Because it'll all come tumbling down if these people are put in charge. And if they double and triple and quadruple your taxes, it will be a whole different ball game. So I'm not putting any pressure on anybody, but in the end, we're going to have a phenomenal economy. And next year, we're going to have a good third quarter. But next year—and I said it before—will be the single greatest year economically that we've ever had, OK?

And if you see that happening—if you see it happening on November third, you don't have the guts to vote against Trump. You—even you—you don't have the guts to vote against Trump. Say, "Wait a minute, darling. My 401(k) is higher than it was the last time. I don't think I want to take a chance." You're not going to want to do that. The stock market has been the best. Think of this—go back one week, and go back fifty days. In that fifty-day period, it's the strongest fifty days in the history of the stock market. Think of it. And your wife or your husband says, "Darling, I love you so much. You are such a great investor." And all you did is just keep the same crap you had the first time, right? "Darling, I love you so much. You've always been a loser. You've always lost money. But now under President Trump, you're one of the greatest financial minds in our country." And all you did was keep your stock.

Now, if you think you're going to run against—oh, they're going crazy. They want the stock market to go down. Even if it costs them money, they want the stock market to go down. Even if it costs them money—and they don't even know why. You know what, they're smart and they're vicious, but they don't know why. I'm telling you, they don't know why. What's wrong with having the strongest military brand in the world? What's wrong with having these great economic numbers? What's wrong with having to close it down? We saved millions of lives. You know, a lot of people say we should have gone herd. Let's go herd. Ask them how are they doing in Brazil. He's a great friend of mine, not good. You heard about Sweden, right? Too much. Ask them how they do it in Sweden. We saved millions of lives, and now it's time to open up, get back to work, OK? Get back to work.

I recently signed groundbreaking criminal justice reform. I secured record and permanent funding for historically black colleges and universities. We slashed regulations and passed massive tax cuts to give black workers a pay raise like they've never, ever gotten before, and lift up black-owned businesses. And I worked closely with a great senator also—friend of theirs, Senator Tim Scott, South Carolina—to create Opportunity Zones, which are doing incredibly. And since then, countless jobs and one hundred billion dollars of new investment—not government investment—have poured into nine thousand of our most distressed neighborhoods anywhere in the country. Nine thousand, never happened before. Tim Scott.

Today, I'm also announcing that I have directed Secretary of the Interior David Bernhardt to place the John Hope Franklin Reconciliation Park here in Tulsa, on the African American Civil Rights Network. So many of my friends have been asking me to do it. So many of my friends, including these great politicians. So we're going to do that. It'll be done very quickly.

We will forever remember and honor the courageous people who helped build this state and this country. Democrats are stoking division in order to distract from their decades of failure on schools, jobs, housing, justice, and crime. In major city public schools run by Democrats, over two-thirds of students are falling behind in reading and math. And I think the numbers are worse than that. But Democrats would rather deny these children the future they deserve, than allow them to attend the charter, public, private, religious, or independent schools of their choice. Pro-choice, pro-choice, pro-choice for schools. It's very popular. But some people, it's like a disaster, because what it does to certain unions that have a lot of power over the Democrats, even though they know it's wrong.

Republicans believe access to education is a civil right. It's a civil right. Twenty of twenty of the most dangerous cities in America are controlled by Democrats. Think of that—twenty of twenty. And so is nearly every major city with a child poverty rate that's over thirty percent. They're controlled by Democrats. We can name every one of them. The murder rate in Baltimore and Detroit is higher than El Salvador, Guatemala, or even Afghanistan. How are they doing, the Democrats running those cities? Your whole country will be like that. In 2018 alone, our police arrested nearly twelve thousand people for murder and manslaughter; twenty-five thousand people for rape; and nearly 1.5 million for assault, violent assault. The Democrats' push against our police will drive up crime and drive up costs at levels you'd never believe. Thousands of innocent lives will be lost. As president, I will always support the incredible men and women of law enforcement.

A vote for Republicans is a vote for better schools, better jobs, safer families, and stronger communities for all Americans. There is [no] limit to what we can together achieve with four more years. With your help, we will lift millions of our citizens from welfare to work, dependence to independence, and poverty to prosperity. That's what's happening. That's what's happening. And that was happening at a level that nobody ever thought they'd see. It was happening before this COVID came in. It was happening at a level that nobody believed possible. And then China sent us the plague. Thank you very much. We will protect Medicare and Social Security for our great seniors. And we'll always protect patients with pre-existing conditions. Always, always. We will appoint more judges to interpret the Constitution as written.

We will end deadly sanctuary cities. We will finish the wall, which has now two hundred twelve miles built. And beautiful, two hundred twelve miles. That's a lot of miles. And let me tell you, you think that was an easy one? That was a tough one. That party was totally unified against building the wall. You know, in the end, they gave up. You know what happened? They realized it was a bad issue for them, because these open borders . . . I love when they fight for open borders, because anybody that wants an open border coming in from rough areas, there's something wrong with those people. So did you notice in the end, it was like, "Just leave us alone. Build your wall; just leave us alone." I said, "Thank you very much."

And we will elect a Republican Congress to create a fair, safe, sane, and lawful system of immigration that puts American workers first. We will revitalize our cities, and we will build gleaming new roads, bridges, tunnels, and airports all across our land. We will enact new trade deals that result in more products proudly stamped with that beautiful phrase, *Made in the USA*. It's so beautiful, so beautiful. Made in the USA. That's happening, too. We have so many plants coming into Michigan and so many other states. We have car plants coming in—would have never come if I wasn't president. Would have never come. We will become the world's premier pharmacy, drug store, and medical manufacturer. That's already started. We're bringing it back. We will keep America out of foolish, stupid, ridiculous foreign wars. We will never hesitate to kill America's terrorist enemies.

When I took over, ISIS was all over the place, and I did something that I felt we should do. And we have now obliterated, we have now captured, one hundred percent of the ISIS caliphate. One hundred. One hundred. And like our depleted military when I took over, like our empty shelves, medically, when I took over, like all of the things that, when I took over, it was a mess. We have done a job. You had to see what ISIS was doing. They were getting bigger, bigger, bigger, bigger, bigger. I came in—smaller, smaller, smaller. "Sir, we've just taken one hundred percent."

We will launch a new age of American ambition in space. And the United States will be the first nation to land on Mars. Good program. You saw the beautiful rocket, three weeks ago, go up. Beautiful.

We will defend privacy, free thought, free speech, religious liberty, and the right to keep and bear arms. And when you see those lunatics all over the streets, it's damn nice to have arms. Damn nice. Interesting how all of a sudden people understand it, right? You couldn't sell it. Now people understand it. The right to keep and bear arms. We'll protect your Second Amendment.

Above all, we will never stop fighting for the sacred values that bind us together as one America. We will support, protect, and defend the Constitution of the United States. We uphold the principle of equal justice under the law. We believe in the dignity of work and the sanctity of life. We believe that faith and family, not government and bureaucracy, are the true American way. We believe that children should be taught to love our country, honor our history, and always salute our great American flag. And we live by the words of our national motto—it will never change—*In God we trust.*

We stand on the shoulders of American heroes who crossed the oceans, blazed the trails, settled the continent, tamed the wilderness, dug out the Panama Canal, laid down the railroads, revolutionized industries. Won two World Wars, defeated fascism and communism, and made America the single greatest nation in the history of the world. And we are making it greater and greater every single day. Proud citizens like you helped build this country. And together, we are taking back our country. We are returning the power to you, the American people. With your help, your devotion, and your drive, we are going to keep on working, we are going to keep on fighting, and we are going to keep on winning, winning, winning.

We are one movement, one people, one family, and one glorious nation under God. America will soon be thriving like never before, because, ladies and gentlemen of Oklahoma, the best is yet to come. Together, we will make America wealthy again, we will make America strong again, we will make America proud again, we will make America safe again, and we will make America great again.

Thank you. Thank you, Oklahoma. Thank you.

American Freedom Exists for American Greatness

MOUNT RUSHMORE NATIONAL MONUMENT,
KEYSTONE, SOUTH DAKOTA

July 3, 2020

Well, thank you very much. Governor Noem, Secretary Bernhardt: we very much appreciate it.

Members of Congress, distinguished guests, and a very special hello to South Dakota. As we begin this Fourth of July weekend, the First Lady and I would wish each and every one of you a very, very happy Independence Day. Thank you.

Let us show our appreciation to the South Dakota Army and Air National Guard, and the US Air Force, for inspiring us with that magnificent display of American air power. And of course, our gratitude, as always, to the legendary and very talented Blue Angels. Thank you very much. Let us also send our deepest thanks to our wonderful veterans, law enforcement, first responders, and the doctors, nurses, and scientists working tirelessly to kill the virus. They are working hard. I want to thank them very, very much.

We're grateful as well to your state's congressional delegation. Senator John Thune. John, thank you very much. Senator Mike Rounds. Thank you, Mike. And Dusty Johnson, Congressman. Hi, Dusty. Thank you. And all others with us tonight from Congress: thank you very much for coming. We appreciate it.

There could be no better place to celebrate America's independence than beneath this magnificent, incredible, majestic mountain monument to the greatest Americans who have ever

259

lived. Today, we pay tribute to the exceptional lives and extraordinary legacies of George Washington, Thomas Jefferson, Abraham Lincoln, and Teddy Roosevelt. I am here as your president to proclaim before the country, and before the world: This monument will never be desecrated. These heroes will never be defaced. Their legacy will never, ever be destroyed. Their achievements will never be forgotten. And Mount Rushmore will stand forever as an eternal tribute to our forefathers and to our freedom.

We gather tonight to herald the most important day in the history of nations—July 4th, 1776. At those words, every American heart should swell with pride, every American family should cheer with delight, and every American patriot should be filled with joy, because each of you lives in the most magnificent country in the history of the world, and it will soon be greater than ever before.

Our Founders launched not only a revolution in government, but a revolution in the pursuit of justice, equality, liberty, and prosperity. No nation has done more to advance the human condition than the United States of America. And no people have done more to promote human progress than the citizens of our great nation. It was all made possible by the courage of fifty-six patriots who gathered in Philadelphia two hundred forty-four years ago and signed the Declaration of Independence. They enshrined a divine truth that changed the world forever when they said, "All men are created equal." These immortal words set in motion the unstoppable march of freedom. Our Founders boldly declared that we are all endowed with the same divine rights, given us by our Creator in Heaven, and that which God has given us, we will allow no one ever to take away ever.

Seventeen Seventy-Six represented the culmination of thousands of years of Western civilization, and the triumph of not only spirit, but of wisdom, philosophy, and reason. And yet, as we meet here tonight, there is a growing danger that threatens every blessing our ancestors fought so hard for, struggled, they bled to secure. Our nation is witnessing a merciless campaign to wipe out our history, defame our heroes, erase our values, and indoctrinate our children. Angry mobs are trying to tear down statues of our Founders, deface our most sacred memorials, and unleash a wave of violent crime in our cities. Many of these people have no idea why they're doing this. But some know exactly what they are doing. They think the American people are weak and soft and submissive. But no, the American people are strong and proud, and they will not allow our country, and all of its values, history, and culture, to be taken from them.

One of their political weapons is cancel culture, driving people from their jobs, shaming dissenters, and demanding total submission from anyone who disagrees. This is the very definition of totalitarianism, and it is completely alien to our culture and to our values, and it has absolutely no place in the United States of America.

This attack on our liberty, our magnificent liberty, must be stopped. And it will be stopped very quickly. We will expose this dangerous movement, protect our nation's children, end this radical assault, and preserve our beloved American way of life. In our schools, our newsrooms, even our corporate boardrooms, there is a new Far-Left fascism that demands absolute allegiance. If you do not speak its language, perform its rituals, recite its mantras, and follow its commandments, then you will be censored, banished, blacklisted, persecuted, and punished. Not going to happen to us.

Make no mistake. This left-wing cultural revolution is designed to overthrow the American Revolution. In so doing, they would destroy the very civilization that rescued billions from poverty, disease, violence, and hunger, and that lifted humanity to new heights of achievement, discovery, and progress. To make this possible, they are determined to tear down every statue, symbol, and memory of our national heritage.

That is why I am deploying federal law enforcement to protect our monuments, arrest the rioters, and prosecute offenders to the fullest extent of the law.

I am pleased to report that yesterday, federal agents arrested the suspected ringleader of the attack on the statue of the great Andrew Jackson in Washington, DC. And in addition, hundreds more have been arrested. Under the executive order I signed last week pertaining to the Veterans Memorial Preservation Memorial and Recognition Act and other laws, people who damage or deface federal statues or monuments will get a minimum of ten years in prison. And obviously, that includes our beautiful Mount Rushmore.

Our people have a great memory. They will never forget the destruction of statues and monuments to George Washington, Abraham Lincoln, Ulysses S. Grant, abolitionists, and many others. The violent mayhem we have seen in the streets and cities that are run by liberal Democrats in every case, is the predictable result of years of extreme indoctrination and bias in education, journalism, and other cultural institutions. Against every law of society and nature, our children are taught in school to hate their own country, and to believe that the men and women who built it were not heroes, but that were villains. The radical view of American history is a web of lies, all perspective is removed, every virtue is obscured, every motive is twisted, every fact is distorted, and every flaw is magnified until the history is purged and the record is disfigured beyond all recognition. This movement is openly attacking the legacies of every person on Mount Rushmore. They defiled the memory of Washington, Jefferson, Lincoln, and Roosevelt. Today, we will set history, and history's record straight.

Before these figures were immortalized in stone, they were American giants in full flesh and blood. Gallant men whose intrepid deeds unleashed the greatest leap of human advancement the world has ever known. Tonight, I will tell you—and most importantly, the youth of our nation—the true stories of these great, great men.

From head to toe, George Washington represented the strength, grace, and dignity of the American people. From a small volunteer force of citizen farmers, he created the Continental Army out of nothing and rallied them to stand against the most powerful military on earth. Through eight long years, through the brutal winter at Valley Forge, through setback after setback on the field of battle, he led those patriots to ultimate triumph. When the Army had dwindled to a few thousand men at Christmas of 1776, when defeat seemed absolutely certain, he took what remained of his forces on a daring nighttime crossing of the Delaware River. They marched through nine miles of frigid darkness, many without boots on their feet, leaving a trail of blood in the snow. In the morning, they seized victory at Trenton after forcing the surrender of the most powerful empire on the planet at Yorktown. General Washington did not claim power but simply returned to Mount Vernon as a private citizen.

When called upon again, he presided over the Constitutional Convention in Philadelphia and was unanimously elected our first president. When he stepped down after two terms, his former adversary, King George, called him the greatest man of the age. He remains first in our hearts to this day. For as long as Americans love this land, we will honor and cherish the father of our country, George Washington. He will never be removed, abolished. And most of all, he will never be forgotten.

Thomas Jefferson, the great Thomas Jefferson, was thirty-three years old when he traveled north to Pennsylvania and brilliantly authored one of the greatest treasures of human history—the Declaration of Independence. He also drafted Virginia's constitution and conceived and wrote the Virginia Statute for Religious Freedom—a model for our cherished First Amendment. After serving as the first secretary of state and then vice president, he was elected to the presidency. He ordered American warriors to crush Barbary pirates. He doubled the size of our nation with the Louisiana Purchase. And he sent the famous explorers Lewis and Clark into the West on a daring expedition to the Pacific Ocean. He was an architect, an inventor, a diplomat, a scholar, the founder of one of the world's great universities and an ardent defender of liberty. Americans will forever admire the author of American freedom, Thomas Jefferson. And he, too, will never, ever be abandoned by us.

Abraham Lincoln, the savior of our Union, was a self-taught country lawyer who grew up in a log cabin on the American frontier. The first Republican president, he rose to high office from obscurity, based on a force and clarity of his anti-slavery convictions. Very, very strong convictions. He signed the law that built the Transcontinental Railroad. He signed the Homestead Act, given to some incredible scholars as—simply defined, ordinary citizens—free land to settle anywhere in the American West. And he led the country through the darkest hours of American history, giving every ounce of strength that he had to ensure that government of the people, by the people, and for the people, did not perish from this earth. He served as commander-in-chief of the US Armed Forces during our bloodiest war—the struggle that saved our Union and extinguished the evil of slavery. Over six hundred thousand died in that war. More than twenty thousand were killed or wounded in a single day in Antietam. At Gettysburg, one hundred fifty-seven years ago, the Union bravely withstood an assault of nearly fifteen thousand men and threw back Pickett's Charge.

Lincoln won the Civil War. He issued the Emancipation Proclamation. He led the passage of the Thirteenth Amendment, abolishing slavery for all time. And ultimately, his determination to preserve our nation and our Union cost him his life. For as long as we live, Americans will uphold and revere the immortal memory of President Abraham Lincoln.

Theodore Roosevelt exemplified the unbridled confidence of our national culture and identity. He saw the towering grandeur of America's mission in the world, and he pursued it with overwhelming energy and zeal. As a lieutenant colonel during the Spanish–American War, he led the famous Rough Riders to defeat the enemy at San Juan Hill. He cleaned up corruption as police commissioner of New York City, then served as the governor of New York, vice president, and at forty-two years old, became the youngest ever president of the United States.

He sent our great new naval fleet around the globe to announce America's arrival as a world power. He gave us many of our national parks, including the Grand Canyon. He oversaw the construction of the awe-inspiring Panama Canal. And he is the only person ever awarded both the Nobel Peace Prize and the Congressional Medal of Honor. He was American freedom personified in full. The American people will never relinquish the bold, beautiful, and untamed spirit of Theodore Roosevelt.

No movement that seeks to dismantle these treasured American legacies can possibly have a love of America at its heart. Can't happen. No person who remains quiet at the destruction of this resplendent heritage can possibly lead us to a better future. The radical ideology attacking our country advances under the banner of social justice. But in truth, it would demolish both justice and society. It would transform justice into an instrument of division and vengeance, and it would turn our free and inclusive society into a place of a repression, domination, and exclusion.

They want to silence us, but we will not be silenced. We will state the truth in full, without apology. We declare that the United States of America is the most just and exceptional nation ever to exist on earth. We are proud of the fact that our country was founded on Judeo-Christian principles, and we understand that these values have dramatically advanced the cause of peace and justice throughout the world. We know that the American family is the bedrock of American life. We recognize the solemn right and moral duty of every nation to secure its borders, and we are building the wall. We remember that governments exist to protect the safety and happiness of their own people. A nation must care for its own citizens first. We must take care of America first. It's time. We believe in equal opportunity, equal justice, and equal treatment for citizens of every race, background, religion, and creed. Every child of every color, born and unborn, is made in the holy image of God.

We want free and open debate, not speech codes and cancel culture. We embrace tolerance, not prejudice. We support the courageous men and women of law enforcement. We will never abolish our police or our great Second Amendment, which gives us the right to keep and bear arms. We believe that our children should be taught to love their country, honor their history, and respect our great American flag. We stand tall, we stand proud, and we only kneel to Almighty God. This is who we are. This is what we believe. And these are the values that will guide us as we strive to build an even better and greater future.

Those who seek to erase our heritage want Americans to forget our pride and our great dignity so that we can no longer understand ourselves or America's destiny. In toppling the heroes of 1776, they seek to dissolve the bonds of love and loyalty that we feel for our country and that we feel for each other. Their goal is not a better America; their goal is to end America.

In its place, they want power for themselves. But just as patriots did in centuries past, the American people will stand in their way, and we will win, and win quickly, and with great dignity. We will never let them rip America's heroes from our monuments or from our hearts. By tearing down Washington and Jefferson, these radicals would tear down the very heritage for which men gave their lives to win the Civil War. They would erase the memory that inspired those soldiers to go to their deaths, singing these words of the "Battle Hymn of the Republic": "As he died to make men holy, let us die to make men free, while God is marching on."

They would tear down the principles that propelled the abolition of slavery, and ultimately around the world, ending an evil institution that had plagued humanity for thousands and thousands of years. Our opponents would tear apart the very documents that Martin Luther King used to express his dream, and the ideas that were the foundation of the righteous movement for civil rights. They would tear down the beliefs, culture, and identity that have made America the most vibrant and tolerant society in the history of the earth.

My fellow Americans, it is time to speak up loudly and strongly and powerfully, and defend the integrity of our country. It is time for our politicians to summon the bravery and determination of our American ancestors. It is time. It is time to plant our flag and to protect the greatest of this nation for citizens of every race, in every city, in every part of this glorious land. For the sake of our honor, for the sake of our children, for the sake of our Union, we must protect and preserve our history, our heritage, and our great heroes. Here tonight, before the eyes of our forefathers, Americans declare again, as we did two hundred forty-four years ago, that we will not be tyrannized, we will not be demeaned, and we will not be intimidated by bad, evil people. It will not happen.

We will proclaim the ideals of the Declaration of Independence, and we will never surrender the spirit and the courage and the cause of July fourth, 1776. Upon this ground, we will stand firm and unwavering. In the face of lies meant to divide us, demoralize us, and diminish us, we will show that the story of America unites us, inspires us, includes us all, and makes everyone free. We must demand that our children are taught once again to see America as did Reverend Martin Luther King when he said that the Founders had signed a promissory note to every future generation. Doctor King saw that the mission of justice required us to fully embrace our founding ideals. Those ideals are so important to us—the founding ideals.

He called on his fellow citizens not to rip down their heritage, but to live up to their heritage. Above all, our children from every community must be taught that to be American is to inherit the spirit of the most adventurous and confident people ever to walk the face of the earth. Americans are the people who pursued our manifest destiny across the ocean, into the uncharted wilderness, over the tallest mountains, and then into the skies, and even into the stars.

We are the country of Andrew Jackson, Ulysses S. Grant, and Frederick Douglas. We are the land of Wild Bill Hickock and Buffalo Bill Cody. We are the nation that gave rise to the Wright brothers, the Tuskegee Airmen, Harriet Tubman, Clara Barton, Jesse Owens, George Patton, General George Patton, the great Louis Armstrong, Alan Shepard, Elvis Presley, and Muhammad Ali. And only America could have produced them all. No other place.

We are the culture that put up the Hoover Dam, laid down the highways, and sculpted the skyline of Manhattan. We are the people who dreamed the spectacular dream—it was called Las Vegas—in the Nevada desert, who built up Miami from the Florida marsh, and who carved our heroes into the face of Mount Rushmore. Americans harnessed electricity, split the atom, and gave the world the telephone and the Internet. We settled the Wild West, won two World Wars, landed American astronauts on the moon. And one day very soon, we will plant our flag on Mars.

We gave the world the poetry of Walt Whitman, the stories of Mark Twain, the songs of Irving Berlin, the voice of Ella Fitzgerald, the style of Frank Sinatra, the comedy of Bob Hope, the power of the Saturn V rocket, the toughness of the Ford F-150, and the awesome might of the American aircraft carriers.

Americans must never lose sight of this miraculous story. We should never lose sight of it. Nobody has ever done it like we have done it. So today, under the authority vested in me as president of the United States, I am announcing the creation of a new monument to the giants of our past. I am signing an executive order to establish the National Garden of American Heroes, a vast outdoor park that will feature the statues of the greatest Americans to ever live.

From this night, and from this magnificent place, let us go forward, united in our purpose and rededicated in our resolve. We will raise the next generation of American patriots. We will write the next thrilling chapter of the American adventure. And we will teach our children to know that they live in a land of legends, that nothing can stop them, and that no one can hold them down. They will know that, in America, you can do anything, you can be anything, and together, we can achieve anything.

Uplifted by the titans of Mount Rushmore, we will find unity that no one expected. We will make strides that no one thought possible. This country will be everything that our citizens have hoped for, for so many years, and that our enemies fear, because we will never forget that the American freedom exists for American greatness. And that's what we have, American greatness. Centuries from now, our legacy will be the cities we built, the champions we forged, the good that we did, and the monuments we created to inspire us all.

My fellow citizens, America's destiny is in our sights. America's heroes are embedded in our hearts. America's future is in our hands. And, ladies and gentlemen, the best is yet to come.

This has been a great honor for the First Lady and myself to be with you. I love your state. I love this country. I'd like to wish everybody a very happy Fourth of July. To all, God bless you. God bless your families. God bless our great military. And God bless America. Thank you very much. Thank you.

Presidential Nomination Acceptance Speech

REPUBLICAN NATIONAL CONVENTION,
CHARLOTTE, NORTH CAROLINA

August 27, 2020

Thank you very much. Friends, delegates, and distinguished guests: I stand before you tonight, honored by your support, proud of the extraordinary progress we have made together over the last four incredible years, and brimming with confidence in the bright future we will build for America over the next four years.

We begin this evening, our thoughts are with the wonderful people who have just come through the wrath of Hurricane Laura. We are working closely with state and local officials in Texas, Louisiana, Arkansas, Mississippi, sparing no effort to save lives. While the hurricane was fierce—one of the strongest to make landfall in one hundred and fifty years—the casualties and damage were far less than thought possible only twenty-four hours ago. And this is due to the great work of FEMA, law enforcement, and the individual states. I will be going this weekend. And congratulations for that great job out there. We really appreciate it. We are one national family, and we will always protect, love, and care for each other.

Here tonight are the people who have made my journey possible, and filled my life with so much joy.

For her incredible service to our nation and its children, I want to thank our magnificent First Lady. I also want to thank my amazing daughter Ivanka for that introduction. And to all of my children and grandchildren— Ivanka, please stand up. I love you more than words can express. I know my brother Robert is looking down on us right now from Heaven. He was a great brother, and was very proud of the job we are doing. We love you, Robert.

Let us also take a moment to show our profound appreciation for a man who has always fought by our side, and stood up for our values—a man of deep faith and steadfast conviction: our Vice President, Mike Pence. Mike is joined by his beloved wife—a teacher and military mom—Karen Pence. Thank you, Karen.

My fellow Americans:

Tonight, with a heart full of gratitude and boundless optimism, I proudly accept this nomination for president of the United States.

The Republican Party, the party of Abraham Lincoln, goes forward united, determined, and ready to welcome millions of Democrats, Independents, and anyone who believes in the greatness of America and the righteous heart of the American people.

In a new term as president, we will again build the greatest economy in history—quickly returning to full employment, soaring incomes, and record prosperity. We will defend America against all threats and protect America against all dangers. We will lead American into new frontiers of ambition and discovery. And we will reach for new heights of national achievement. We will rekindle new faith in our values, new pride in our history, and a new spirit of unity that can only be realized through love for our country. Because we understand that America is not a land cloaked in darkness, America is the torch that enlightens the entire world.

Gathered here at our beautiful and majestic White House—known all over the world as the People's House—we cannot help but marvel at the miracle that is our Great American Story. This has been the home of larger-than-life figures like Teddy Roosevelt and Andrew Jackson, who rallied Americans to bold visions of a bigger and brighter future. Within these walls lived tenacious generals like Presidents Grant and Eisenhower, who led our soldiers in the cause of freedom. From these grounds, Thomas

Jefferson sent Lewis and Clark on a daring expedition to cross a wild and uncharted continent. In the depths of a bloody civil war, President Abraham Lincoln looked out these very windows, upon a half-completed Washington Monument, and asked God, in His Providence, to save our nation. Two weeks after Pearl Harbor, Franklin Delano Roosevelt welcomed Winston Churchill, and just inside, they set our people on a course to victory in the Second World War.

In recent months, our nation, and the entire planet, has been struck by a new and powerful invisible enemy. Like those brave Americans before us, we are meeting this challenge. We are delivering lifesaving therapies and will produce a vaccine before the end of the year. Or maybe even sooner. We will defeat the virus, end the pandemic, and emerge stronger than ever before.

What united generations past was an unshakable confidence in America's destiny, and an unbreakable faith in the American people. They knew that our country is blessed by God and has a special purpose in this world. It is that conviction that inspired the formation of our Union, our westward expansion, the abolition of slavery, the passage of civil rights, the space program, and the overthrow of fascism, tyranny, and communism.

This towering American spirit has prevailed over every challenge and lifted us to the summit of human endeavor.

And yet, despite all of our greatness as a nation, everything we have achieved is now in danger. This is the most important election in the history of our country.

At no time before have voters faced a clearer choice between two parties, two visions, two philosophies, or two agendas.

This election will decide whether we save the American Dream, or whether we allow a socialist agenda to demolish our cherished destiny.

It will decide whether we rapidly create millions of high-paying jobs or whether we crush our industries and send millions of these jobs overseas, as has foolishly been done for many decades.

Your vote will decide whether we protect law-abiding Americans or whether we give free reign to violent anarchists, and agitators, and criminals who threaten our citizens.

And this election will decide whether we will defend the American way of life, or whether we allow a radical movement to completely dismantle and destroy it. It won't happen.

At the Democrat National Convention, Joe Biden and his party repeatedly assailed America as a land of racial, economic, and social injustice. So tonight, I ask you a simple question: How can the Democrat Party ask to lead our country when it spends so much time tearing down our country?

In the Left's backward view, they do not see America as the most free, just, and exceptional nation on earth. Instead, they see a wicked nation that must be punished for its sins.

Our opponents say that redemption for you can only come from giving power to them. This is a tired anthem spoken by every repressive movement throughout history.

But in this country, we don't look to career politicians for salvation. In America, we don't turn to government to restore our souls. We put our faith in Almighty God.

Joe Biden is not the savior of America's soul. He is the destroyer of America's jobs. And if given the chance, he will be the destroyer of American greatness.

For forty-seven years, Joe Biden took the donations of blue-collar workers, gave them hugs, and even kisses, and told them he felt their pain. And then he flew back to Washington and voted to ship their jobs to China and many other distant lands. Joe Biden spent his entire career outsourcing their dreams and the dreams of American workers, offshoring their jobs, opening their borders, and sending their sons and daughters to fight in endless foreign wars—wars that never ended.

Four years ago, I ran for president because I could not watch this betrayal of our country any longer. I could not sit by as career politicians let other countries take advantage of us on trade, borders, foreign policy, and national defense. Our NATO partners, as an example, were very far behind in their defense payments. But at my strong urging, they agreed to pay one hundred and thirty billion dollars more a year—the first time in over twenty years that they upped their payments. And this one hundred and thirty billion dollars will ultimately go to four hundred billion dollars a year. And Secretary General Stoltenberg, who heads NATO, was amazed after watching for so many years, and said that President Trump did what no one else was able to do.

From the moment I left my former life behind—and it was a good life—I have done nothing but fight for you.

I did what our political establishment never expected, and could never forgive—breaking the cardinal rule of Washington politics. I kept my promise.

Together, we have ended the rule of the failed political class—and they are desperate to get their power back by any means necessary. You've seen that. They are angry at me because, instead of putting them first, I very simply said, "America first."

Days after taking office, we shocked the Washington establishment and withdrew from the last administration's job-killing Trans-Pacific Partnership. I then approved the Keystone XL and Dakota Access Pipelines, ended the unfair and very costly Paris Climate Accord, and secured, for the first time, American energy independence. We passed record-setting tax and regulation cuts, at a rate nobody had ever seen before. Within three short years, we built the strongest economy in the history of the world.

Washington insiders asked me not to stand up to China. They pleaded with me to let China continue stealing our jobs, ripping us off, and robbing our country blind. But I kept my word to the American people. We took the toughest, boldest, strongest, and hardest-hitting action against China in American history by far.

They said that it would be impossible to terminate and replace NAFTA. But again, they were wrong. Earlier this year, I ended the NAFTA nightmare and signed the brand-new US–Mexico–Canada Agreement into law. Now, auto companies and others are building their plants and factories in America, not firing their employees and not deserting us for other countries.

In perhaps no area did the Washington special interests try harder to stop us than on my policy of pro-American immigration. But I refused to back down. And today, America's borders are more secure than ever before. We ended catch and release, stopped asylum fraud, took down human traffickers who prey on women and children, and we have deported twenty thousand gang members, and five hundred thousand criminal aliens. We have already built three hundred miles of border wall, and we are adding ten new miles every single week. The wall will soon be complete, and it is working beyond our wildest expectations.

We are joined this evening by members of the Border Patrol union, representing our country's courageous border agents. Thank you very much for being here. Thank you. Brave, brave people. You see, this country loves our law enforcement. They do. They really do. Love and respect.

When I learned that the Tennessee Valley Authority laid off hundreds of American workers and forced them to train their lower-paid foreign replacement, I promptly removed the chairman of the board. And now, those talented American workers have been rehired, and are back providing power to Georgia, Alabama, Tennessee, Kentucky, Mississippi, North Carolina, and Virginia. They have their old jobs back, and some are here with us this evening. Please stand. You went through a lot. Please stand. Thank you. Thank you very much, You've been through a lot. Thank you very much.

Last month, I took on Big Pharma—you think that's easy? It's not—and signed orders that will massively lower the cost of your prescription drugs, and give critically ill patients access to lifesaving cures. We passed the decades-long-awaited Right to Try. We also passed VA Accountability and VA Choice. Our great veterans—we're taking care of our veterans. Ninety-one percent approval rating this month—the VA, given by our veterans. First time anything like that's ever happened.

By the end of my first term, we will have approved more than three hundred federal judges, including two great new Supreme Court justices. To bring prosperity to our forgotten inner cities, we worked hard to pass historic criminal justice reform, prison reform, Opportunity Zones, and long-term funding of historically black colleges and universities, and—before the China virus came in—produced the best unemployment numbers for African Americans, Hispanic Americans, and Asian Americans ever recorded. And I say, very modestly, that I have done more for the African American community than any president since Abraham Lincoln, our first Republican president. And I have done more in three years for the black community than Joe Biden has done in forty-seven years. And when I'm reelected, the best is yet to come.

When I took office, the Middle East was in total chaos. ISIS was rampaging, Iran was on the rise, and the war in Afghanistan had no end in sight. I withdrew from the terrible, one-sided Iran nuclear deal. Unlike many presidents before me, I kept my promise, recognized Israel's true capital, and moved our embassy to Jerusalem. But not only did we talk about it as a future site, we got it built. Rather than spending one billion dollars on a new building, as planned, we took an already-owned, existing building in a better location—real estate deal, right?—and opened it at a cost of less than five hundred thousand dollars. Many things like that the government is doing right now. We also recognized Israeli sovereignty over the Golan Heights, and this month we achieved the first Middle East peace deal in twenty-five years. Thank you to UAE, thank you to Israel. In addition, we obliterated one hundred percent of the ISIS caliphate and killed its founder and leader, Abu Bakr al-Baghdadi. Then, in a separate operation, we eliminated the world's number-one terrorist, Qasem Soleimani.

Unlike previous administrations, I have kept America out of new wars—and our troops are coming home. We have spent nearly 2.5 trillion dollars on completely rebuilding our military, which was very badly depleted when I took office, as you know. This includes three separate pay raises for our great warriors. We also launched the Space Force, the first new branch of the United States military since the Air Force was created almost seventy-five years ago.

We have spent the last four years reversing the damage Joe Biden inflicted over the last forty-seven years.

Biden's record is a shameful roll call of the most catastrophic betrayals and blunders in our lifetime. He has spent his entire career on the wrong side of history. Biden voted for the NAFTA disaster, the single worst trade deal ever enacted. He supported China's entry into the World Trade Organization, one of the greatest economic disasters of all time. After those Biden calamities, the United States lost one in four manufacturing jobs. The laid-off workers in Michigan, Ohio, New Hampshire, Pennsylvania, and many other states, they didn't want Joe Biden's hollow words of empathy—they wanted their jobs back.

As vice president, he supported the Trans-Pacific Partnership, which would have been a death sentence for the US auto industry. He backed the horrendous South Korea trade deal, which took many jobs from our country, and which I've reversed and made a great deal for our country. He repeatedly supported mass amnesty for illegal immigrants. He voted for the Iraq War. He opposed the mission to take out Osama bin Laden. He opposed killing Soleimani. He oversaw the rise of ISIS, and cheered the rise of China as "a positive development" for America and the world. Some positive development. That's why China supports Joe Biden and desperately wants him to win, I can tell you that, upon very good information.

China would own our country if Joe Biden got elected. Unlike Biden, I will hold them fully accountable for the tragedy that they caused—all over the world, they caused.

In recent months, our nation and the world has been hit with a once-in-a-century pandemic that China allowed to spread around the globe. The could have stopped it, but they allowed it to come out. We are grateful to be joined tonight by several of our incredible nurses and first responders. Please stand and accept our profound thanks and gratitude. Many Americans, including me, have sadly lost friends and cherished loved ones to this horrible disease. As one nation, we mourn, we grieve, and we hold in our hearts forever the memories of all of those lives that have been so tragically taken. So unnecessary. In their honor, we will unite. In their memory, we will overcome.

And when the China virus hit, we launched the largest national mobilization since World War Two. Invoking the Defense Production Act, we produced the world's largest supply of ventilators. Not a single American who has needed a ventilator has been denied a ventilator, which is a miracle. Good job heading the task force by our great vice president. Thank you very much, Mike. Please, please stand up. We shipped hundreds of millions of masks, gloves, and gowns to our frontline healthcare workers. To protect our nation's seniors, we rushed supplies, testing kits, and personnel to nursing homes. We gave everything you can possibly give, and we're still giving it, because we're taking care of our senior citizens. The Army Corps of Engineers built field hospitals, and the Navy deployed our great hospital ships.

We developed, from scratch, the largest and most advanced testing system anywhere in the world. America has tested more than every country in Europe put together, and more than every nation in the Western Hemisphere combined. Think of that. We have conducted forty million more tests than the next closest nation, which is India.

We developed a wide array of effective treatments, including a powerful antibody treatment known as "convalescent plasma"—you saw that on Sunday night, when we announced it—that will save thousands and thousands of lives. Thanks to advances we have pioneered, the fatality rate—and you look at it, and you look at the numbers—has been reduced by eighty percent since April. Eighty percent.

The United States has among the lowest case fatality rates of any major country anywhere in the world. The European Union's case fatality rate is nearly three times higher than ours, but you don't hear that. They don't write about that. They don't want to write about that. They don't want you to know those things. Altogether, the nations of Europe have experienced a thirty percent greater increase in excess mortality than the United States. Think of that.

We enacted the largest package of financial relief in American history. Thanks to our Paycheck Protection Program, we have saved or supported more than fifty million American jobs. That's one of the reasons that we're advancing so rapidly with our economy. Great job. As a result, we have seen the smallest economic contraction of any major Western nation, and we are recovering at a much faster rate than anybody. Over the past three months, we have gained over nine million jobs and that's a record in the history of country.

Unfortunately, from the beginning, our opponents have shown themselves capable of nothing but a partisan ability to criticize. When I took bold action to issue a travel ban on China, very early indeed Joe Biden called it hysterical and xenophobic. And then I introduced a ban on Europe, very early again. If we had listened to Joe, hundreds of thousands more Americans would have died.

Instead of following the science, Joe Biden wants to inflict a painful shutdown on the entire country. His shutdown would inflict unthinkable and lasting harm on our nation's children, families, and citizens of all backgrounds.

The cost of the Biden shutdown would be measured in increased drug overdoses, depression, alcohol addiction, suicides, heart attacks, economic devastation, job loss and much more. Joe Biden's plan is not a solution to the virus, but rather it's a surrender to the virus.

My administration has a very different approach. To save as many lives as possible, we are focusing on the science, the facts, and the data. We are aggressively sheltering those at highest risk—especially the elderly—while allowing lower-risk Americans to safely return to work and to school, and we want to see so many of those great states be opened by Democrats. We want them to be open. They have to be open. They have to get back to work. They have to get back to work, and they have to get back to school.

Most importantly, we are marshalling America's scientific genius to produce a vaccine in record time. Under Operation Warp Speed, we have three different vaccines in the final stage of trials right now—years ahead of what has been achieved before. Nobody thought it could ever be done this fast. Normally, it would be years, and we did it in a matter of a few months. We are producing them in advance, so that hundreds of millions of doses will be quickly available.

We will have a safe and effective vaccine this year. And together, we will crush the virus.

At the Democrat Convention, you barely heard a word about their agenda. But that's not because they don't have one. It's because their agenda is the most extreme set of proposals ever put forward by a major party nominee. Joe Biden may claim he is an "ally of the Light," but when it comes to his agenda, Biden wants to keep us completely in the dark. He doesn't have a clue.

He has pledged a four trillion-dollar tax hike on almost all American families, which will totally collapse our rapidly improving economy, and once again, record stock markets hat we have right now will also collapse. That means all of your 401(k)s. That means all of the stocks that you have. On the other hand, just as I did in my first term, I will cut taxes even further for hardworking moms and dads. I will not raise taxes, I will cut them, and very substantially. We will also provide tax credits to bring jobs out of China, back to America. And we will impose tariffs on any company that leaves America to produce jobs overseas. We'll make sure our companies and jobs stay in our country, as I've already been doing, or quite some time, if you've noticed. Joe Biden's agenda is "Made in China." My agenda is "Made in the USA."

Biden has promised to abolish the production of American oil, coal, shale, and natural gas—laying waste to the economies of Pennsylvania, Ohio, Texas, North Dakota, Oklahoma, Colorado, and New Mexico—destroying those states—absolutely destroying those states and others. Millions of jobs will be lost, and energy prices will soar. These same policies led to crippling power outages in California just last week. Everybody saw that. Tremendous power outage. Nobody's seen anything like it, but we saw that last week in Calfornia. How can Joe Biden claim to be an "ally of the Light," when his own party can't even keep the lights on?

Joe Biden's campaign has even published a one-hundred-ten-page policy platform—you can't get away from this—co-authored with far-left Senator Crazy Bernie Sanders. The Biden-Bernie manifesto calls for suspending all removals of illegal aliens, implementing nationwide catch and release, and providing illegal aliens with free taxpayer-funded lawyers. Everybody gets a lawyer. Come on over to our country. Everybody has a lawyer. We have a lawyer for you. That's what we need is more lawyers. Joe Biden recently raised his hand on the debate stage and promised he was going to give away your healthcare dollars to illegal immigrants, which is going to bring massive numbers of immigrants into our country. Massive numbers will pour into our country in order to get all of the goodies that they want to give—education, healthcare—everything. He also supports deadly sanctuary cities that protect criminal aliens. He promised to end national security travel bans from Jihadist nations. And he pledged to increase refugee admissions by seven hundred percent. This is in the manifesto. The Biden plan would eliminate America's borders in the middle of a global pandemic. And he's even talking about taking the wall down. How about that?

Biden also vowed to oppose school choice and close all charter schools, ripping away the ladder of opportunity for black and Hispanic children.

In a second term, I will expand charter schools and provide school choice to every family in America. And we will always treat our teachers with the tremendous respect that they deserve. Great people. Great, great people.

Joe Biden claims he has empathy for the vulnerable—yet the party he leads supports the extreme late-term abortion of defenseless babies, right up to the moment of birth. Democrat leaders talk about moral decency, but they have no problem with stopping a baby's beating heart in the ninth month of pregnancy.

Democrat politicians refuse to protect innocent life, and then they lecture us about morality and saving America's soul. Tonight, we proudly declare that all children, born and unborn, have a God-given right to life.

During the Democrat Convention, the words "Under God" were removed from the Pledge of Allegiance—not once, but twice. We will never do that. The fact is, this is where they're coming from. Like it or not, this is where they're coming from.

If the Left gains power, they will demolish the suburbs, confiscate your guns, and appoint justices who will wipe away your Second Amendment and other constitutional freedoms.

Biden is a Trojan horse for socialism. If Joe Biden doesn't have the strength to stand up to wild-eyed Marxists like Bernie Sanders and his fellow radicals—and there are many, there are many many—we see them all the time—it's incredible, actually—then how is he ever going to stand up for you? He's not.

The most dangerous aspect of the Biden platform is the attack on public safety. The Biden–Bernie manifesto calls for abolishing cash bail, immediately releasing four hundred thousand criminals onto your streets and into your neighborhoods.

When asked if he supports cutting police funding, Joe Biden replied, "Yes, absolutely." When Congresswoman Ilhan Omar called the Minneapolis Police Department a cancer that is "rotten to the root," Biden wouldn't disavow her support and reject her endorsement. He proudly displayed it shortly, later, on his website—displayed it in big letters..

Make no mistake, if you give power to Joe Biden, the radical Left will defund police departments all across America. They will pass federal legislation to reduce law enforcement nationwide. They will make every city look like Democrat-run Portland, Oregon. No one will be safe in Biden's America.

My administration will always stand with the men and women of law enforcement. Every day, police officers risk their lives to keep us safe. And every year, many sacrifice their lives in the line of duty.

One of these incredible Americans was Detective Miosotis Familia. She was part of a team of American heroes called the NYPD, or New York's Finest. I was very, very proud to get their endorsement, just the other day. Great people. Great, great people. If they were allowed to do their job, you'd have no crime in

New York. Rudy Giuliani knows that better than anybody. Thank you, Rudy. Three years ago, on Fourth of July weekend, Detective Familia was on duty in her vehicle when she was ambushed just after midnight, and murdered by a monster who hated her purely for wearing the badge.

Detective Familia was a single mom. She'd recently asked for the night shift so she could spend more time with her kids. Two years ago, I stood in front of the US Capitol, alongside those beautiful children and held their grandmother's hand as they mourned their terrible loss, and we honored Detective Familia's extraordinary life—it was extraordinary.

Detective Familia's three children are with us this evening. Genesis, Peter, Delilah, we are so grateful to have you here tonight. Thank you very much for coming. Thank you very much. I promise you that we will treasure your mom in our memories forever.

We must remember that the overwhelming majority of police officers in this country—and that's the overwhelming majority—are noble, courageous, and honorable. We have to give law enforcement—our police—back their power. They are afraid to act. They are afraid to lose their pension. They are afraid to lose their jobs. And by being afraid, they are not able to do the job that they so desperately want to do for you. And those who suffer most are the great people who they protect and who they want to protect at an even higher level.

When there is police misconduct, the justice system must hold wrongdoers fully and completely accountable. And it will. But we can never have a situation where things are going on as they are today. We must never allow mob rule. We can never allow mob rule. In the strongest possible terms, the Republican Party condemns the rioting, looting, arson, and violence we have seen in Democrat-run cities all, like Kenosha, Minneapolis, Portland, Chicago, and New York, and many others, Democrat-run.

There is violence and danger in the streets of many Democrat-run cities throughout America. This problem could easily be fixed if they wanted to. Just call. We're ready to go in. We'll take care of your problem in a matter of hours. Just call. We have to wait for the call. It's too bad we have to, but we have to wait for the call. We must always have law and order. All federal crimes are being investigated, prosecuted, and punished to the fullest extent of the law.

When the anarchists started ripping down our statues and monuments, right outside, I signed an order—ten years in prison—and it was a miracle—it all stopped. No more statues. They said, "That's just too long" as they looked at a statue. "I think we'll rip it down," and they they said, "Ten years in prison, I think that's too long. Let's go home.

During their convention, Joe Biden and his supporters remained completely silent about the rioters and criminals spreading mayhem in Democrat-run cities. They never even mentioned it during their entire convention. Never once mentioned. Now they're starting to mention it, because their poll numbers are going down like a rock in water. It's too late, Joe. In the face of left-wing anarchy and mayhem in Minneapolis, Chicago, and other cities, Joe Biden's campaign did not condemn it; they donated to it. At least thirteen members of Joe Biden's campaign staff donated to a fund to bail out vandals, arsonists, looters, and rioters from jail.

Here tonight is the grieving family of retired police captain David Dorn, a thirty-eight-year veteran of the Saint Louis Police Department, a great man and a highly respected man by all. In June, Captain Dorn was shot and killed as he tried to protect a store from rioters and looters, or, as the Democrats would call them, "peaceful protesters." They call them "peaceful protesters." We are honored to be joined tonight by his wonderful wife, Ann, and beloved family members Brian and Kielen. To each of you: we will never forget the heroic legacy of Captain David Dorn. Thank you very much for being here. Thank you. Thank you very much. Great man, great man.

As long as I am president, I will defend the absolute right of every American citizen to live in security, dignity, and peace.

If the Democrat Party wants to stand with anarchists, agitators, rioters, looters, and flag-burners, that is up to them. But I, as your president, will not be a part of it. The Republican Party will remain the voice of the patriotic heroes who keep America safe and salute the American flag.

Last year, over one thousand African Americans were murdered as result of violent crime in just four Democrat-run cities. The top ten most dangerous cities in the country are run by Democrats and have been for many decades. Thousands more African Americans are victims of violent crime in these communities. Joe Biden and the Left ignore these American victims. I never will.

If the radical Left takes power, they will apply their disastrous policies to every city, town, and suburb in America. Just imagine if the so-called peaceful demonstrators in the streets were in charge of every lever of power in the US government. Just think of that.

Liberal politicians claim to be concerned about the strength of American institutions. But who exactly is attacking them? Who is hiring the radical professors, judges, and prosecutors? Who is trying to abolish immigration enforcement, and establish speech codes designed to muzzle dissent? In every case, the attacks on American institutions are being waged by radical Left.

Always remember: they are coming after me, because I am fighting for you. That's what's happening. And it's been going on since before I even got elected. And remember this: They spied on my campaign, and they got caught. Let's see now what happens.

We must reclaim our independence from the Left's repressive mandates. Americans are exhausted trying to keep up with the latest list of approved words and phrases, and the ever-more restrictive political decrees. Many things have a different name now, and the rules are constantly changing. The goal of cancel culture is to make decent Americans live in fear of being fired, expelled, shamed, humiliated, and driven from society as we know it. The Far Left wants to coerce you into saying what you know to be false, and scare you out of saying what you know to be true. It's very sad.

But on November third, you can send them a very thundering message they will never forget.

Joe Biden is weak. He takes his marching orders from liberal hypocrites who drive their cities into the ground while fleeing far from the scene of the wreckage. These same liberals want to eliminate school choice, while they enroll their children in the finest private schools in the land. They want to open our borders while living in walled-off compounds and communities in the best neighborhoods in the world. They want to defund the police, while they have armed guards for themselves.

This November, we must turn the page forever on this failed political class. The fact is, I'm here [turns around and points to the White House]. What's the name of that building? But I'll say it differently: The fact is we're here, and they're not. To me, one of the most beautiful buildings anywhere in the world, and it's not a building, it's a home, as far as I'm concerned. It's not even a house, it's a home. It's a wonderful place with an incredible history. But it's all because of you. Together, we will write the next chapter of the Great American Story.

Over the next four years, we will make America into the manufacturing superpower of the world. We will expand Opportunity Zones bring home our medical supply chains, and we will end go right after China. We will not rely on them one bit. We are taking out business out of China. We are bringing it home. We want out business to come home.

We will continue to reduce taxes and regulations at levels not seen before.

We will create ten million jobs in the next ten months. And it will be higher than that.

We will hire more police, increase penalties for assaults on law enforcement, and surge federal prosecutors into high-crime communities.

We will ban deadly sanctuary cities, and ensure that federal healthcare is protected for American citizens—not for illegal aliens.

We will have strong borders. And I've said for years, without borders, we don't have a country. Don't have a country. Strike down terrorists who threaten our people, and keep America out of endless and costly foreign wars.

We will appoint prosecutors, judges, justices who believe in enforcing the law—not enforcing their own political agenda—which is illegal.

We will ensure equal justice for citizens of every race, religion, color, and creed.

We will uphold your religious liberty and defend your Second Amendment right to keep and bear arms. And if we don't win, your Second Amendment doesn't have a chance, I can tell you that. I have totally protected it.

We will protect Medicare and Social Security.

We will always, and very strongly, protect patients with pre-existing conditions. And that is a pledge from the entire Republican Party.

We will end surprise medical billing, require price transparency, and further reduce the cost of prescription drugs and health insurance premiums—they are coming way down.

We will greatly expand energy development, continuing to remain number one in the world, and keep America energy independent. And for those of you that still drive a car, look how low your gasoline bill is. You haven't seen that in a long time.

We will win the race to 5G and build the world's best cyber and missile defense—already under construction.

We will fully restore patriotic education to our schools and always protect—we will always, always protect—free speech on college campuses. And we'll put a very big penalty in. If they do anything having to do with your free speech, colleges have to pay a tremendous, tremendous financial penalty, and again, it's amazing how open they've been lately.

We will launch a new age of American ambition in space. America will land the first woman on the moon. And the United States will be the first nation to plant its beautiful flag on Mars.

This is the unifying national agenda that will bring our country together.

So tonight, I say again to all Americans: This is the most important election in the history of our country. There has never been such a difference between two parties, or two individuals, in ideology, philosophy, or vision, than there is right now.

Our opponents believe that America is a depraved nation.

We want our sons and daughters to know the truth: America is the greatest and most exceptional nation in the history of the world.

Our country wasn't built by cancel culture, speech codes, and soul-crushing conformity. We are not a nation of timid spirits. We are a nation of fierce, proud, and independent American patriots.

We are a nation of pilgrims, pioneers, adventurers, explorers, and trailblazers who refused to be tied down, held back, or in any way reined in. Americans have steel in their spines, grit in their souls, and fire in their hearts. There is no one like us on earth.

I want every child in America to know that you are part of the most exciting and incredible adventure in human history. No matter where your family comes from, no matter your background—in America, anyone can rise. With hard work, devotion, and drive, you can reach any goal and achieve every ambition.

Our American ancestors sailed across the perilous ocean to build a new life on a new continent. They braved the freezing winters, crossed the raging rivers, scaled the rocky peaks, trekked the dangerous forests, and worked from dawn till dusk. These pioneers didn't have money. They didn't have fame. But they had each other. They loved their families, they loved their country, and they loved their God!

When opportunity beckoned, they picked up their Bibles, packed up their belongings, climbed into their covered wagons, and set out West for the next adventure. Ranchers and miners, cowboys and sheriffs, farmers and settlers—they pressed on past the Mississippi to stake a claim in the Wild Frontier.

Legends were born—Wyatt Earp, Annie Oakley, Davy Crockett, and Buffalo Bill.

Americans built their beautiful homesteads on the Open Range. Soon, they had churches and communities, then towns, and with time, great centers of industry and commerce. That is who they were. Americans build the future; we don't tear down our past.

We are the nation that won a revolution, toppled tyranny and fascism, and delivered millions into freedom. We laid down the railroads, built the great ships, raised up the skyscrapers, revolutionized industry, and sparked a new age of scientific discovery. We set the trends in art and music, radio and film, sport and literature—and we did it all with style, and confidence, and flair. Because that is who we are.

Whenever our way of life was threatened, our heroes answered the call. From Yorktown to Gettysburg, from Normandy to Iwo Jima, American Patriots raced into cannon blasts, bullets, and bayonets, to rescue American liberty. They had no fear

But America didn't stop there. We looked into the sky and kept pressing onward. We built a six million-pound rocket and launched it thousands of miles into space. We did it so that two brave patriots could stand tall and salute our wondrous American flag planted on the face of the moon.

For America, nothing is impossible.

Over the next four years, we will prove worthy of this magnificent legacy. We will reach stunning new heights. And we will show the world that, for America there is a dream, and it is not beyond your reach.

Together, we are unstoppable. Together, we are unbeatable. Because together, we are the proud citizens of the United States of America. And on November third, we will make America safer, we will make America stronger, we will make America prouder, and we will make America greater than ever before. I am very, very proud to be the nominee of the Republican Party. I love you all.

God bless you and God bless America. Thank you.

Supreme Court Nominee, Amy Coney Barrett

THE WHITE HOUSE, WASHINGTON, DC

September 26, 2020

Thank you very much. Thank you. Thank you.

I stand before you today to fulfill one of my highest and most important duties under the United States Constitution: the nomination of a Supreme Court justice. This is my third such nomination after Justice Gorsuch and Justice Kavanaugh. And it is a very proud moment, indeed.

Over the past week, our nation has mourned the loss of a true American legend. Justice Ruth Bader Ginsburg was a legal giant and a pioneer for women. Her extraordinary life and legacy will inspire Americans for generations to come.

Now we gather in the Rose Garden to continue our never-ending task of ensuring equal justice and preserving the impartial rule of law.

Today, it is my honor to nominate one of our nation's most brilliant and gifted legal minds to the Supreme Court. She is a woman of unparalleled achievement, towering intellect, sterling credentials, and unyielding loyalty to the Constitution: Judge Amy Coney Barrett.

We're also joined by Amy's husband, Jesse—thank you, Jesse, very much—and their seven beautiful children. Congratulations to you all. A very special day.

With us as well are the First Lady—thank you, First Lady—along with Vice President Mike Pence and his amazing wife, Karen. Thank you very much, Mike.

Judge Barrett is a graduate of Rhodes College and the University of Notre Dame Law School. At Notre Dame, she earned a full academic scholarship, served as the executive editor of the Law Review, graduated first in her class, and received the law school's award for the best record of scholarship and achievement.

Upon graduation, she became a clerk for Judge Laurence Silberman on the US Court of Appeals for the District of Columbia. Amy then received one of the highest honors a young lawyer could have, serving as a clerk on the Supreme Court for Justice Antonin Scalia. A highly—a very highly respected law professor at Notre Dame wrote to Justice Scalia with a one-sentence recommendation: "Amy Coney is the best student I ever had." That's pretty good. Justice Scalia hired her shortly thereafter.

And we are honored to have his wonderful wife, Maureen—where is Maureen?—Maureen Scalia, with us today. Thank you. And our great secretary of labor, thank you very much. Thank you, Mister Secretary. Very good genes in that family, I will say. Very good genes.

Before joining the bench, Judge Barrett spent fifteen years as a professor at the University of Notre Dame Law School. She was renowned for her scholarship, celebrated by her colleagues, and beloved by her students. Three times, she was selected at Notre Dame, Distinguished Professor of the Year.

When I nominated Judge Barrett to serve on the US Court of Appeals for the Seventh Circuit in 2017, every law clerk from her time at the Supreme Court endorsed her and endorsed her nomination, writing, quote: "We are Democrats, Republicans, and Independents . . . yet we write to support the nomination of Professor Barrett to be a Circuit Judge . . . . Professor Barrett is a woman of remarkable intellect and character. She is eminently qualified for the job."

And I can tell you, I did that, too. I looked and I studied, and you are very eminently qualified for this job. You are going to be fantastic. Thank you. Really fantastic.

The entire Notre Dame Law facility and faculty—everybody, everybody at that school also . . . we got so many letters—also wrote letters of support of Amy's nomination to the Seventh Circuit. They wrote, in effect: "Despite our differences, we unanimously agree that our constitutional system depends upon an independent judiciary staffed by talented people devoted to the fair and impartial administration of the rule of law. And we unanimously agree that Amy is such a person."

For the last three years, Judge Barrett has served with immense distinction on the federal bench. Amy is more than a stellar scholar and judge; she is also a profoundly devoted mother. Her family is a core part of who Amy is. She opened her home and her heart, and adopted two beautiful children from Haiti. Her incredible bond with her youngest child—a son with Down syndrome—is a true inspiration.

If confirmed, Justice Barrett will make history as the first mother of school-aged children ever to serve on the US Supreme Court. That's good.

To her children, Emma, Vivian, Tess, John Peter, Liam, Juliet, and Benjamin: thank you for sharing your incredible mom with our country. Thank you very much.

Amy Coney Barrett will decide cases based on the text of the Constitution as written. As Amy has said, "Being a judge takes courage. You are not there to decide cases as you may prefer. You are there to do your duty and to follow the law wherever it may take you." That is exactly what Judge Barrett will do on the US Supreme Court.

I want to thank the members of the Senate. We have so many of them here today. Thank you very much. I see you in the audience, and you're so proud. But I want to thank you for your commitment, and to providing a fair and timely hearing. I know it will be that.

Judge Barrett was confirmed to the circuit court three years ago by a bipartisan vote. Her qualifications are unsurpassed—unsurpassed—and her record is beyond reproach. This should be a straightforward and prompt confirmation. It should be very easy. Good luck. It's going to be very quick. I'm sure it'll be extremely non-controversial. We said that the last time, didn't we? Well, thank you all very much. And thank you for being here. That's really great. Thank you.

I further urge all members of the other side of the aisle to provide Judge Barrett with the respectful and dignified hearing that she deserves—and frankly, that our country deserves. I urge lawmakers and members of the media to refrain from personal or partisan attacks.

And the stakes for our country are incredibly high. Rulings that the Supreme Court will issue in the coming years will decide the survival of our Second Amendment, our religious liberty, our public safety, and so much more.

To maintain security, liberty, and prosperity, we must preserve our priceless heritage of a nation of laws, and there is no one better to do that than Amy Coney Barrett.

Law and order is the foundation of the American system of justice. No matter the issue, no matter the case before her, I am supremely confident that Judge Barrett will issue rulings based solely upon a fair reading of the law. She will defend the sacred principle of equal justice for citizens of every race, color, religion, and creed.

Congratulations again to Judge Barrett. I know that you will make our country very, very proud. Please, Amy, say a few words.

On the Violence at the Capitol

THE WHITE HOUSE, WASHINGTON, DC

January 13, 2021

My fellow Americans:

I want to speak to you tonight about the troubling events of the past week. As I have said, the incursion of the US Capitol struck at the very heart of our republic. It angered and appalled millions of Americans across the political spectrum.

I want to be very clear. I unequivocally condemn the violence that we saw last week. Violence and vandalism have absolutely no place in our country, and no place in our movement. Making America great again has always been about defending the rule of law, supporting the men and women of law enforcement, and upholding our nation's most sacred traditions and values.

Mob violence goes against everything I believe in, and everything our movement stands for. No true supporter of mine could ever endorse political violence. No true supporter of mine could ever disrespect law enforcement or our great American flag. No true supporter of mine could ever threaten or harass their fellow Americans. If you do any of these things, you are not supporting our movement. You are attacking it, and you are attacking our country. We cannot tolerate it.

Tragically, over the course of the past year, made so difficult because of COVID-19, we have seen political violence spiral out of control. We have seen too many riots, too many mobs, too many acts of intimidation and destruction. It must stop. Whether you are on the right or on the left, a Democrat or a Republican, there is never a justification for violence. No excuses. No exceptions.

America is a nation of laws. Those who engaged in the attacks last week will be brought to justice.

Now I am asking everyone who has ever believed in our agenda, to be thinking of ways to ease tensions, calm tempers, and help to promote peace in our country. There has been reporting that additional demonstrations are being planned in the coming days, both here in Washington and across the country. I have been briefed by the US Secret Service on the potential threats.

Every American deserves to have their voice heard in a respectful and peaceful way. That is your First Amendment right. But I cannot emphasize that there must be no violence, no law-breaking, and no vandalism of any kind. Everyone must follow our laws and obey the instructions of law enforcement.

I have directed federal agencies to use all necessary resources to maintain order. In Washington, DC, we are bringing in thousands of National Guard members to secure the city and ensure that a transition can occur safely and without incident.

Like all of you, I was shocked and deeply saddened by the calamity at the Capitol last week. I want to thank the hundreds of millions of incredible American citizens who have responded to this moment with calm, moderation, and grace. We will get through this challenge, just like we always do.

I also want to say a few words about the unprecedented assault on free speech we have seen in recent days. These are tense and difficult times. The efforts to censor, cancel, and blacklist our fellow citizens are wrong, and they are dangerous. What is needed now is for us to listen to one another, not to silence one another. All of us can choose, by our actions, to rise above the rancor and find common ground and shared purpose. We must focus on advancing the interests of the whole nation, delivering the miracle vaccines, defeating the pandemic, rebuilding the economy, protecting our national security, and upholding the rule of law.

Today, I am calling on all Americans to overcome the passions of the moment and join together as one American people. Let us choose to move forward, united for the good of our families, our communities, and our country.

Thank you. God bless you. And God bless America.

Farewell Address

THE WHITE HOUSE, WASHINGTON, DC

January 19, 2021

My fellow Americans:

Four years ago, we launched a great national effort to rebuild our country, to renew its spirit, and to restore the allegiance of this government to its citizens. In short, we embarked on a mission to make America great again—for all Americans.

As I conclude my term as the forty-fifth president of the United States, I stand before you, truly proud of what we have achieved together. We did what we came here to do—and so much more.

This week, we inaugurate a new administration and pray for its success in keeping America safe and prosperous. We extend our best wishes, and we also want them to have luck—a very important word.

I'd like to begin by thanking just a few of the amazing people who made our remarkable journey possible.

First, let me express my overwhelming gratitude for the love and support of our spectacular First Lady, Melania. Let me also share my deepest appreciation to my daughter Ivanka, my son-in-law Jared. And to Barron, Don, Eric, Tiffany, and Lara: you fill my world with light and with joy.

I also want to thank Vice President Mike Pence, his wonderful wife, Karen, and the entire Pence family.

Thank you as well to my chief of staff, Mark Meadows; the dedicated members of the White House Staff and the Cabinet; and all the incredible people across our administration who poured out their heart and soul to fight for America.

I also want to take a moment to thank a truly exceptional group of people: the United States Secret Service. My family and I will forever be in your debt. My profound gratitude as well to everyone in the White House Military Office, the teams of Marine One and Air Force One, every member of the Armed Forces, and state and local law enforcement all across our country.

Most of all, I want to thank the American people. To serve as your president has been an honor beyond description. Thank you for this extraordinary privilege. And that's what it is—a great privilege and a great honor.

We must never forget that, while Americans will always have our disagreements, we are a nation of incredible, decent, faithful, and peace-loving citizens who all want our country to thrive and flourish and be very, very successful and good. We are a truly magnificent nation.

All Americans were horrified by the assault on our Capitol. Political violence is an attack on everything we cherish as Americans. It can never be tolerated.

Now, more than ever, we must unify around our shared values and rise above the partisan rancor, and forge our common destiny.

Four years ago, I came to Washington as the only true outsider ever to win the presidency. I had not spent my career as a politician, but as a builder looking at open skylines, and imagining infinite possibilities. I ran for president because I knew there were towering new summits for America, just waiting to be scaled. I knew the potential for our nation was boundless, as long as we put America first.

So I left behind my former life and stepped into a very difficult arena, but an arena, nevertheless, with all sorts of potential, if properly done. America had given me so much, and I wanted to give something back.

Together, with millions of hardworking patriots across this land, we built the greatest political movement in the history of our country. We also built the greatest economy in the history of the world. It was about America First, because we all wanted to make America great again. We restored the principle that a nation exists to serve its citizens. Our agenda was not about right or left. It wasn't about Republican or Democrat, but about the good of a nation, and that means the whole nation.

With the support and prayers of the American people, we achieved more than anyone thought possible. Nobody thought we could even come close.

We passed the largest package of tax cuts and reforms in American history. We slashed more job-killing regulations than any administration had ever done before. We fixed our broken trade deals, withdrew from the horrible Trans-Pacific Partnership and the impossible Paris Climate Accord, renegotiated the one-sided South Korea deal, and we replaced NAFTA with the groundbreaking USMCA—that's Mexico and Canada—a deal that's worked out very, very well.

Also—and very importantly—we imposed historic and monumental tariffs on China. Made a great new deal with China. But before the ink was even dry, we and the whole world got hit with the China virus. Our trade relationship was rapidly changing, billions and billions of dollars were pouring into the US, but the virus forced us to go in a different direction.

The whole world suffered, but America outperformed other countries economically because of our incredible economy, and the economy that we built. Without the foundations and footings, it wouldn't have worked out this way. We wouldn't have some of the best numbers we've ever had.

We also unlocked our energy resources and became the world's number one producer of oil and natural gas, by far. Powered by these policies, we built the greatest economy in the history of the world. We reignited America's job creation and achieved record-low unemployment for African Americans, Hispanic Americans, Asian Americans, women—almost everyone.

Incomes soared, wages boomed, the American Dream was restored, and millions were lifted from poverty in just a few short years. It was a miracle. The stock market set one record after another, with a hundred forty-eight stock market highs during this short period of time, and boosted the retirements and pensions of hardworking citizens all across our nation. 401(k)s are at a level they've never been at before. We've never seen numbers like we've seen—and that's before the pandemic and after the pandemic.

We rebuilt the American manufacturing base, opened up thousands of new factories, and brought back the beautiful phrase "Made in the USA."

To make life better for working families, we doubled the child tax credit and signed the largest-ever expansion of funding for childcare and development. We joined with the private sector to secure commitments to train more than sixteen million American workers for the jobs of tomorrow.

When our nation was hit with the terrible pandemic, we produced not one, but two vaccines with record-breaking speed. And more will quickly follow. They said it couldn't be done, but we did it. They call it a medical miracle. And that's what they're calling it right now: a medical miracle.

Another administration would have taken three, four, five, maybe even up to ten years to develop a vaccine. We did in nine months.

We grieve for every life lost, and we pledge in their memory to wipe out this horrible pandemic, once and for all.

When the virus took its brutal toll on the world's economy, we launched the fastest economic recovery our country has ever seen. We passed nearly four trillion dollars in economic relief, saved or supported over fifty million jobs, and slashed the unemployment rate in half. These are numbers that our country has never seen before.

We created choice and transparency in healthcare, stood up to big pharma in so many ways, but especially in our effort to get favored-nations clauses added, which will give us the lowest prescription drug prices anywhere in the world.

We passed VA Choice, VA Accountability, Right to Try, and landmark criminal justice reform.

We confirmed three new justices of the United States Supreme Court. We appointed nearly three hundred federal judges to interpret our Constitution as written.

For years, the American people pleaded with Washington to finally secure the nation's borders. I am pleased to say we answered that plea and achieved the most secure border in US history. We have given our brave border agents and heroic ICE officers the tools they need to do their jobs better than they have ever done before, and to enforce our laws and keep America safe.

We proudly leave the next administration with the strongest and most robust border security measures ever put into place. This includes historic agreements with Mexico, Guatemala, Honduras, and El Salvador, along with more than four hundred fifty miles of powerful new wall.

We restored American strength at home, and American leadership abroad. The world respects us again. Please don't lose that respect.

We reclaimed our sovereignty by standing up for America at the United Nations, and withdrawing from the one-sided global deals that never served our interests. And NATO countries are now paying hundreds of billions of dollars more than when I arrived just a few years ago. It was very unfair. We were paying the cost for the world. Now the world is helping us.

And perhaps most importantly of all, with nearly three trillion dollars, we fully rebuilt the American military—all made in the USA. We launched the first new branch of the United States Armed Forces in seventy-five years: the Space Force. And last spring, I stood at Kennedy Space Center in Florida and watched as American astronauts returned to space on American rockets for the first time in many, many years.

We revitalized our alliances and rallied the nations of the world to stand up to China like never before.

We obliterated the ISIS caliphate and ended the wretched life of its founder and leader, al-Baghdadi. We stood up to the oppressive Iranian regime and killed the world's top terrorist, Iranian butcher, Qasem Soleimani.

We recognized Jerusalem as the capital of Israel, and recognized Israeli sovereignty over the Golan Heights.

As a result of our bold diplomacy and principled realism, we achieved a series of historic peace deals in the Middle East. Nobody believed it could happen. The Abraham Accords opened the doors to a future of peace and harmony, not violence and bloodshed. It is the dawn of a new Middle East, and we are bringing our soldiers home.

I am especially proud to be the first president in decades who has started no new wars.

Above all, we have reasserted the sacred idea that, in America, the government answers to the people. Our guiding light, our North Star, our unwavering conviction, has been that we are here to serve the noble everyday citizens of America. Our allegiance is not to the special interests, corporations, or global entities, it's to our children, our citizens, and to our nation itself.

As president, my top priority, my constant concern, has always been the best interests of American workers and American families. I did not seek the easiest course. By far, it was actually the most difficult. I did not seek the path that would get the least criticism. I took on the tough battles, the hardest fights, the most difficult choices, because that's what you elected me to do. Your needs were my first and last unyielding focus.

This, I hope, will be our greatest legacy: Together, we put the American people back in charge of our country. We restored self-government. We restored the idea that, in America, no one is forgotten, because everyone matters, and everyone has a voice. We fought for the principle that every citizen is entitled to equal dignity, equal treatment, and equal rights, because we are all made equal by God. Everyone is entitled to be treated with respect, to have their voice heard, and to have their government listen. You are loyal to your country, and my administration was always loyal to you.

We worked to build a country in which every citizen could find a great job and support their wonderful families. We fought for the communities where every American could be safe, and schools where every child could learn. We promoted a culture where our laws would be upheld, our heroes honored, our history preserved, and law-abiding citizens are never taken for granted. Americans should take tremendous satisfaction in all that we have achieved together. It's incredible.

Now, as I leave the White House, I have been reflecting on the dangers that threaten the priceless inheritance we all share. As the world's most powerful nation, America faces constant threats and challenges from abroad. But the greatest danger we face is a loss of confidence in ourselves. A loss of confidence in our national greatness.

A nation is only as strong as its spirit. We are only as dynamic as our pride. We are only as vibrant as the faith that beats in the hearts of our people.

No nation can long thrive that loses faith in its own values, history, and heroes, for these are the very sources of our unity and our vitality.

What has always allowed America to prevail and triumph over the great challenges of the past has been an unyielding and unashamed conviction in the nobility of our country and its unique purpose in history. We must never lose this conviction. We must never forsake our belief in America.

The key to national greatness lies in sustaining and instilling our shared national identity. That means focusing on what we have in common: the heritage that we all share.

At the center of this heritage is also a robust belief in free expression, free speech, and open debate. Only if we forget who we are, and how we got here, could we ever allow political censorship and blacklisting to take place in America. It's not even thinkable. Shutting down free and open debate violates our core values and most enduring traditions.

In America, we don't insist on absolute conformity or enforce rigid orthodoxies and punitive speech codes. We just don't do that. America is not a timid nation of tame souls who need to be sheltered and protected from those with whom we disagree. That's not who we are. It will never be who we are.

For nearly two hundred fifty years, in the face of every challenge, Americans have always summoned our unmatched courage, confidence, and fierce independence. These are the miraculous traits that once led millions of everyday citizens to set out across a wild continent and carve out a new life in the great West. It was the same profound love of our God-given freedom that willed our soldiers into battle, and our astronauts into space.

As I think back on the past four years, one image rises in my mind above all others. Whenever I traveled all along the motorcade route, there were thousands and thousands of people. They came out with their families so that they could stand as we passed, and proudly wave our great American flag. It never failed to deeply move me. I knew that they did not just come out to show their support of me, they came out to show me their support and love for our country.

This is a republic of proud citizens who are united by our common conviction that America is the greatest nation in all of history. We are, and must always be, a land of hope, of light, and of glory to all the world. This is the precious inheritance that we must safeguard at every single turn.

For the past four years, I have worked to do just that. From a great hall of Muslim leaders in Riyadh, to a great square of Polish people in Warsaw; from the floor of the Korean Assembly, to the podium at the United Nations General Assembly; and from the Forbidden City in Beijing, to the shadow of Mount Rushmore—I fought for you, I fought for your family, I fought for our country. Above all, I fought for America and all it stands for—and that is safe, strong, proud, and free.

Now, as I prepare to hand power over to a new administration at noon on Wednesday, I want you to know that the movement we started is only just beginning. There's never been anything like it. The belief that a nation must serve its citizens will not dwindle, but instead only grow stronger by the day.

As long as the American people hold in their hearts deep and devoted love of country, then there is nothing that this nation cannot achieve. Our communities will flourish. Our people will be prosperous. Our traditions will be cherished. Our faith will be strong. And our future will be brighter than ever before.

I go from this majestic place with a loyal and joyful heart, an optimistic spirit, and a supreme confidence that for our country and for our children, the best is yet to come.

Thank you, and farewell. God bless you. God bless the United States of America.

We've Left It All on the Field

JOINT BASE ANDREWS, MARYLAND

January 20, 2020

Thank you very much. And we love you—and I can tell you that from the bottom of my heart. This has been an incredible four years. We've accomplished so much together. I want to thank all of my family, and my friends, and my staff, and so many other people, for being here. I want to thank you for your effort, your hard work. People have no idea how hard this family worked—and they worked for you.

They could have had a much easier life. But they just—they did a fantastic job. I just want to thank all of you—everyone.

I want to thank Mark Meadows, who's here someplace—right there. I want to thank Mark. But it's been—it's been something very special. We've accomplished a lot. Our First Lady has been a woman of great grace and beauty and dignity, and so popular with the people. So popular with the people, in fact. Honey, would you like to say a few words?

MELANIA TRUMP: Being your first lady was my greatest honor. Thank you for your love and your support. You will be in my thoughts and prayers. God bless you all. God bless your families. And God bless this beautiful nation.

DONALD TRUMP: What else has to be said. Right?

But what we've done—that's true, honey, great job—what we've done has been amazing, by any standard. We rebuilt the

313

United States military. We created a new force called Space Force. That in itself would be a major achievement for a regular administration. We were not a regular administration.

We took care of the vets—ninety-one percent approval rating. They've never had that before. The vets have given us—the VA—the vets have given us an approval rating like it has never been before. We took care of our vets. And our beautiful vets, they were very badly treated before we came along. And as you know, we get them great service, and we pick up the bill, and they can go out and they can see a doctor if they have to wait long periods of time.

We got it so that we can, sadly, get rid of people that don't treat our vets properly. We didn't have any of those rights before when I came on. So our vets are happy, our people are happy. Our military is thrilled. We also got tax cuts—the largest tax cut and reform in the history of our country, by far.

I hope they don't raise your taxes. But if they do, I told you so.

And if you look at the regulations—which I consider the regulation cuts to be maybe even more important. That's why we have such good—and have had—such good job numbers. The job numbers have been absolutely incredible.

When we started, had we not been hit by the pandemic, we would have had numbers that would never have been seen. Already, our numbers are the best ever. If you look at what happened until February, a year ago, our numbers were at a level that nobody had ever seen before. And even now, we really built it twice. We got hit—nobody blames us for that; the whole world got hit—and then we built it again. And now the stock market is actually substantially higher than it was at its higher point, prior to the pandemic. So it's really—you could say we built it twice.

And you're going to see—you're going to see incredible numbers start coming in, if everything is sort of left alone. Be careful—very complex. Be careful. But you're going to see some incredible things happening. And remember us when you see these things happening. If you would, remember us. Because I'm looking at—I'm looking at elements of our economy that are said to be a rocket ship up. It's a rocket ship up.

We have the greatest country in the world. We have the greatest economy in the world. And as bad as the pandemic was—we were hit so hard, just like the entire world was hit so hard—places that thought they got away with it, didn't get away with it. They're suffering right now.

We did something that is really considered a medical miracle. They're calling it a miracle—and that was the vaccine. We got the vaccine developed in nine months instead of nine years, or five years, or ten years, or a long time. It was supposed to take a long time—many, many years to develop a vaccine. We have two out. We have another one coming almost immediately, and it really is a great achievement. So you should start to see really good numbers over the next few months. I think you're going to see those numbers really skyrocket downward.

And I can only say this: We have worked hard. We've left it all—as the athletes would say—we've left it all on the field.

We don't have to—we don't have to come and say—we'll never say in a month, when we're sitting in Florida—we're not going to be looking at each other and saying, "You know, if we only worked a little bit harder." You can't work harder. And we had a lot of obstacles, and we went through the obstacles.

And we just got seventy-five million votes. And that's a record in the history of—in the history of sitting presidents. That's an all-time record by a lot—by many millions—in the history of sitting presidents. It's been, really, just an honor.

One of the things we're very, very proud of is the selection of almost three hundred federal judges and three great Supreme Court justices. That's a very big number. That's a record-setting number.

And so we've done a lot, and there's still things to do.

The first thing we have to do is pay our respects and our love to the incredible people and families who suffered so gravely from the China virus. It's a horrible thing that was put onto the world. We all know where it came from, but it's a horrible, horrible thing. So be very careful. Be very, very careful. But we want to pay great love—great love—to all of the people that have suffered, including families who have suffered so gravely.

So with that, I just want to say, you are amazing people. This is a great, great country. It is my greatest honor and privilege to have been your president.

I will always fight for you. I will be watching. I will be listening. And I will tell you that the future of this country has never been better. I wish the new administration great luck and great success. I think they'll have great success. They have the foundation to do something really spectacular.

And again, we put it in a position like it's never been before, despite the worst plague to hit since, I guess you'd say, 1917—over a hundred years ago. And despite that, despite that, the things that we've done have been just incredible. And I couldn't have done them—done it without you.

So just a good-bye. We love you. We will be back in some form.

And again, I want to thank our vice president, Mike Pence, and Karen. I want to thank Congress, because we really worked well with Congress—at least, certain elements of Congress. But we really did. We've gotten so much done that nobody thought would be possible. But I do want to thank Congress, and I do want to thank all of the great people of Washington, DC—all of the people that we worked with to put this miracle together.

So have a good life. We will see you soon.

Thank you. Thank you very much. Thank you very much.

Illustration Credits

Cover
President Trump in Springfield, Missouri (August 30, 2017)
White House Photo/Alamy Stock Photo

Frontispiece
Official Presidential Portrait of Donald J. Trump
Government Publishing Office

Trump—The Launch (June 16, 2015)
AP Photo/Reichard Drew, File

Trump tells convention America 1st (July 21, 2016)
The Yomiuri Shimbun via AP Images

US Presidential election acceptance (November 9, 2016)
Paco Anselmi/PA Wire URN:29129632
(Press Association via AP Images)

President Trump delivers his inaugural address
(January 20, 2017)
Yin Bogu/Xinhua/Alamy Live News

President Trump delivers his address at the Israel Museum
(May 23, 2017)
US State Department/Alamy Stock Photo

President Trump in Warsaw, Poland (July 6, 2017)
Anna Ferensowicz/Pacific Press/Alamy Live News

President Trump, Interior Secretary Ryan Zinke, and Energy
Secretary Rick Perry at National Boy Scout Jamboree
(July 24, 2017)
AP Photo/Steve Helber, File

President Trump speaks to with African-American supporters in
Cabinet Room (June 10, 2020)
AP Photo/Patrick Semansky

President Trump speaks during UN General Assembly
(September 19, 2017)
AP Photo/Mary Altaffer

President Trump delivers a statement on Jerusalem
(December 6, 2017)
Sipa USA via AP

President Trump joins West Point cadets during the Army v. Navy
football game (December 14, 2019)
Andrew Caballero-Reynolds/AFP via Getty Images

President Trump speaks with FIFA President Gianni Infantino at
the World Economic Forum (January 21, 2020)
Jim Watson/AFP via Getty Images

President Trump welcomes NASCAR Cup Champion Joey
Logano to White House (April 30, 2019)
Chip Somodevilla/Getty Images

Texas Governor Greg Abbot and President Trump at border security
briefing (June 30, 2021)
Joel Martinez/The Monitor via AP, Pool

President Trump acknowledges guests during State of the Union
address (February 5, 2019)
Planetpix/Alamy Live News

Queen Elizabeth II and President Trump at event to mark 75th
anniversary of D-Day (June 5, 2019)
AP Photo/Matt Dunham

President Trump and commander of US Space Command,
Air Force General John W. Raymond (August 29, 2019)
DoD photo by Lisa Ferdinando/Alamy Stock Photo

President and Mrs. Trump depart White House for Georgia
(December 5, 2020)
Al Drago/Stringer/Getty Images

President Trump awards Presidential Medal of Freedom to
wrestler Dan Gable (December 7, 2020)
Doug Mills-Pool/Getty Images

President Trump honors US Military Academy football team at
White House (May 6, 2019)
Cheriss May/Nur Photo via Getty Images

President Trump speaks during a campaign rally in Tulsa,
Oklahoma (June 20, 2020)
AP Photo/Sue Ogrocki

President Trump and First Lady Melania Trump at Mount
Rushmore National Memorial (July 3, 2020)
AP Photo/Alex Brandon

President Trump at 121st Army-Navy football game
(December 12, 2020)
AP Photo/Andrew Harris

President Trump, First Lady Melania Trump, Amy Coney Barrett
and her husband Jesse on Blue Room balcony at the White
House (October 26, 2020)
AP Photo/Alex Brandon

President Trump in Oval Office during an event commemorating
the repatriation of Native American remains from Finland
(September 17, 2020)
Saul Loeb/AFP via Getty Images

President Trump and First Lady Melania Trump make their way to
Marine One before departing the White House (January 20, 2021)
Mandel Ngan/AFP via Getty Images

President Trump and First Lady Melania Trump at Andrews
Air Force Base (January 20, 2021)
AP Photo/Luis M. Alvarez